LOGIC
AND
MATHEMATICS

LOGIC AND MATHEMATICS

EDITED BY

JOHN H. PIET

AND

AYODHYA PRASAD

COSMO PUBLICATIONS

2000 INDIA

LOGIC AND MATHEMATICS

First COSMO Print 2000

ISBN 81-7755-011-x

This indipendent and complete volume has been derived from the set -
Encyclopaedia of ETHICS AND LOGIC

Published by
MRS. RANI KAPOOR
for COSMO PUBLICATIONS Div. of
GENESIS PUBLISHING PVT. LTD.
24-B, Ansari Road,
Darya Ganj,
New Delhi-110 002, INDIA

Composed at
Cosmo Publications

Printed at
Mehra Offset Press

CONTENTS

1. The Principles of Logic and Mathematics 1

- The Principles of Logic: Aximos or Rules?
- Can a line be drawn between Logic and Mathematics?

2. On the Ways and Means by which the Mind arrives at Mathematical Evidence 17

3. On Synthetic Judgments *a Priori* other than Mathematical, or on the *a Priori* Connections of the Understanding, or Logical Conceivability 33

4. Of Transcendental Logic Positively 51

5. Constructing a Logical Calculus 81

- Introduction
- Schematic letters
- Variables
- Dummy letters
- Connectives
- Formulae
- Sequents
- The role of Formation rules
- The role of Interpretation rules
- The role of Derivation rules
- Languages, Systems, Calculi

— Classification of Calculi
— Metalogical notation
— Defnitions
— Some properties of Relatins

6. Using a Logical Calculus 109

— Introduction
— Truth and correctness
— Deductive correctness
— Criterion of deductive correctness
— From: sentences versus schemata
— From: sentences versus propositions
— Validity: languages
— Validity: contexts
— Validity: domains
— Validity: worlds
— The definition of 'valid sequent'
— Proof
— Alternative route
— The power of Logic

7. Formation Rules and Definitions 163

— Syntax refined
— Formulating the rules
— Symbolic definitions
— Scope
— Indemnities
— Other people's rules

8. Interpretation Rules 185

— Formulating the rules for letters
— Formulating the rules for connectives
— Formulae into schemata
— Truth conditions and meaning
— Pure semantics
— Metatheorems on truth
— Other people's rules

9. Derivation Rules for Sequents 217

— Natural deduction
— Formulating the rules
— Sequent-derivations
— Metatheorems on derivability.
— Abridged derivations
— Other people's rules

10. Derivation Rules for Formulae 251

— Axiomatic systems
— Formulating the rules
— Fomula-derivations
— Metatheorems on derivability
— Abridged derivations
— Other people's rules

11. Modal 277

— A sample argument
— Modalities
— Kinds of Modality
— Modal Speakers
— Alternative situations and kinds of modality
— Modality and validity
— A note of caution

Chapter-1

The Principles of Logic and Mathematics

Chapter 1

1. THE PRINCIPLES OF LOGIC: AXIOMS OR RULES?

Before the 1930s it was taken for granted that any body of established truths must be a development from fundamental truths and any system of theorems (if one desisted from a truth-claim) must develop out of postulates. In both cases the initial principles are axioms in the sense that they state that something is so (on the basis of intuition or as a free choice) and that they are used to derive all other statements. An essential feature of an axiom is that it takes a grip on reality. What is held in this grip will vary from science to science because the difference in subject-matter between sciences will appear in their sets of axioms. But, as axioms, the initial principles always have in common that they are an apprehension—through intuition or postulation—or what is so.

Curiously enough the suitability of axiomatization for logic itself has been called in question although mathematical logic, since the time of Boole, has been perfecting the general study of axiomatics, and since the time of Frege has been perfecting the specific application of the method to logic. Kneale points out:

> It must be confessed, however, that there is something strange in talk about axioms of logic, whether these are supposed to be few, as in Frege's system, or infinitely many, as in von Neumann's. Before Frege's day logicians thought it their business to consider how theorems followed from axioms in studies such as geometry, but they did not commonly try to present logic itself as a deductive system with axioms and theorems. Frege was not, of course, the first to maintain that some logical principles could be derived from others. For Aristotle reduced all valid syllo-

> gisms to *Barbara* or *Celarent*, and Chrysippus deduced complex moods from his indemonstrables. But Frege, following some suggestions of Leibniz and Boole, offered a system in which the axioms and theorems are not truths about what follows from what but logical truisms of the same status as the law of non-contradiction and the law of excluded middle.(*The Development of Logic*, p.530)

Frege's deductive system of logic had many lineal descendants, notably that of Russell and Whitehead in the *Principia Mathematica* and those in Polish logic, before the question was asked: why should logic be conceived as having axioms at all?

It was quite natural that Frege and other mathematicians would extend to the codification and certification of logical truths a method that was very successful in mathematics. It was doubly natural that Frege and Russell would suppose that since (as they thought) arithmetic is conceptually a part of logic, there must be some fundamental logical axioms through which arithmetic merges as a deductive system, into logic. However, with the work of Wittgenstein and Post in 1921, it became clear that in propositional logic, since logical truths coincide with the tautologies certified by truth tables, axiomatization is rendered unnecessary. More importantly it has been seen to be misleading:

> This became apparent in the 1930's, as a result of the pioneering work of Rudolf Carnap in formal syntax and Tarski in formal semantics. Their studies served, among other things, to clarify the distinctions between a theory and the logic in which it is formalized and between the syntactical and the semantical characterizations of logic. The danger is that the axiomatization of logic. The danger is that the axiomatization of logic tends to create the presumption that logic is merely another theory to be axiomatized, like a geometry or an algebra. This, of course, is not so. The axiomatization of a geometry pre-supposes a logic that governs the deducing of theorems from geom-

etrical axioms. This logic, when made explicit, is found to consist of *inference rules*: 'logical axioms', unlike the 'proper axioms' of the axiomatized (mathematical) theories, do not in fact enter as premises in any of the deductions in these systems. (Albert E.Blumberg: article on Modern Logic, *Encyclopedia of Philosophy*, vol. 5, pp. 24-5)

Logic is not simply one system of knowledge that can be brought into coordinate and cumulative relationships with other systems. Its principles pervade all other systems, are indeed formalizations of the rational deductive processes they observe. And for this reason most contemporary logicians feel that logic receives its full and proper characterization only when it is given a natural deduction format. A theory of logic, on this view, is an attempt to identify the deep dynamisms which determine our deductions of what is true in everyday life and in science.

In the natural deduction approach a primary grip is taken not on the world but on rationality: what are initially formalized are natural deduction movements, deep movements of reason under the impulse of nature. A logic developed from such principles presents itself as an intensive analysis of rationality, a detailed elaboration of rational dynamisims. Such a logic does not provide extra axioms or truisms for other systems but it can be said to pervade all other systems in so far as they have a rational deductive character, logic being a grammar of their rationality.

It is not an unreasonable tribute to Boole to say that the natural deduction format of logic achieved an objective towards which he was groping although he misconceived it as a higher mathematics. In *The Mathematical Analysis of Logic* he emphasized the need for a contextless calculus, a calculus of deductive reasoning elaborated in abstraction from all contexts. And he expressed the view that the principles of such a calculus would formalize laws to which mental operations as human deductive processes are subject and thus would be revealing the constitution of the human mind:

They who are acquainted with the present state of the theory of Symbolical Algebra, are aware, that the validity of the processes of analysis does not depend upon the interpretation of the symbols which are employed, but solely upon the laws of their combination. Every system of interpretation which does not affect the truth of the relations supposed, is equally admissible, and it is thus that the same process may, under one scheme of interpretation represent the solution of a question on the properties of numbers, under another, that of a geometrical probloem, and under a third, that of a problem of dynamics or optics. This principle is indeed of fundamental importance...But the full recognition of the consequences of this important doctrine has been, in some measure, retarded by accidental circumstances... Thus the abstractions of the modern Analysis, not less than the ostensive diagrams of the ancient Geometry, have encouraged the notion, that Mathematics are essentially, as well as actually, the Science of Magnitude ...That to the existing forms of Analysis a quantitative interpretation is assigned, is the result of the circumstances by which those forms were determined, and is not to be construed into a universal condition of Analysis. It is upon the foundation of this general principle, that purpose to establish the Calculus of Logic, and that I claim for it a place among the acknlowledged forms of Mathematical Analysis, regardless that in its object and in its instruments it must at present stand alone.(Introduction. pp. 3-4)

It appeared to me that although Logic might be viewed with reference to the idea of quantity, it had also another and a deeper system of relations. If it was lawful to regard it from *without*, as connecting itself through the medium of Number with the intuitions of Space and Time, it was lawful also to regard it from *within*, as based upon facts of another order which have their abode in the constitution of the Mind ... The laws we have to examine are the laws of one of the most important of our mental faculties. The mathematics we have to construct are the mathematics of

> the human intellect.... Nor will it lessen the interest of this study to reflect that every peculiarity which they will notice in the form of the Calculus represents a corresponding feature in the constitution of their own minds. (Preface, p.l; Introduction, p. 7)

Of course the language of Boole does remind us at times of Psychologism, a general attitude and detailed doctrine prevalent in the last century and quite alien to the spirit of the new mathematical logic. The general attitude had indeed dominated Europe since 1600 and helped to create the so-called classical logic of the period, 1600-1900. This logic functioned as a science of mental operations in much the same way as latin grammar was a science of latin sentences: it presented itself as a normative science or art of thinking and its natural fruit was better thinking. At the beginning of the nineteenth century a general philosophical position developed which regarded psychology as the fundamental philosophical discipline and identified philosophic method with self-observation: when the laws of the development of the human soul are understood with certainty and clarity, then also a clear and full knowledge of philosophic disciplines is achieved. In Germany the term, *Psychologism*, came to be used in reference to this philosophy. Indeed two of its strongest and most explicit advocates were the German philosophers Jakob Friedrich Fries and Friendrich Eduardo Beneke, who presented it as a radical departure from Kantian doctrine. Towards the middle of the centruy the philosophy was applied to both logic and mathematics reducing their content to psychic elements of subjective experience. Many logicians accepted this reduction of their discipline and not only on the Continent of Europe but also in England (strongly in the logic of Bradley and Bosanquet, more ambivalently in that of Mill) the logical tradition was anti-mathematical.

At the same time, the modern renaissance of logic as an exact science beginning with Boole continued without interruption, and towards the end of the century the Neo-Kantian opposition to psychologism was developed systematically. Thus refutations of psychologism were written by both philosophers and logicians, the classic ones being by Lotze, Frege and Husserl:

> The psychological act of thinking is, according to Lotze, completely distinct from the content of thought. The psychological act exists only as a determinate temporal phenomenon, whereas the content has another mode of being-validity. A decade later Gottlob Frege defended the same point of view....'Never take a description of the origin of an idea for a definition, or an account of the mental and physical conditions through which we become conscious of a proposition for a proof of it. A proposition may be thought, and again it may be true; never confuse these two things. We must remind ourselves, it seems, that a proposition no more ceases to be true when I cease to think of it than the sun ceases to exist when I shut my eyes.'*(Die Grundlagen der Arithmetik,* Introduction) The systematic critique of psychologism in the fields of logic and mathematics is an important part of Husserl's *Logische Untersuchungen...* Later in his career Husserl wrote, in terms very close to Frege's 'To refer to it [a number] as a mental construct is an absurdity, an offence against the perfectly clear meaning of arithmetical discourse, which can at any time be perceived as valid, and precedes all theories concerning it.' (*Ideen,* Sec.22) He warned against the tendency to 'psychologize the eidetic'—that is, to identify essences, which are the authentic objects of knowledge, with the simultaneous consciousness of these essences. (Ibid.,Sec.61) (Nicola Abbagnano: article on Psychologism in *The Encyclopedia of Philosophy,* vol.6)

In retrospect one can see that the early mathematical logicians were at a disadvantage in having to refute Psychologism:they developed logic on the basis of its affinity to mathematics but did not discover and utilize broader possibilities of development. The natural deduction approach has corrected this limitation, making explicit links logic has with philosophy and psychology. It is an authentic development of mathematical logic which is quite alien to the excesses of Psychologism. Its LAF's are no more mental entities than propositions are linguistic sentences: they formalize natural rule content as propositions formalize thought content. The formalized rules are intuitively rational and since they are rationality-preserving they can be operated purely syntactically with the guarantee that what is, syntactically, a correct theorem will also be, semantically, a valid implication.

Thus the natural deduction approach presents rationality as the essential preoccupation of logic. It presents logical truth in the form of consequence, as an expression and working out of rationality rather than as a correspondence, with fact. In this presentation, the corpus of logical truth is both a deductive system and a netwoek of paradigms for deductions in all other systems. It is a grammar of proof and as Boole said: 'In one respect, the science of Logic differs from all others; the perfection of its method is chiefly valuable as an evidence of the speculative truth of its principles.' (*The Mathematical Analysis of Logic,* Preface)

In summary it is fair to say that the concept of rule has come to have a central place in metalogic.The concept of logical necessitation has been enriched by formalizing it as an inescapable expression of rationality. The causality operating in cogent reasoning has been clarified by demonstrating the intrinsic power of natural deduction movements to evolve into whole deductive systems. And in general, logicians believe that appropriate principles for logic are rules: in this format logic (1) presents itself as a science certified, ultimately, by the nature of reason; (2) explains how, as a deductive system evolved from rules, it can pervade all reasoning situations in life and in science as the authority for inference-licenses. However, it will be a matter for philosophy of logic to explore how and in what ultimate sense logic not only expresses rationality but also achieves truth, i.e. conforms to fact. The axiomatization of logic which has been systematically perfected in modern times leaves one in no doubt that logic cannot be completely understood except as a corpus of truth.

II. CAN A LINE BE DRAWN BETWEEN LOGIC AND MATHEMATICS?

Perhaps the most striking feature of mathematics as an intellectual discipline is the enormous variety of the problems with which it deals...This variety, coupled with a lack of clear-cut criteria for what forms the subject matter of mathematics, makes large-scale syntheses and unifications extremely difficult to achieve. One must also beware of unifications of such exalted generality as to be trivial and avoid syntheses so rigid that they constrain future growth and developments. It should be noted that the only serious attempt in recent years to present the whole of mathematics from a unified point of view, that of the Bourbaki group, was criticized on *both* of these grounds.(*Mathematics and Logics* by Mark Kac and Stanislaw Ulam, p.108)

During the last century mathematicians turned their attention to the problem of synthesis and to the foundations of mathematics. The amount of mathematical material in existence was vast and there was a great variety of mathematical notions, nevertheless over centuries the method of proof and the format of organization had hardly changed. There was still the selection of axioms and the repeated application of well-defined rules with a consequent array of theorems describing properties and relations of the mathematical objects that were being studied. Becoming increasingly committed to the ideal of rigour in the construction of proofs and more reliant on logical analysis, mathematicians subjected traditional axiomatics to exhaustive logical analysis and made it more and more efficient and perfect. As a consequence axiomatic thinking was employed in all parts of mathematics with new interest, power and scope. The elegance and success of the results provided both experience and encouragement for attempts to axiomatize the whole of mathematics.

This work on the axiomatization of mathematics coupled with interest in its foudations was the occasion of the origion, with Frege, of *Logicism.* This was the view that mathematics is a branch of logic and it received its best known exposition in the detailed reduction achieved by Russell and Whitehead in their *Principia Mathematica.* In his *Principles of Mathematics* Russell summed up the logistic thesis as floolws:

> Pure Mathematics is the class of all propositions of the form 'p implies q' where p and q are propositions containing one or more variables, the same in the two propositions, and neither p nor q contains any constants except logical constants. And logical constants are all notions definable in terms of the following: implication, the relation of a term to a class of which it is a member, the notion of *such that,* the notion of relation, and such further notions as may be involved in the general notion of propositions of the above form. In addition to these mathematics *uses* a notion which is not a constituent of the propositions which it considers, namely the notion of truth.(p.3)

In other words the whole of classical mathematics can be systematized *within* a logical calculus: the axioms of mathematics leading us back to those of the logical calculus, the truth conditions of the mathematical system to the truth conditions of the primitive logical signs, all mathematical concepts to purely logical ones—so that it becomes impossible to say where logic ends and mathematics begins; indeed it becomes clear that it is merely practical convenience which maintains any distinction between these two subjects.

Before Frege, mathematics had discovered that all mathematical signs can be defined on the basis of the signs of the theory of natural number, and for Frege numbers are logical entities which we can find by correlating the extensions of concepts:if correlation reveals concepts which are similar in extension these concepts may be said to have the same number. It is true that number is not a property of external things; it is 'independent of our sensation, intuition and imagination and of all construction of mental pictures and of memories of earlier sensations' (*Grundlagen,* 36[c]); but it is *given to reason* as a set of all similar classes and sheer rationality forces us to accept statements expressing laws of number. It is because numerical thinking is a pure exercise of rational insight that it is essentially logical.

Such a view relies, of course, on the concept of class being so rational as to be immune to paradox. In our treatment of Russell's paradox of classes we have seen that this is not so, that throughout history philosophers and logicians have disputed the grounds of classal thinking, and that set theory in particular has had to defend itself from paradox by special axioms rather than to present itself as self-guaranteeing through the inherent rationality of the concept, set.

Commenting in general on the logistic approach, Mostowski says:

> This seemed to be an excellent program, but when it was put into effect,it turned out that there is simply no logic strong enogh to encompass the whole of mathematics. Thus what remained from this program is a reduction of mathematics to set theory. This can hardly be said to be a satisfactory solution of the problem of foundations of mathematics since among all mathematical theories it is just the theory of sets that requires clarification more th-an any other. (*Thirty years of Fondational Studies,* Intr-oduction)

It is important to remember that the study of the foundations of mathematics as a whole is so general and so much concerned with the process of deduction rather than with its fruits, that it has not had a profound effect on the main body of mathematics. The discovery of non-Euclidean geometries and the study of the foundations of geometry has played a more vital part in modern mathematics and in science generally.

Opposing Logicism, Hilbert and Bernays proposed to

systematize classical mathematics as a mere calculus and not to involve mathematics with ideas of logic in a framework of truth and falsehood. Their view is called Formalism and the resulting calculus is callled metamathematics. It is purely syntactic in character, a theory of mathematics solely as a formal system, and, while not denying that a fuller presentation of the foundations of mathematics would involve considerations of truth and falsity they are concerned with proof of consistency and even regard this as the main task of metamathematics. Of course in providing a proof of consistency one shows that a true interpretation and application of a calculus is logically possible. However, so far a proof has been provided for only a certain part of arithmetic. In their proofs formalists are Boolean in spirit, insisting on the value and power of a consistent, foolproof symbolism and on the sufficiency of combinatorial processes of thought no more complicated than that involved in seeing that two things and two things make four things.

Evaluating this view, Mostowski says:

> the formalism of Hilbert set up a program which required, first that the whole of mathematics be axiomatized and, secondly, that these axiomatic theories be then proved consistent by using very simple combinatorial arguments. As it has turned out, this program is not realizable; and even if it were, it would hardly satisfy philosophically minded mathematicians because of the inevitable arbitrariness of the axioms. (Ibid)

The final view is that of *Intuitionism* which originated with Brouwer(1912). There is room for this kind of approach once one asks the question: as an interpreted system is mathematics simply an instrument of deduction within fields of empirical knowledge, or is it a system of knowledge, of information, of sentences with factual content.For the intuitionist the latter is emphatically the case. As a system mathematics symbolizes mathematical thought, i.e. thought 'by which individuals organize phenomena in their most general aspect to satisfy their needs. Hence it is not enough to have a symbolism for mathematical thoughts; they are independent of the particular language used to express them. What is absolutely necessary is that the language should significantly express thoughts. We must be able to stop at every point in mathematics and see the state of affairs which is expressed as clearly as we can see the fact that to a heap of objects, no matter how many, it would always be possible to add one more and again one more in a never-ending process. Knowledge of this particular process, the possibility of indefinitely extending a series of objects by the addition of extra members, which may be expressed alternatively with sufficient precision for present purposes as direct knowledge of the sequence of the natural numbers, is termed "Urintuition" (basic intuition) by Brouwer; it is fundamental and irreducible in his philosophy.' (Max Black: *The Nature of Mathematics,* p. 10)

Only propositions with a clear intuitive meaning are admissible into mathematics; general propositions which cannot be tested for truth by any known procedure are simply not admissible. Presumably, on this basis, computerization can vastly extend the body of mathematical knowledge but the latter will always be traceable ultimately to pure intuition and mathematics must always be regarded as a special field of mental activities. Mostowski comments as follows:

> [intuitionism] views mathematics in isolation from other branches of science and insists on restricting the notions and methods used in mathematics to the most elementary and intuitive ones. For these reasons, few mathematicians have joined the intuitionistic school.(Ibid.)

How can one sum up the *status quaestionis* at this point of time? A significant development has happened within logic since the 1930s: it is generally held now that a natural deduction format displays the character of logic most properly and fully: logic is essentially semantic, and evolution and formalization of rationality; it is a science generated from rules, unique in being free of axiomatic boundaries. The contention of Logicism can be evaluated now by the criterion: can mathematical material be entirely organized within the natural deduction format? We have seen that a long history of controversy about the key concept, class, seems to imply could not situate mathematical material within the purely rule-governed system of logic: it seems to require stipulated conditions or axiomatic control to be rendered immune to paradox. The other two foundational approaches, Formalism and Intuitionism, do not contend that logic and mathematics are a continuum in form and content. Formalism works within mathematics at its syntactic organization, without prejudging the nature or extent of isomorphism with lofic; Intuitionism accepts a dividing line between mathematics and all other disciplines, and seeks to explain it in terms of unique empirical foundations.

As long as systematization and axiomatization coincided it was impossible to draw a line between logic and mathematics: they are so alike in rigour, clarity, simplicity and in the use of a formalistic method. But once logic presents itself as purely rule-governed system a line appears and mathematics shows itself as a body of essentially axiomatic disciplines which uses rules and paradigms of logic, although it does so in a more immediate, general and aesthetic way than other sciences. To use a modern metaphor, sciences are deductive and probative in character because they are programmed to be so: the true source of this programme is in logic.

Chapter-2

Of the Ways and Means by which the Mind Arrives at Mathematical Evidence

Chapter 2

1. We are certain, inasfar as we know that it is impossible that the knowledge should be false.[1] Certainty, however, is to be distinguished from evidence. Two positions may be equally certain and yet the one have the advantage in being more evident. Thus: the certainty is as great in the calculations of algebra as in the demonstrations of geometry; but the latter are confessedly accompanied with a greater evidence, and the truth in both is capable of being rendered more evident than the truths of metaphysics, on the one hand, while on the other, than the truths of induction or the knowledge derived from experience. [Not] by their certainty, for we cannot say that they are more certain.A truth may be more or less evident but in certainty there are no degrees.[2] What is it, then, that gives the certainty to mathematical truths? And secondly, what is it that gives to the mathematics generally their greater evidence (which, however, is not equal in all its branches? And thirdly, therefore, what is it that (the certainty being one and the same in all) makes the evidence in geometry greater than that of arithmetic, and the evidence of arithmetic greater than that of the higher calculus? First. In order to understand a thing we must know all its component parts, and to be certain that we understand it, we must be certain that all the parts that belong to the thing are present to our mind, and that no others are imagined to be there. This process, be which we determine that nothing is wanting, and nothing intruded, is called in technical logic the "exhaustion of the terms".[3] Within our own memory, theoretical chemists believed themselves to understand the nature of muriatic acid,[4] that is, they believed themselves to have enumerated all its components or constituents, to the exclusion of all that were not such, in the terms oxygen in combination with a peculiar base. A more exact analysis and multiplied experiments caused them to believe that water was present in all cases,and that no means existed

of its entire detachment. It was then thought safer—in other words, it was thought that the nature of muriatic acid was more intelligible—by admitting water as a component part. And for more than thirty years, during which time, too, chemistry was most zealously and most successfully cultivated, the favourite science of the age, all the chemists of the civilised world coincided in this assurance as grounded on the evidence of the senses, or on inferences so immediate and necessary as to be no more than the exponents of the phenomena or the phenomena themselves generalised in the conception and this conception expressed in words. They asserted, in short, that the position "muriatic acid is composed of oxygen with an unknown base and water" was the true and only *meaning* of the phenomena and that there was no other way of conceiving the facts experimentally ascertained. And yet at the close of this period it was (or what for our purpose is the same, it was and is believed to have been) incontrovertibly shown that pure muriatic acid contains neither water, nor oxygen, nor an unknown base.[5] Add, too, that after the *experimentum crusics*,[6] the decisive proof of the accuracy of Scheele's opinion respecting the simplicity of the oxymuriate[7] had been published by Sir H. Davy,[8] the founder of philosophic, as Wollaston[9] of scientific, chemistry, the truth was not acknowledged till after a long and obstinate controversy, in which the English chemists were by no means unanimous in receiving it, while the Scottish, German, and French chemists were almost unanimous in its rejection. And even at last the balance was determined, it is probable, by the discovery of an analogous body, viz. the iodine.[10] It is not without deep interest that I can reflect that the French or Lavoisier's system, the adhesion to which occasioned this reluctance, is founded on as gross a *quid pro quo*[11] and equivoque as is to be found in the *elenchi* or sophisms exposed in the old books of logic, viz. the confusion of a power or principle with the body in which it appeared to be most predominant or in which it manifested itself most obviously.[12] On the very same ground on which Lavoisier made oxygen the principle of acidification, and thereby of combustion, he might have made platinum the power of gravity and elevated musk into universal repulsion.

2. The first distinction, therefore, the first characteristic prerogative of the mathematician, is that having first demanded a power which no man can deny, he begins by making his own terms. In all philosophical and historical disquisition the definition most properly should form the conclusion, as the result of the reasoning. If the writer commences with it, it is either by anticipation for the purpose of determining the reader's thought to the especial object proposed by the enquirer, as if a man pointing with his finger to the distance should say, "keep in this direction and at yonder point you will see a building", which the speaker proceeds to describe in its main characteristics. Strictly speaking, these should rather be called "declarations" than "definitions". In the mathematics, on the contrary, I begin with the definition. By the postulates I assert my power of productive action; by the definitions I determine what the product shall be and by what name it shall be known. These elementary products and the simplest constructions and integrations of the same are my definitions. By an act of my will I think four straight lines that enclose a plane space so that the opposite sides shall not be parallel, and I call the figure that results from this construction a trapezium.[13] To this I confine myself; I say nothing of anything out of myself as corresponding to it. There may, for aught I know, be many bodies that might in part be described in the same words, but these bodies may have many other and, perhaps, more essential characters. But this creation of my own is this and this only. These components and this composition constitute the trapezium. And to suppose myself deceived, or to pretend any the least doubt, would convict me of the same absurdity as that of the simpleton in one of our old plays, whom the poet introduces fresh from the wonders and sight-baffling sights of a pretended magician and which have left him so doubtful respecting the evidence of his senses, and so proud of his newly acquired scepticism, that speaking of a blazing fire he

exclaims, "This fire does not really burn; it only seems to burn; but it does not really seem, it only seems to seem."[14] Now there might be some pretence for the first scruple, but the second contradicts itself. The man that sees a ghost *actually* sees it, though it may not at all follow that really there was any ghost to be seen. Now in the mathematics the producing act and the product are one and indivisible. A cone may signify elsewhere what you will, but the geometrician speaks of a cone which he himself has created by voluntarily presenting to himself a right-angled triangle that turns round on one side. It is therefore a synthesis, a composition, a construction.[15] The construction takes place, the product has its birth and existence within the mind. It is therefore a synthesis *ab intra.*[16] But this power must be presupposed in order to the possibility of contemplating the outward objects in similar relations. It is therefore a synthesis *a priori*. It is necessary; for it is impossible and a contradiction to affirm that he has not exercised the act which he is exercising, or that the product can be other than it is. And lastly it is universal; for he knows infallibly and on the very same principle that he possesses this as a man, not as an individual, that he can with certainty anticipate the same result from every other man, that is, rational and intelligent being having the faculty of sense, on the single condition of inducing him to make the attempt. (*Vide the Menon* of Plato.)[17]

3 But secondly, and which distinguishes the mathematical evidence from the logical, as the former contradistinguishes it from the experimental, the mathematician *always* and essentially reasons intuitively. It is not only a synthesis *a priori;* but a synthesis *a priori* of intuitions, which (the act and the product being one) are themselves intuitions *a priori*. The conceptions of the logician and the philosopher may be accompanied with intuitions mixed or pure, may be illustrated by them; but those of the mathematician *must* be presented *intuitively*. *Immediate* presentation *et in concreto*, in contradistinction from the knowing a thing *mediately* by representative marks ob-

tained by abstraction (which the logicians call *in abstracto* as the antithesis to *in concreto*)[18], is *essential* in mathematical evidence and *makes* the evidence mathematical. Now to contemplate our knowledge *in concreto* and this by an *act* of the mind is what we mean by construction. I contemplate my face *in concreto* in the looking-glass, but the concrete or image is no act of mine as far as I am conscious—and within the bounds of consciousness alone we are now moving. My mind is passive to the impression on my eye. We need only demonstrate the simplest proposition in Euclid to be made [to] know how different this is from the contemplation of the concrete by means of a constructive act.

4. But here the difficulty seems rather to increase than. diminish; how is it possible to contemplate anything, to have the intuition of an object, except by the immediate presence of the object; and what is this but experience, or at least the matter of fact of which experience is composed, but of which the intuitions in question are to be independent? And truly, if the intuition in question were of that kind that it represented the things or self-subsistents as they are in themselves, it would be impossible otherwise than by experience. For what is contained in the object of itself I can know only as far as such object is present or given to me. It would be something worse than absurd to suppose in a finite mind the power of creating anything out of itself; but what I cannot create for myself I must have given to me if I am to have it at all. I confess that even under the condition of this datum it is altogether incomprehensible how my intuition of a present object should enable me to know it as it is in itself, or to know anything more than the relations in which I myself stood to the object thus given. For the attributes or properties of a thing cannot pass over,like emigrants into my soul or sentient being. If, however, the possibility of this be taken for granted, still this intuition could not take place *a priori;* for this would imply a right destructive of all reason and all philosophy-the right of asserting at will the commencement of a thing at any

particular time without any assignable ground, cause, or occasion. In fact [this is] the doctrine of Malebranche and of some other Cartesians [who] have taken refuge in the hypothesis of inspiration or immediate acts of divine agency—which may be *piety,* which may even be *truth;* but which most certainly is not *logic,* or philosophy logically deduced.[19] In our knowledge *a posteriori,* or the image in the mind correspondent to the outward object consequent on the presence of that object, the fact may bear down the want of insight into the possibility of the fact. At all events it does not contradict the principle of the sufficient reason, or any other universal principle real or formal, which would be the case in the assertion of an intuition *a priori* of an object which is yet distinct from the object itself and its correspondent.

5. There remains therefore but one way in which it is possible that my intuition should, in its universal forms, be antecedent to the presentation of the object, and certain of my particular intuitions being independent of any outward object, viz. if the intuition and these particular constructions of the same contain nothing else but the forms of the sense, the sense itself in short, considered apart from the sensibility, the form in my own mind as the subject is anterior to all actual impressions from without as being that which predetermines within certain bounds the mode in which outward objects can be contemplated by me. In short, knowledge *a priori* is possible, but *possible* then only when the knowledge and the object known, the *scire* and the *scitum,* are one and the same.

6. We have now only to refer to the preceding chapters on space and time as the universal forms,[20] *that* of the outward, *this* of the inward sense, and then to any, the simplest, operation in mathematics, geometrical or arithemetical, in proof and illustration of the productive imagination by which the intuition of space and that of time are variously combined or constructed, to have afforded a complete solution of our three first questions, viz. "How are *a priori* knowledge, or synthetic judgments not experiential, possible?" Secondly, "How mathematical knowledge

in particular, as forming one class of synthetic judgments *a priori,* is possible?" And thirdly, "Wherein do these judgments differ essentially from others that are likewise both synthetic and *a priori,* that is, what is, the essential distinctive character of pure mathematics?"

7. Of the ordinary and indispensable proceedings of the mathematicians, let the following be taken as the illustrative instances. That a space, as far as it is the space, and not a boundary of any other space, has three dimensions, and that space in the absolute is a truth grounded on the position that not more than three lines can cut each other at right angles in one point. But this proposition cannot be proved out of any conceptions. It cannot be logically concluded or deduced but rests altogether and immediately on the intuition: we *see* that so it is, and this [is] a pure intuition, an intuition *a priori,* arising out of the intuitive faculty itself, because it is a certainty accompanied with a sense of the impossibility of the contrary; because we do not confine ourselves [to affirming] that so it is in this instance and so it has been hitherto in all my experience, and in that of all other men as far as I know, and I see no reason for supposing that it will be otherwise in future, which is the utmost that knowledge founded on experience could warrant or excite, but so it must be, and if contemplated in sense it cannot be contemplated otherwise. But that such intuitions are pure and *a priori* is likewise proved, because the geometrician can, and often does, require that a line should be produced infinitely (*in indefinitum*) or that a series of changes, a series of spaces left behind in a given motion, should be continued *ad infinitum*—postulates which presuppose a presentation or intuition (or if I may use the language of the Cartesians without implying my assent to its appropriateness or expediency), *an innate idea* of space and time which subsists wholly in the intuitive faculty itself, as far as it exercises its power unaided and unbounded by anything out of itself [21]. In the same manner all the proof of the perfect equality of two given figures rests wholly on the immediate

intuition of their entire coincidence, or that they cover each other in all points, which as an image indeed might have been derived from experience, but not as a necessary truth[22]. It was the inadvertence to this distinction that misled the late Dr. Beddoes to the strange assertion that the evidences of the mathematician are of the same kind, derived from the same sources, derived from the same means, as those of the chemist[23]. To the strange position before mentioned, even suppose two bodies to be made [to] cover each other before our eyes, yet what could we say but that these bodies, as far [as] *I* see, coincide. In order to determine whether the equality grounded on this coincidence is a *necessary* and universal consequent, I must construct it in my own mind, and in *this* construction it is that I find the impossibility of the contrary. In fact the very words, "if these two surfaces cover each other they are equal", have no proper or immediate reference to the *bodies*. For I have no reason to suppose the existence or even the possibility of any two bodies or surfaces absolutely equal to each other, and if such did exist, yet I have certainly no means of ascertaining it, nor should I have, though my eyes were ten times more microscopic than Mr. Pope supposes those of the fly to be.[24] The true meaning of the words refers to the constructive faculty itself, not to the image,no, not even to the image in the fancy, which is no other than the mental diagram, both it and that drawn on the slate or paper being alike pictures of the mathematical line generated by the mathematical points and of the mathematical surfaces generated by the lines, which, as the very definitions are sufficient to show, are acts and products of the active and productive imagination.

8. What the use of the picture is in aid of the evidence, and how little it is essential to the certainty of the intuition, we may find in going through any arithmetical operation—that 3×3 = 9 and 3×9 = 27 we determine in the first instance by the law of succession in ourselves, that is, by the intuition of time, and this [is] sufficient for certainty as long as we can attend to the progression with the recollection of what went before, or some mark representative of the same and a substitute for

the recollection more secure than the recollection itself, the names, I mean, of each unit expressing and involving all that in the line of time had gone before; but yet in order to extend and facilitate the construction and for the purpose of increased evidence we express the intuitions of time by those of space. A 9 we call the square, and 27, the cube of 3; but which no more alters the nature of the former process or prevents it from being constructed intuitively, that is, a truth immediately grounded in the form and constructive power of the inner sense itself, than the notes of music cease to be auditual and successive by being entitled sharps and flats. The student, if acquainted with fluxions and the processes of integration and of differentials, will find the happiest and most perfect exemplification of the relations which the two forms of the outer and inner sense, that is, of space and time, are capable of bearing to each other. We reason algebraically and above all infinitesimally in order to give rapidity and sense of difference to our reasoning, and we translate it, where it is practicable, geometrically, that is, into the intuitions of space, in order to give it totality and greater evidence.

9. We have seen, likewise that the intuitions of time are higher and more comprehensive than those of space, the constructions of space, that is, figure, being inconceivable exclusively of the inner sense, while these may exist for themselves. In order to form a line we imagine the successive motion of a point; and to form a figure the lines must be finite in one direction at least; and if the figure is to be complete, a circle, square, ellipse, etc, and dependent for its degree of evidence on the forms of the outward sense, the component lines must be finite altogether. But figure is not necessary to the conception of motion, and it is by the sense of succession, that is, under the universal form of time, that we arrive at the motion *ad indefinitum,* whence we may comprehend the greater affinity which the intuitions of time and the constructions of the same have to the conceptions of the understanding than takes place in pure geometry. The higher we advance in the higher calculus, or in what is mathematically called the tran-

scendental analysis, the more does the mathematical reasoning resemble the logical, differing from it, indeed, in this respect, that though the reasoning be in *abstracto,* yet this abstraction must be a certainty that intuitions, or at least there must be capable of being resolved into intuitions, or at least there must be a certainty that intuitions are the grounds and constituents of the certainty. Otherwise it would cease to be mathematical and be merely logical. The preceding remark supposes a greater acquaintance with the higher mathematics than I am entitled to suppose that my reader possesses or in fact than I myself possess, if the remark requires anything more than simply to know from other authority that so it is, and to understand that from the nature of the thing so it ought to be.[25]

Footnotes

1. The sentence is from *Untersuchung* Betrachtung III 1: VS II 35.
2. Cf CN III 3455: "Two kinds of proof equal in certainty yet leaving the mind in very different states—these may be called the Algebraic & Geometrical proofs—in the one you see it is so, and so it must be—in the other, you see likewise, *how* it is so, & why it cannot be otherwise-".Cf the distinction made between certainty and positiveness in *Friend* (*CC*) II 7, *CN* II 3095, and *CL* III 48.
3. *Exhaustio terminorum.*
4. Now called hydrochloric acid or hydrogen chloride.
5. See Humphry Davy "On the Fallacy of the Experiments in Which Water Is Said to Have Been Formed by the Decomposition of Chlorine" *Phil Trans* CVIII (1818)169-71.
6. The "crucial experiment", or "acid test".
7. Karl Wilhelm Scheele (1742-86), Swedish chemist, whose analysis of manganese dioxide in 1774 led him to the isolation of chlorine.
8. A reference to Humphry Davy's Bakerian lecture of 15 Nov 1810—"On Some of the Combinations of Oxymuriatic Gas and

Oxygene..."*Phil Trans* CI (1811) 1-35. Davy particularly discusses the impropriety of the term "oxymuriatic acid" ("its great discoverer", he says, "called it dephlogisticated marine acid") and proposes instead "chlorine" or "chloric gas" (p 32). C was an indefatigable reader of the *Phil Trans,* knew Davy well, and took a keen interest in his work. C appears to have felt personally involved with this discovery, however; on the endpapers of Steffens *Geognostisch-geologische Aufsätze*, he has written: "Long before Sir H. Davy's attempts to establish the independent existence of the Oxymuriatic as Chlorine, I had anticipated it a priori...."

9. William Hyde Wollaston (1766-1828). C refers to one of his articles in a note on the flyleaf of Tennemann III. His tribute to Wollaston is less personal; see *CL* v 410 (early Feb 1825): "I have not the honor of any such acquaintance with Dr Woolaston, having only occasionally met him at dinner parties...."Cf *Friend* (CC) I 471.

10. See Humphry Davy's lecture of 20 Jan 1814, "Some Experiments and Observations on a New Substance...." *Phil Trans* CIV (1814) 74-93. Davy names the new substance "iodine" (p 91) and credits Courtois—Bernard Courtois (1777-1838)—with having discovered it about two years earlier.

11. "A mistaken substitution".

12. Cf *CN* II 3192 (Dec 1807), in which the French chemists' misapplication of the names "hydrogen" and "oxygen" is referred to.

13. C's example is taken from *Untersuchungen* Betrachtung I § 1: VS II 5-6.

14. The original of this remark appears in a letter of Moses Mendelssohn's in F.H. Jacobi *Ueber die Lehre des Spinoza*...(Breslau 1789) 86: " Lessing lässt, in einem seiner Lustspiele, jemanden, der Zauberey zu sehen glaubt, von einem brennenden Lichte sagen: Dieses Licht brennt nicht wirklich, es scheint nur zu brennen; es scheint nicht wirklich, es scheint nur zu scheinen." ("Lessing, in one of his comedies, has someone who believes he is seeing sorcery say of a burning light: this light does not really burn, it only seems to burn; it does not really seem, it only seems to seem.") The comedy in question is the fragment *Die*

Matrone von Ephesus, first published in Lessing *Theatralische Nachlass* (Berlin 1784); the remark occurs in the first scene, and the offerer of the suspect flame is a supposed ghost. C's substitution of a "pretended magician" and his "wonders and sight-baffling sights", whether deliberate or forgetful, has the advantage of applying the incident to an old joke about theories of perception. See e. g. *Guardian* No 24 (8 Apr 1713) and *Spectator* No 242 (7 Dec 1711)—both by Steele. The *Guardian* story is used for its philosophical implications by Dugald Stewart in "Dissertation First..." *Supplement to the Fourth, Fifth, and Sixth Editions* of the Encyclopaedia *Britannica* (Edinburgh 1824 6 vols)I 97.

15. The example of the cone is from *Untersuchungen* Betrachtung I $ 1: VS II 6.

16. "From within".

17. *Meno* 82B-85B. Cf *BL* ch 12 (1907) I 173: "Socrates in Plato show, that an ignorant slave may be brought to understand and of himself to solve the most difficult geometrical problem." Cf *Friend (CC)* I 457.

18. E.g. Leibniz *Theodice* Preliminary Discourse $ 63 (quoting Bayle):"the reason of man, or *reason in concreto* and... reason in general, or reason *in abstracto*".

19. Nicolas Malebranche (1638-1715). C cites him in *BL* ch 12 (1907) I 187 to the effect that we see all things in God, but on that occasion he is merely paraphrasing Schelling (*System des transcendentalen Idealismus* 319). He refers to him in *CL* II 679 and *CN* III 3974. Cf Kant's similar dismissal of Malebranche ("Principiorum...elucidatio" $ 3 II prop xiii usus par 6: VS IV 171 and De *mundi sensibilis atque intelligibilis forma et principiis* $ 22 scholion:VS II 473-4).

20. Ch IV above, Pp 150-73].

21. Paragraph 7 up to this point is freely translated from Kant *Prolegomena* $ 12 (1783) 55-6.

22. The sentence is based on *Prolegomena* $ 13 (1783) 57. Cf above, pp 160ff.

23. See above, p 15 n 1.

24. Essay on Man ep I lines 193-4. Cf C's reference to the eyes of the

Aranea prodigiosa and to Baker's *Microscopic Experiments* in *AR* (1825) 158 and n.

25. For C's regret at knowing so little mathematics, see his marginal note in Böhme *Works* published in *CN* II 2894n.

Chapter-3

On Synthetic Judgments *a priori* Other Than Mathematical, or on the *a priori* Connections of the Understanding, or Logical Conceivability

Chapter 3

1. We have seen, then, that MATHEMATICAL SCIENCE is grounded in the intuitive faculty itself, and consists of the acts and products of this faculty, that is, pure intutions ans constructions *a priori;* and that in this view, and this alone, we are enabled to comprehend how the positions or judgments of the mathematician should be *synthetic,* no less than the judgments a *posteriori* (that is, the combinations ascertained by *experience*),and yet necessarily certain and apodictic, which no judgments merely experiential are or can be. We have arrived at this insight by the transcendental deduction of our conception time and space as the universal forms of the sense, that is, of the sentient faculty considered abstractly from its objects; and we see that without this deduction, and without granting, moreover, the postulate which it suggests to us, that whatever is presented to our senses (to the *outward* senses in space, and to the *inner* sense in time) is contemplated and apprehended as it *appears* to us, not as it is in itself (*ut res* PHAENOMENALIS *et subjectiva, non ut res in se-et seorsim a mente subsistens*)[1]. We might indeed have found ourselves compelled to admit the *fact* of mathematical certainty, but how such a fact is *possible* we must have remained ignorant. We might have *known* it, but we could not have *understood* it. And lastly we have learnt the distinction between certainty and evidence; more than this is beyond the bounds of logic, either common or critical; the attempt if made at all belong to *noetic*, or the doctrine of ideas.

2. The time is gone by when a few misinterpreted metaphors and symbolic expressions of the divine philosopher[2] induced the visionary platonist to attempt the explanation of spiritual mysteries, and make discoveries in the spiritual words,by means of geometrical figures and mathematical numbers, and to find the originals and first parents of our human diagrams in

celestial realities, angelic triangles, and arch-angelic circles. I need not in the present age instruct the reader that *mathematical* truths as the forms of the sense are exclusively applicable to the objects of the senses, and that these forms are realised, or possess a reality more than subjective, only as far as the observations of experience are found coincident therewith; and with what fortunate success our astronomic discoveries and both the discoveries and inventions in mechanics and statics bear witness. As little does the reader require to be informed that the mathematic is most applicable to those appurtenances or attributes of external nature that are most homogeneous with itself, viz. that which is most general and capable of being abstracted and generalised, [such] as extent, mass, weight, and motion. Before we proceed it will be expedient to guard against an error into which the frequent mention of pure and mixed intutions, that is, immediate perceptions of the modifications of extension and succession, might mislead the student, as if in mathematical reasoning these were the only constituents. It will be useful, I say, to look somewhat more narrowly into the famous adage common to the Aristotelian school and that of Epicurus, "Nihil in intellectu quod non *prius* in sensu" –and not so much for the purpose of guarding against its undue extension by adding the Leibnizian postscript, "praeter ipsum intellectum",[3] which we have already done in general and the particular explanation of which is the subject of the present chapter; but with especial reference to the word *prius*. "There is nothing in the understanding which was not previously in the sense",which, to an incautious mind at least, might seem to infer that, though in the exercise of reason there can be no conceptions formed independently of perceptions, yet we may reason by perceptions, that is, possess intuitive knowledge without the aid of conceptions. The error indeed would yield to the first attentive reflection, and wtih a thoughtful reader therefore could only be momentary. For it would give to the mathematician the power of knowing and of demonstrating his propositions, but deny him that of understanding them. The true distinctive character of mathematical science lies in the necessary construction and essential constructibility of its conceptions in the forms of intuition. The presence of conceptions therefore is as truly presupposed as that of intuitions. In fact each suppose the other. And not only does this hold true in the instance of those conceptions which are properly intended in the Aristotelian adage and of which alone the assertion can be truly made, viz. the *quotquot* IN *intellectu;*[4] but likewise to those purely formal, which are included in Leibniz's cautionary addition. "praeter ipsum intellectum". Examine any synthetic judgment of whatever kind (or we might submit them all to an exact analysis). and we shall find, though in opposition to the common opinion, that they never consist of intuitions alone that are merely combined by an act of *comparison* or *equation* into one judgment; but that the synthetic judgment would be impossible if, over and above the conception abstracted from the intuitions, whether it be the image of an outward object or the image itself considered as an object, there did not like wise supervene a *pure* conceptions of the understanding, not derived from any from of sense of representment of the senses, under which conception the former (those viz. abstracted from the object of the senses, of expressed in the forms of the sense itself) are taken up or subordinated (which process is by the logicians technically called subsumption, or the act of subsuming). And when the conceptions and intuitions are thus subsumed under some pure conception, some one of the inherent and constituent forms of the understanding, then first are thay capable of being combined into a judgment that has real validity and significancy.[5] And observe that this reality, or objectivity in the secondary sense of the word is not confined to judgments *a posteriori* or to what we affirm or deny on grounds of experience. Let the image be the offspring of the intuitive faculty itself and the immediate product of its imaginative power called into action. Still, yet even here, the mind itself is assumed as the substance, the substratum of the form, and as far as this can be universally and permanently assumed in contradistinction from individual peculiar and contingent [considerations], the truths resulting are equivalent to those in which the substance or substratum of the forms is other than the subject engaged in contemplating them, or the mental subject, and because the two result are equal they have been expressed by the same name as judgments possessing objective validity. The reader will excuse me that I so readily avail myself of bringing back to his recollection explanations that have been so frequently given before, but the more nearly he approaches to the conclusion of our logical disquistions, the more should his mind be prepared and predisposed to see and understand the utmost boundary as well as the legitimate extent of the antithesis, subject and object, subjective and objective; and that, both in the one term and in the other, different, may, at first sight contradictory, senses, that at different times are expressed by one and the same word, are not to be attributed to any removable defect in the technical language of the science, or to an injudicious choice of equivocal terms;but from the necessary indifference of both in the point producing (or on each side produced into) the line of which they are the differentials or opposite poles: *opposita semper unigena. In omni opposition datur suppositum in quo(seu, tenus quod) oppostia unum sunt. Thesis = antithesis in aliqua prothesi.*[6] Terms that can be rightly opposed to each other in the evolution of a truth must be identical in the root, that is, radically one. These are different ways of expressing the same principle, a principle of paramount importance in philosophy no less than in logic, pregnant as an idea and infallible as a criterion.

3. We have said that synthetic judgments in no instance consist of intuitions merely nor of conceptions formed from them, but that in all cases, whether the judgments [be] *a priori or a posteriori*, there must be some pure conception of the understanding as the ground and condition of the former; even the position of the pure mathematic in its simplest axioms form no exception.That the straight line is the shortest between two points presupposes that the line is subsumed under the conception of qantity, which most assuredly is no mere

intuition but has its seat wholly in the understanding and in this instance exercises an appropriate function. There is first the intuition- the line, to wit—now this line cannot be reflectively contemplated but in relation to the judgments which the mind may form respecting it. And the conception in this instance determines this judgment in respect of the *quantity* of the line by which I judge that in any given image a number (plurality, multeity) of homogeneous points or spaces is contained in the unity of a given intution.[7] The exceedingly abstract character of the words which on subjects so universal and abstract as the present must needs be, e.g., points, lines surface, etc, give [s] the appearance of a difficulty which really does not exist in the conception itself.

4. Let the student try the experiment whether he can present a given line to his mind without some determination in his mind of its being longer of shorter, that is, containing more or less of an homogeneous extension, more or fewer of an indefinite multitude of homogeneous points, which it is in his power to conceive singly and successively, and so far as *many* that are nct *one* but which here he contemplates as co-present, continuous, and as the *many* in *one*. But this unity depends, he will find, on determining the *quantum* of the *many* that have become *one*. Now this is not in the line; for it is out of our power to think it long or short, more or less, except in comparison with some other, but this again holds equally true or that other and of ecah and every possible intuition *ad infinitum*. But that which exists neither in A nor in B, and yet is such that without it neither A nor B can be contemplated at all, or consciously known as existing, must of necessity exist in C as a relation of A and B taken comparatively to some principle of comparison in C itself. Here, that is, in C, as the subject or mind contemplating A and B, there is no focus in which any imaginable rays converge and become intense. That which neither A nor B possess [es], neither A nor B can irradiate or give forth. The utmost that can be said [is] that it was called forth in C in consequence of A and B

falling at one time under his contemplation, which is indeed proved further by the fact that one of the objects may have been noticed for the first and last time twenty years ago and in China, the other at the present moment and in Peru,[8] and the conception of their comparative quantity will take place equally well. But comparative supposes positive, and every finite a previous indefinite. We cannot conceive waves without a sea, lake, or river, nor a sea, lake, or river without the preconception of water, as the common term. The very terms "more" or "less" , "larger" or "smaller", with all their definite determinants, of number, weight, and measure, inches, feet, miles, pints, gallons, etc, etc presuppose that of which thay are at once *measures* and parts, measures of *quantity* and themselves quantities, not parts, from the co-existence or proximity of which a whole results, as in a heap of corn or any other mere aggregate; but parts that owe their existence and their possibility to a pre-existing All, an ευ και παυ *ejusdem generis*,[9] to which they have the same relation as the thoughts to the mind, as spaces to space itself, etc.

5. Might I again interrupt for a moment the disquisition, in order to address the student as if he were indeed present, I would say, "Do not let the newness and strangeness of these speculations discourage you or lead you to suppose that there is any difficulty in the thoughts themselves, anything abstruse in that which is really meant, otherwise than as all efforts are troublesome to which we are unaccustomed. They are hard only because they are strange. The unexpected, the unusual, oppresses and overbears us. And hence the origin of the word *'insolent', insolens, quod maxime insolitum.*[10] Abstraction, indeed, in its highest degrees and when the process is not favoured by the senses (as in abstracting a colour, redness, for instance, from the many and diverse bodies thay are so coloured, but on the contrary we have to abstract from all the accidents of sense), is the most arduous function of the understanding, and the minds able and disposed to exercise it are comparatively rare. 'Peu de têtes sont faites pour une abstraction absolue,

c'est à dire, pour une attention qui n'est dirigee qu'a l'etre. Mais la vérité ne sauroit nous venir de dehors elle est en nous.'[11] In other words, to abstract adequately is hard, but in scientific pursuits there is no getting at the truth without it. If we would emancipate ourselves from the tyranny of appearances, we must abstract. The abstraction, however sufficient for our present purposes, is trifling compared with what is required in the higher branches of the mathematics, and even with regard to the degree in which it must be exerted in making the experiment of the line in the last paragraph but one. If having read the paragraph two or three times attentively you either miss the meaning or find it dim and flitting and that it escapes a steadfast grasp, in this and in other similar cases I would advise you to desist from the effort and pass on. The few passages in which this is likely to occur, where there exists an actual wish to understand my words and a proportional vigour and continuity of attention, are in no instance, I flatter, indispensable. What follows or what has gone before may perhaps supersede the necessity of the particular argument or illustration, while the latter, perhaps, may have the same effect for some other reader with respect to a paragraph in which you had found no dificulty, but on the contrary a furtherance and the very light you were seeking. Desist, I say, from *trying* to understand; for first, it may not be necessary, and secondly, it is most probable that as so often happens with regard to names it will start up of its own accord when you are not thinking of it."

6. Retrace our recent exposition of quantity, and of quantities that are parts and measures of quantity. You observe at first sight thay it cannot be *things* that are here spoken of and thus described, but *thoughts*, or modes and powers of thinking. If by a thing be meant a possible object of the senses, a whole, that is of necessity antecedent to its parts. cannot be a thing; it is impossible, for it is the very definition of a sensible whole that it is the sum, limit, and common result of its constituent parts. And therefore in direct contrast with

a *whole* of the former kind, that which precontains its parts. This the student will have suspected from the instances given, [such] as the mind and its thoughts, space and the spaces, as compared with the illustrations and similes, the sea, for instance, and the waves, if what is said were to be understood of the things themselves and not of our thoughts respecting them. If I propose to myself in humble imitation of Archimedes the question of the number of drops in tub of water,[12] it is most certain that the universal or, if I might borrow a more expressive and more English [word] from our sister language the German, the allcommon (*allgemein*) term " water" precedes the given whole, namely the vessel of water, and the vessel, that is the given total quantity, goes before the conception of the drops, and predetermines their number, though physically and matter of fact the vessel may have been put in the rain and the drops have been antecedent to the whole that results from them or which they have made. Do not misconceive me, I do not say that a whole necessarily antecedent to its parts must always be mere thought or *ens logicum*: for such a whole must life be, and every particular life. But I say that it cannot be an object of the senses, and must therefore be a subject, or some act, mode or attribute of a subject, whether it be a subject simply, as life or a subject having its object in itself, that is, the mind, or some determinate act or product of the life or mind.

7. When, therefore, I say that every particular conception of quantity which I attach to particular intuitions pure or experiential presupposes the universal conception "quantity", and this as innate and *a priori*, I can by the latter form have but one meaning, viz. that my mind is so constituted as of necessity to contemplate objects in this particular relation to itself, that as a machine moving in a particular way, predetermined by the construction of the machine itself, describes of itself a particular figure and impresses this on any impressible body that comes under its action, so in the mind itself there is a self-determining predispositions to contemplate objects in certain ways, and as far as they are its objects, to contemplate

these its own acts and products in them.

8. "Well! This", the student may reply," we can understand, and in this sense, as you have yourself informed us, Mr. Locke himself admits the existence of innate conceptions under the name of determinate predispositions of the mind. But with what propriety are they called "conceptions", pure general, *a priori* "conceptions"? Even as in your former expostions of space and time, with what propriety is the power of contemplating objects immediately as objects of sense and the predetermination of that power-or more shortly, with what propriety is the law of the intuitive faculty itself entitled an intuition? If in addition to what has been already urged by me in a former chapter, in which the subject was elucidated by the kaleidoscope, any answer is necessary,I know not how to reply but by the uncourteous way of retorting the question. With what greater propriety can thay be called anything else but pure general conceptions? Nay! in strict propriety and with austere precision what else can they be called? Reflect for a moment, but first permit me to impose on you the trouble of turning back to and attentively reperusing the contents of [Part One Chapter II] a what do we mean by a conception? Can we mean any more than the mind conceiving more or less determinately, more or less singly? I may form a conception of this ruby, or of a ruby, or of precious stones in general. In what other way am I to express these three several acts to which the mind by another simultaneous act of reflection gives unity and fixation? The result thus substantiates, or understood, or having an understanding given to it, becomes the product of the former act: but a single conception, a particular and a general? Or, if I composed the series of more links, I might give to the highest and most comprehensive the name of "universal". Now it is evident that as these characteristic names do not refer to the things in themselves, but wholly to my thoughts and to the way in which I arrange them, the names themselves are variable in their application so far that, when I say, an "universal conception". I mean only that the conception includes all of that space or number which I have

circumscribed or secluded. E.g.: this ruby, a ruby a precious stone, a stone. The latter would here be an universal conception, but if I had chosen to think yet more comprehensively and had added the conception " an oxide", the term" universal " must have been transferred to this, the conception " stone" would have become generic, that of "a precious stone" specific, that of "a ruby" particular, etc. If, then, we are entitled to call a conceiving and its mental porduct,, which neither is nor possibly can be any more than an act self-known, a "conception", what can a mode of conceving mean more than a series of such conceptions? Or what the faculty of conceiving in this particular mode other than a generalised term, an *ens logicum*, expressing at once the sum total of these acts, their particular character, and the mind as the agent? All language originates in reflection, and it is only by means of this reflection, by which we represent the mind as a whole consisting of all its thoughts as its parts, that we can form any conception of mind at all. And if it were true that the human mind was limited to the impresions on the sensibility, to the forms of the sense, to the conceptions generalised from both these as the objects of the understanding, and lastly to the acts of the reflection itself generalised and reflected on, if this were indeed true, our conception of the mind would stop there. The mind could be thought of by us only as a watch, a house, or any other mechanical whole,as the resulting mass of its constituent parts, and in fact more than this could neither be directly demonstrated nor coercively concluded from premises that a man can be made to admit as truths passively known and the knowledge of which it is not in his power to deny mentally or other wise than in words. Such, for instance, are the fundamental principles of geometry, and supposing the integrity of the senses, such are the facts of immediate experience. If I can but once place the object before his eyes, I can but once place the object before his eyes, I can compel the man to know that I have a hand and five fingers and that I hold it up in such and such a direction. His free will is not at all brought into act. Hence, in asserting the existence of a whole antecedent and constitutive of its parts, I not merely assert a something which by no effort of sence or understanding I could have acquired, and of which no logic will enable me legitimately to conclude for the information of another, but in using the terms supplied by the understanding, I incur, or at least border closely on, a contradiction; for I speak of a whole the constituent parts of which are in no moment all present or all existing. But if, sensible of this, I substitute the phrase of "productive unity" as that which gives existence, I venture on a thought which, while it necessarily escapes the notice of the sense, contradicts the first axioms of the understanding, which as imperiously demands the stuff for the form, as the form for the stuff, and in whose creation a chaos necessarily precedes the world. From such contradictions there is but one way of escaping, viz. by assuming, by WILLING to assume, that the truth passeth all understanding, and that a contradiction exists in the heterogeneity of the faculty, not in the object; or rather in the misapplication of the faculty to an object for which it was neither adapted nor intended. It is a Gordian knot which it is incomparably more to our interest to cut than untie, even if the latter were as easy as it is in fact impossible. Above all let it be remembered that to draw strict conclusions from lax and accommodated terms is an outrage on the first principles of ratiocination. But if not *strict*, then no logical conclusions at all. For logic has no degrees. That which is not *strictly* logical is not logical; and how can a thing be at once logical and illogical? And what can be more illogical than to use the same terms in one sense in the premise and in another in the deduction?

9. In that higher department of logic which we are now investigating, we have two objects in view: first, to learn what the understanding in connection with the forms of sense and the affections of the sensibility *can* do; and secondly, and of no less practical importance, what it canitldo.The former we may call the sphere of the understanding; and this alone is the rightful sphere of logic. As *ligicians*, therefore, and even in opposition to our *philosophic* creed, we may take it as the total

sphere of the human mind; and we are induced to treat it as such not only because by thus insulating the subject we may contemplate it more distinctly; but likewise and chiefly because we cannot compel an opponent to admit the contrary by arguments purely speculative or on premises which it is not in his power to deny if it should be his choice. As long as we remain within the circle of a theoretic science—if I may venture on a pleonasm for the sake of additional clearness— we must confine ourselves to that which can be theoretically and scientifically proved, and in the present instance therefore to the understanding, sense, and sensibility. But though we are incompetent to give a scientific proof of any other and higher source of knowledge, it is equally true that no logic requires us to assert the negative, or enables us to disprove that a position which is neither theoretically undeniable nor capable of being logically *concluded* may nevertheless be morally *convincing* or even philosophically evident.

10. There is one thing, however, that logic does peremptorily prescrib—or rather it is a requisition of common sense, the giving effect to which is one main end of the study of logic—namely, that whatever term we use, and whether we assert of deny a reality correspondent thereto, we should use it in some fixed and appropriate sense and consequently that we should predefine it when there is any chance of its being understood in any other sense. For this reason, therefore, and without even starting the question respecting their existence, I hold myself bound to inform the reader what and what alone I mean by "ideas". Those truths, namely supposing such to exist, the knowledge and acknowledgment of which require the whole man, the free will, no less than the intellect, and which are therefore not merely speculative, nor yet merely practical, but both in one, I propose to call "ideas" simply because, of all the other meanings that have been attached to the word, I do not know one which has not already a word of its own more expressive, more appropriate, and far less liable to be mistaken. And it may perhaps be thought an additional recommendation to this proposal that its general adoption would

do away with the half-meanings which seem to have rendered the word "idea" an especial favourite [with many] out of whose vocabulary it might be dropped without their sustaining the least damage or inconvenience.[13]

11. It will be expedient, however, to observe that the ideas are not distinguished from the notions of the senses, the intuitions of the sense, and the conceptions and notions of the understanding by their being referred to another and higher source; for this ideas have in common with all the TRUTHS of REASON. Now though ideas must needs be truths of reason, truths of reason are not all necessarily ideas. There are such that have their source in the speculative (or theoretical) reason alone, and these I have termed principles—principles of reason inseparable connected with the human understanding as a foundation is with its edifice, but yet like the foundation presupposed, and therefore not included in the latter; for what is assumed as the precondition of the understanding must in the order of thought be taken as antecedent to the same, even though there were not another and more obvious ground for referring these principles to the reason, that they are absolutely universal and unconditionally applicable, that is equally valid, whether we apply them to matter or spirit, to beast, man, angel, or Deity. I will add the following remark, not so much for its intrinsic value, though even in this respect it may not be found useless, as that it leads us back at once to our proper subject. If these, as a portion of that light which is to the understanding what the material light is to the eye, and so far therefore extrinsic, be termed principles of reason, there would seem to be no impropriety if the forms belonging to the understanding on which the exercise of its functions is grounded, were called analogously the principles of the understanding, and in like manner if the universal forms of the intuitive faculty were entitled the principles of sense, and should this be thought a more natural or more readily intelligible expression than that of "pure conceptions" and "pure intuitions", there can be no objection to the change capable of outweighing its convenience- provided only that the point be

considered as a question of taste and expediency and by no means a correction required by the nature of the things meant-provided that it does not lead us unaware into the error of supposing a conception to be a something in nature different from conceiving, or conceiving a something different from the mind that so conceives. And now then we return to the scientific and didactic, our subject being henceforward, directly and exclusively, of the human under—standing and its constitution, that is, the elements of transcendental logic, in the strict and most proper sense of the term, and as a positive science.

Footnotes

1 Literally, "as an apparent and as subsisting from the subjecting thing, not as a thing in itself mind."

2. Plato.

3. "Exrcpt the understanding itself." Leibniz *Nouveaux essais* bk II ch 1§ 8 (var). See above, P 134 n 2.

4. "As many things as are *in* the understanding."

5. Cf Kant *Prolegomena* § 20 (1783) 83, and, for what follows, Cf 82-3.

6. "Opposites are always of the same genus. In every opposition a suppositum is given in which (or insofar as which) opposites are one. Thesis = antithesis in some prothesis".

7. Paragraph 3 up to this point is from Kant *Prolegomena* § 20 (1783) 84.

8. An echo of C's favourite example of redundancy—Johnson's *The Vanity of Human Wishes* lines 1-2.See *CL* IV 685 and n.

9. "Homogeneous one and all".

10. "Insolent, because most unusual". C is pointing out that "insolent" (Latin *insolens*) is derived from the negative prefix *in* and *soleo* ("I am accustomed"), so that its original meaning was "what is very unexpected or unusual".

11. "Few minds are suited to absolute abstraction, that is, to directing their attention exclusively to being. But the truth cannot come to us from without, it is within us." The passage is attrib-

uted to Spinoza by Hemsterhuis in an imaginary dialogue; it appears, accompanied by a translation into German, in Jacobi *Ueber die Lehre des Spinoza*...123-4. C has reversed the order of the sentences and moved the "mais" from one to the other accordingly.

12. A reference to Archimedes' testing of Hiero's crown or a confusion of his work on hydraulics with his calculation of the possible number of grains of sand in the universe? Cf *SM (CC)* 51n.

13. Cf C D r V 369-70 (310) and 376 (314).

Chapter-4

Of Transcendental Logic Positively

Chapter 4

1. The understanding is the substantiative power, that by which we give and attribute substance and reality to phenomena and raise them from mere affections and appearances into objects communicable and capable of being anticipated and reasoned of. The way in which the understanding effects this is by judging according to certain principles and forms inherent in its own constitution.

2. The understanding therefore may be defined as the faculty of judging; for it understands only as far as it judges that to such and such appearances there belongs a ground, an hypostasis, or supporting reality.

3. The proper and immediate substance, or hypostasis, is the understanding itself—the three words being indeed the literal rendering each of the other, or the Greek, Latin, and English sounds of the same mental word. We may, therefore, distinguish *power* from *faculty* in the present instance so far as to say that the understanding is the substantiative power. The substantiative power is its essence; or rather the latter is the meaning of the former. But this power again may be considered in relation to its proper characteristic end and object; and in this point of view we may say that the understanding or substantiative power of the mind is likewise, or exercises itself as, the faculty of judging, and namely of judging concerning the substantiality of phenomena in that further sense in which substantiality is the same with objectivity, or correspondency to a real object. Therefore we said that the understanding hath a twofold character. It gives and it attributes substance. The first is its essential act, without which it could not act at all; there would be nothing for it to act on. We mean the same power when we speak of the unity of consciousness. It follows, therefore, that all objects of understanding must be likewise and previously *entia logica,* or logical entities, having their

substance in the understanding itself; but it does not follow that all logical entities are *entia realia*, that is, having a correspondence to realities out of the mind.

4. It has been shown in a preceding chapter[1] that this substantiation consists in the power and necessity of reflecting under the forms of quantity, quality, relation, and (in especial relation to the reflective acts themselves and rather as a syllepsis of the three former) mode or, to speak scholastically, modality.What the understanding cannot conceive responsively to the *quantum*, the *quale*, in what case or relation and in what mode the understanding itself is placed, it cannot conceive at all. Consequently the understanding cannot judge of its own different judgings in any other way of by any other rule. We are now speaking of the mind, not in respect to the *quid est*, or what it is, but to the *quo fungitur*, or what offices does it discharge, in other words, not with regard to its constitutive but its functional powers. And if in this sense it be rightly defined the faculty of judging, our first question must be, "In what way are these judgings characterised?" Are they capable of being distinguished, classed, and specified? And in order to this, it has been shown under the necessity of substantiating the acts of judging into logical entities and to contemplate the act as a product, the judging as a judgment.

5 (a) Dry as this subject is, and as the writer himself feels it to be, it is yet of such extensive application that the student will be well repaid for the trouble of impressing it on his memory, for it lies at the bottom of universal grammar as well as of logic. In order to reflect on any series or collection of similar acts, we convert the verb or participle into a noun; thus, to determine the character of a given continuous act of moving, we represent it under the abstract term "velocity". And even so, any given act of judging must be represented as a particular judgment. And when we affirm anything universally, without exception or confining what we affirm to any part or particular number, the so judging is on the same principles called an universal judgment.

5(b) What we would examine steadily we must first fix-even though, as in the instance of the firefly fixed in the microscope and examined by daylight, we too often destroy the essential quality that had excited the desire of examining it at all.[2] But this makes the difference between logic and philosophy, and the knowledge of the difference is, as we have before had occasion to remark, not the least among the uses of transcendental logic. The student therefore will soon overcome the strangeness of finding the character of objects relatively to the human understanding predicated of the judgments themselves and severally assigned to them as their characteristic names. He will see that this is no figure of speech, no arbitrary pedantry of Scholastic logic, but that from the constitution of the human mind it cannot be otherwise. When a verb has been changed into a noun, it must observe the proprieties and cases of a noun.To continue the metaphor, we must decline the *entia logica* in the present case, the judgments concerning objects, by the same accidents or predicaments as the *entia realia*, or the objects, themselves concerning which we judge. And there will be this further advantage, that the process will serve as a test or proof of our former position; for if it have been truly asserted by us that quantity, quality, relation, and modality are the sum of the constituent forms or most general and innate conceptions of the understanding, we shall be able to class all the possible judgments according to one or the other of these. No sort of judgment or way of judging will be adducible which will not have been found characterised under one or other of these four predicaments as being one or other of the three species comprised under each.

6. N.B. The singular circumstance of this threefold division or trichotomy obtaining throughout the analysis of the mind, and which the founder of the critical philosophy contents himself with noticing as being singular and worthy of notice, and which he supposes himself to have noticed first,[3] may be found in a much earlier writer, our own celebrated Richard Baxter. Any attempt to explain it would be out of its place in the present

disquisition. It is a primary datum of the understanding, the *way in which* we reflect, proved to us by the pure *products* of reflection, as the existence of the *forma formans* must in every case be manifested by and in the *forma formata*, but [is] not to be explained by them.[4] Its purpose is to *account* for the results of reflection, and it would be preposterous to expect that these should account for it. Briefly, in common logic the fact has no interest: in transcendental logic it is a necessary element, but its explanation belongs to neither, as transcending the faculty of which the one gives the results and the other the analysis.

7 Here the student may expediently halt for a moment and, before he proceeds to the analysis of the understanding in the detail of its constituent members, collect and bring to his distinct consciousness a few positions from preceding chapters that may assist in warding off any confusion or misconception of the terms adopted in that which is to follow.

[Memento I]

8. First, words, that in their proper and primary sense express relations of space, are likewise used sometimes *for* and sometimes inclusive of the relations of time. The language of *sight* is transferred to the affections and object of the other senses, and of the inward *experience*. (See Aesthetic Chapter *ad finem.*)[5] In disciplining his mind one of the first rules should be to lose no opportunity of tracing words to their origin, one good consequence of which will be that he will be able to use the *language* of sight without being enslaved by its affections. He will at least secure himself from the delusive notion that what is not *imageable* is likewise not *conceivable.* To emancipate the mind from the despotism of the eye is the first step towards its emancipation from the influences and intrusions of the senses, sensations, and passions generally. Thus most effectually is the power of abstraction to be called forth, strengthened, and familiarised, and it is this power [of] abstraction that chiefly distinguishes the human understanding

from that of the higher animals, and in the different degrees in which this power is developed the superiority of man over man mainly consists. Hence we are to account for the preference which the divine Plato gives to expressions taken from the objects of the ear, as terms of music and harmony, and in part at least for the numerical symbols in which Pythagoras clothed his philosophy.[6]

9. On this principle I do not object to the extension of the term "image" (or "idea" in Hume's usage) from the *re*-presentations of the sight to the analogous relicts of the other senses-and if other reasons had not induced me to reject the *Humian* terminology of "impressions" and "ideas", the same concession would have been made to the phrase "auditual and tactual *ideas*"—a phrase, the use of which by one of our greatest living philosophers, then in the early morning of his manhood, and his fame only beginning to dawn did, as I well remember, give occasion of surprise and scandal to a veteran metaphysician in my presence.[7]

10. (a) I will conclude this first Memento by the following extract from the Latin dissertation delivered by Immanuel Kant, 20th August, 1770, on taking his degree as professor ordinarius of logic and metaphysic, the (afterwards justly celebrated) physician and physiologist Marcus Hertz,[8] the friend and townsman of Moses Mendelssohn, being the respondent; and I cannot too earnestly recommend the student by careful and repeated perusal to impress the contents both on his memory and his understanding.[9]

10. (b) "Hinc patet, qui fiat, ut *cum* irrepraesentabile et *impossibile* vulgo ejusdem significatus habeantur,conceptus tam *Continui*, quam *Infiniti*, a plurimis rejiciantur, quippe quorum, *secundum leges cognitionis intuitivae*, repraesentatio est impossibilis. Quanquam autem harum e non paucis scholis explosarum notionum, praesertim prioris, caussam hic non gero, maximi tamen momenti erit monuisse: gravissimo illos errore labi, qui tam perversa argumentandi ratione utuntur. Quicquid enim *repugnat* legibus intellectus et rationis [,utique est

impossibile; quod autem, cum rationis][10] purae sit objectum, legibus cognitionis intuitivae tantummodo non subest, non item. Nam hic dissensus inter facultatem *sensitivam et intellectualem* [...] nihil indigitat, nisi, *quas mens ab intellectu acceptas fert ideas abstractas, illas in concreto exsequi et in Intuitus commutare saepenumero non posse.* Haec autem reluctantia *subjectiva* mentitur, ut plurimum, repugnantiam aliquam objectivam, et incautos facile fallit, limitibus, quibus mens humana circumscribitur, pro iis habitis, quibus ipsa rerum essentia continetur."

Memento II

11 "Image" involves the existence of a correspondent. Hence, though I should not object to the word in the same extension in which Mr. Hume and his followers use "ideas", as opposed to (or at least distinguished from) "impressions", I would not ordinarily employ it to express the *pure* constructions of the intuitive faculty, that is, the immediate products of its productive acts. I would say, the image of a thing, but not (except for illustration, *et* PER REGULAM *falsi*[11] as it were) the image as the thing. If there be felt an uncouthness, which the student finds it difficult to overcome, in the use of the plural term, "intuitions", for the mathematical concretes (e.g. the figures of pure geometry) I should prefer "theoremes" (θεωρημα, *contemplamen*), and in this sense the word actually occurs in one of the noblest passages of Plotinus,[12] or "forms", or even "sensuous ideas", to "images".

Memento III

12. We commenced by adopting the old division of knowledge into the theoretic, or intellective, and the practical, or that which respects the acts of the will, the judgments of conscience, the rules of conduct, and the laws of the practical reason; and it was settled that, as far as the present enquiry was concerned, our attention was to be given exclusively to the former, that is, the theoretic.

13. It was next determined that we should confine our inquisition to the data presented to us by *reflection*, and as they appear to us in the act of reflecting; or to the immediate inferences from these made necessary by the laws of reflection. What these laws are is a subject for future enquiry, but be they what they may, it is easy to imagine some superior being capable of contemplating at once an individual mind and its objects, of judging how far and in what manner the objects are modified for the human mind by its own mechanism, and lastly of looking at the objects independent of such modification. Now he who disclaims all pretensions to any prerogative of this kind, or who, though believing that a *substitute* or a something *analogous* to it subsists even for the human intelligence, nevertheless *abstracts* (that is, voluntarily withdraws his attention) from it and agrees to reason as though no such power existed, is said to *stand on the point of reflection*. And here we agreed to take our position, that is, to take things as they appeared from the point of reflection, and to assume nothing that by sense and reflection, alone we could not have discovered to exist. And as every disjunctive position is more readily recollected and acquires the semblance at least of additional clearness when a distinct name is assigned to that from which it is disjoined, we contradistinguish the point on which we do *not* stand from the point on which we do stand by designating the former as the "ideal point" and the latter as the "point of reflection".

Memento IV

14. Our next step was that of abstracting from all objects existing out of the mind—and these *collectively* we entitled the "objective"; and this is the primary sense of the word as *technically* used. What remained, and to which alone our attention was to be given, we consented to call the "subject", or the "subjective" collectively.

Memento V

15(a) Yet not all that might be comprised under this head did we propose to comprehend in our specific enquiry. In the subject itself we abstracted from the *affections* of the sensibility, and the passive impressions on the senses, and agreed to regard the sensibility (in this *restricted* sense and the self-active power of sentiency *not* included) as the common boundary, or neutral ground, of the objective and subjective. What remained after this last abstraction we found to be the powers of perceiving and conceiving, the faculty of contemplating *in concreto*, and that of *thinking* generally or *in abstracto*. I contemplate the essential properties of the triangle; I think of the Divine Attribute. The first we named THE SENSE or "intuitive" power, the second THE UNDERSTANDING or "reflective"faculty. The knowledges possessed by the understanding, whether derived from the sense (that is, grounded on "intuitions") or acquired by reflection on its own acts and processes, these and these only are the admissible data of our intended disquisition and form the subject matter of logic.

15(b) But we were made aware that among the data of reflection there were a few the peculiar character of which suggested, even if it did [not] necessitate, the assumption of a higher origin than either of the two faculties, taken with the abstractions above noticed; and that in point of fact the understanding in all its acts does *presume* them, as the indispensable conditions of its own existence as well as of its exercise of each particular function. These, therefore, as having the distinctive character of absolute universality and unconditional necessity (that is, not merely necessary in relation to the human sense and understanding), we named "principles" and (yet *without deserting the point of reflection*) "principles *of reason*". For they are *data* of the understanding, made known to us in and by reflection, though there may be ground for considering [them] as the offspring of a higher source, which for distinction's sake we named "the reason". Of these principles we found no more than two, entitled the "principles of identity and incompatibility"; and in thus admitting them as principles of reason, we were made distinctly [to] understand that as *logicians* and from the point on which, as such, we had placed ourselves, we meant no more by "reason itself"; then the source of absolute principles,as inferred from the fact of their existence.

16. P.S. The knowledge thus obtained by the understanding we entitled "discursive", in distinction from the "intuitive" knowledge given by the sense; the understanding itself being named by elder logicians the "discursive" faculty, and, as far as its processes are grounded on the principles above mentioned, by our great dramatic poet "discourse of reason".[13]

Memento VI

17. Having thus separated the sense from the sensibility, and the subjective, now comprising the sense and the understanding, from the objective, and further the sense, as the source of *intuitive* knowledge, from the understanding, as the source of *discursive* knowledge, we took the latter as the especial subject of the science we had chosen for our present study. The temple of Truth has two main portals, the first and more magnificent being the science of intuition, or MATHEMATICS, the other and narrower but not less necessary, the science of discourse and the discursive faculty, or LOGIC.

Memento VII

18(a). The very title of our science leads us naturally to the two parts into which it is subdivided: viz. first, the necessary *forms* and connections of all legitimate discourse and the *rules* generalised from the same, resulting indeed from the constitution of the discursive faculty itself, but evident of themselves and therefore capable of being given independently of the knowledge of the latter; and secondly, the analysis of the understanding in order to a knowledge of its constitution.

Which, however,could not have been effected or made intelligible without a previous analysis of the sense: both conjunctively taken forming the science of *transcendental* analysis, so called from the character of its aim and object, which is to rise from the *knowledge or matter* of consciousness to the *faculty* by which it is known or presented.

18(b). The former of these two main divisions we passed through under the name of the "common" or "syllogistic logic", or the "logical canon";and of the latter, first introduced as the pure "logical criterion", and then more definitely named the "science of transcendental analysis" comprised under two heads, "transcendental aesthetic", or the analysis of the pure sense, or *faculty* of intuition, and "transcendental logic", or the analysis of the understanding, or discursive faculty. We have completed the first head (namely the aesthetic) and prepared for the accomplishment of the remainder by a large declaration of the historical origin and true nature of the question, an exact exposition of the terms to be employed in its solution, and by such other notices and reminiscences as seemed calculated to facilitate our progress either directly and, as it were, *propulsively*, or indirectly, by the removal of possible obstacles, misconceptions—for instance, the errors of prejudice and the mistakes of inadvertence.

18(c). There remains then but one additional Memento, if it may be so named; it being in part only retrospective and in part preliminary—but equally with the seven preceding belonging to the purpose of this review of our past labours, as being preparative for the work immediately before us.

Memento VIII

19. Hitherto the understanding (see Memento V) has been only negatively defined by its distinction from the sense. It is a faculty of knowledge that is not sensuous. (N.B. As we took the sense abstractedly from the sensibility, so in order to distinguish the adjective corresponding to the two terms we adopted the unusual but highly sanctioned word "sensuous"

for the former and appropriated to the latter more common word, namely, "sensual", though without any mixture of the moral meaning ordinarily connected with it.[14] We should use the word, if we used it at all, as expressive of the *kind* and not of any excess or *blamable degree*, though even in *kind* we have generally included it in the wider term of "empirical", having at the commencement—*vide* Memento v-abstracted from the sensibility, and put the sensual relatively to our science on the same ground with the outward objective.)

20. The understanding is an unsensuous faculty of knowing, or whereby knowledge is acquirable. Now independently of the sense we can have no intuition or intuitive knowledge. Consequently the understanding is not a faculty of intuition; its knowledge is not intuitive, not sensuously presentable or constructed *in concreto*. In plain English, we do not perceive by means of the understanding. But besides perceptions (that is, intuitions pure or mixed) there exists no other way of knowing, or sort of knowledge, but by means of conceptions. Therefore the knowledge of every understanding that is the same with the human is a knowledge by means of conceptions, not *intuitive* but *discursive*[15] (*vide* Memento VI). "In varios docto discurritur ordine gyros".(Claudian.)[16] Our perceptions as far as they are sensual are grounded on the affections of the sensibility; as far as they are the pure and immediate products of the intuitive faculty, in which sense we, for distinction's sake, have most commonly called them "intuitions", they are grounded on the productivity or productive acts of the sense. It will be expedient therefore to carry on the same purpose of distinct terminology by grounding the conceptions on the functions of the understanding. This latter term is a word in common usage, and we must all, therefore, have some conception of what is meant by it, more or less precise, more or less in our power to communicate. This, however, will not suffice for the exact analyst. He must ascertain the full, distinct, and proper meaning of the word, and then determine whether it apply in the instance before him and this, too, adequately, so far at least as to justify its selection as the best and most

applicable word.

21(a). We have already had occasion to distinguish the unity of totality, the oneness which we connect with the conception of a whole—of a watch, for instance—and which we may denominate the consequent or resulting unity, from the productive or producible unity—that of the proper germ, or *heart*, or plantule of a seed, apart from its lobes, eye, and coat, as the ground and productive principle of the future whole, and which we may call the "antecedent" unity. (Not forgetting, however, that the antecedence here spoken of is a priority in order of thought, and [not] necessarily a priority in time, and that as a memento of this we have recommended the occasional substitution of the phrase, *ab intra or ab intimo*[17] *for* that of *a priori*.)

21(b). This twofold unity is comprised in the definition of the term "constitution", *Constitutio fit ubicunque unum e pluribus* (= *unitas* CONSEQUENS) *et plura in uno sunt* (= *unitas antecedens*).[18] And the relation of the latter to the former [is described] in the some-what unpoetic line of a philosophic poem accidentally lying open before me,

-the constitutive one
present to all that doth make all one whole.[19]

We have only to add that, as the result or consequent is necessarily a harmony of differences, the antecedent must be a unity of differential powers; for though an effect is not always an adequate or exhaustive measure of the cause, yet whatever exists in the result as an effect or product must have been contained in the antecedent as an attribute or productive power. And this is what the Scholastic logicians meant by "*existing eminently*", *Quicquid existit in consequenti realiter, vel manifeste, existit in suo antecedente eminenter*.[20] Nor does a plurality of interdistinguishable attributes in the antecedent interfere with the conception of its unity. Far rather it is requisite to its being conceived; for without distinction conception cannot exist, and in this consists the important difference of positive unity or oneness from indistinguishable unicity or negative sameness.

22(a). Having thus removed, we trust, all ambiguity from the two extreme terms, we shall pursue the attempt with the word in question as an intermediate between both and then illustrate the whole by an example, premising only, what must indeed be evident on the first serious reflection, that every such attribute, considered as a differential force, must of necessity be contemplated as an unity. Else it would not be the attribute of an antecedent one but a factor or component part of a consequent whole.Hence as it is a distinct unity manifesting a *difference*, so must it be a reduction of differences to a distinct and several unity, or, to use the technical and more precise term already explained, it is that by which any number of *differents* are at once *differenced* and subsumed under a several unity. Now this is a FUNCTION.[21] And the function of a power is the unity of any given class or series of its actions by which a difference is manifested and communicated. And observe that this unity, though we could not have conceived it but by the aid of abstraction, is, however, not to be conceived as being itself a mere generalisation or expression of coexistence; for this would be in effect to fall into the delusion exposed ([?σοφισμα]) and convert actions into things separate from the agent or supposed to constitute the agent as the result of their composition.

22(b). On the other hand, however, a different error lies in our way against which it is no less important that we should be on our guard—an error sufficiently glaring, indeed, when it has been once detected and presented in its nakedness, but which under various disguises and by means of indistinct and fluctuating conceptions has imposed on doctors of no small celebrity and lies at the bottom of more than one theory, physiological and medical as well as psychological and metaphysical. I allude to the confusion between distinct inherence and dividuous or separate subsistency and to the consequent treatment of the attributes and faculties of a mind as if they were so many several minds in miniature. In like manner with respect to the understanding itself and its co-ordinate faculty of sense, metaphysical writers have too often expressed themselves as if they were speaking of so many different *persons*, the *homunculi* as it were, of which the integral man was composed, and thus seem to renew the whimsy of the old homoeomerists, according to whom the heart was an architectural structure of little hearts.[22] But still more obviously does this confusion remind us of the craniological theory, at all events of a very frequent misconception of the same, in which the various convolutes of the brain not only act the part of so many several brains, but of so many several and altogether different souls actuating and as it were playing upon them—the total brain representing the orchestra in which some thirty and odd musicians are seated each in his own stall and at his own several instrument.[23]

23. There are many things not necessary and yet not superfluous, and in this list we may place the repetition of the same caution in proportion to the frequency with which the error guarded against is likely to occur. On this account we are not unwilling to be again reminded that, as men or as philosophers, we do not speak even of the understanding itself; no,nor even of the mind including both sense and understanding, as of the man or personal being; but as an attribute of each individual person common to him and to all other men, as far as they are *men*, that is, possess the characteristics of *human* nature. Only as our particular science had for its exclusive object the mind abstractedly (*vide* above, pp 110-11 and we are therefore understood to speak as *logicians* merely, for *us*, I say, and as long as we are understood to be using a *technical* language, the *mind* is the vicegerent and representative of the man or of the soul. And we personify the mind without incurring or occasioning delusion. Thus in the administration of justice, the ultimate power and *real substantive* is supposed to be the king, and the court is the representative of the royal person; yet we speak of the court itself as of a person and assign to it all the forms, acts, and attributes of personality. And observe, this is no mere generalisation (or, as the grammarians say, a

noun of multitude); the court is a real personal power, and that power a real unity. And we have only to contemplate a court exercising at different times several different sorts and forms of judicial law, and we shall have the example or illustration that our subject requires. We have seen that it is a true personal power and likewise a true unity; but not a true personal or individual unity. What then is this unity? We reply that it is the unity of the action by which the representative of a more comprehensive or manifold power exercises a given portion of that power, or that power in a given direction and determination, and in this unity of action corresponds to the personal unity from which its personal power is derived and of which it is consequently the representative. Now this is a "function", and the algebraic use of the term is substantially the same with that here given. First a variable undeterminate quantity is assumed = X. With these, other quantities having determinate and invariable values are joined, and the expressions that result from such conjunction are called "functions" of X. Now a function comprehending several functions whether in *co*-ordination or *sub*ordination may be distinguished from the ultimate power and personal unity whose function it is by the name of "functionary", and this may be allowably done whether the manifold function be placed in a single individual, as in the instance of the Lord Chancellor, or in many persons, as the House of Lords or the Board of Admiralty, or lastly, by the law of reflection which we have elsewhere called "substantiation", in a personal power or faculty. Thus if it were my intention to carry the analysis no farther I should say that the sense and the understanding were functions of the soul; but, if I meant to enter into the analysis of the understanding into its component powers, then, to avoid confusion and in obedience to the old adage, "qui bene distinguit, bene docet",[24] I might find it expedient to designate the component powers, alone as functions and to impersonate the understanding itself as the functionary. It is a matter of indifference as long as we are aware that it is a matter of words, decided wholly and exclusively by considerations of convenience. But above all as long as we see and understand that the *function* is *the unity of the action*, whether we are thinking of the functions of the Lord Chancellor or of the Court of Chancery, in both alike we abstract from personal individuality. But though the function be the unity of the action only, yet it is an antecedent and not a resulting unity (*unitas collectiva*), an active and communicating, not [a] passive or received. Therefore it was said that though we arrived at the thought by aid of abstraction it was still something more than a mere abstract, and, if we may call in the aid of analogy and of the sense, in the attempt to master and fix this conception, only substituting the spontaneous for the mechanical, we might refer to the movements which without much impropriety we might consider as the functions of Brewster's kaleidoscope, or Mr.Asa Spencer's geometrical lathe, by which an endless variety of beautiful patterns is successively produced, transferred, and retransferred.[25] For here too [there is] a unity of the act, and this real, antecedent, and operative.

24(a). We may now, with increased confidence in the intelligibility of our words, repeat that images are grounded on affections of the sensibility; pure intuitions on the productive self-representing energies of the sense; and the conceptions on the functions of the understanding. Again, the acts of the will and of the reason, when we speak of the reason not as a presence only but as an agency (though perhaps it would be better to say the acts of the man), are characterised as voluntary, the functions of the understanding as spontaneous. Our conceptions therefore originate in the spontaneity of the thinking or conceiving faculty, and now what use does or can the understanding make of these its conceptions? A moment's reflection convinces us that it neither does nor can make any other use of them but that of judging thereby. And as no representation refers otherwise than mediately to the object and immediately to the intuition or affection, it follows *a fortiori* that a conception never refers immediately to an object but to some other representation of the same which may be either image or perhaps some previous conception. This, then, being understood, we can be at no loss in defining a judgment of the understanding.A judgment is the *mediate* knowledge of a thing and consequently the representation of a representation of that thing.

24(b). In every judgment there is a conception that is common to, that is, equally predicable of, a number of things, and this number comprehends likewise a certain given representation which latter is then referred immediately to the object in point. A single example will suffice to give the meaning of these words. I judge that all bodies are partible, and in this judgment, "All bodies are partible", the conception of partibility, or that which can be divided into parts, is applicable to several other conceptions,but out of these it is here especially referred to the conception of "body", and this conception again to certain appearances and affections which have occurred to us. These which are the ultimate immediate objects of our consciousness are represented or mediately presented by the conception of partibility. All judgments are therefore functions of unity in our representations or official acts by which a unity is effected among our representations, inasmuch as that instead of an immediate representation, and of course therefore a representation *in concreto*, a higher one comprising (or, in logical language, comprehending under it) these and others is employed in order to the knowledge of the object, whereby several possible knowledge (cognitions) are contracted into one. But all acts of the understanding subsequent to the operation essential to and one with the faculty itself and implied in the term "understanding", subsequent to that, namely, for which we have appropriated the term "substantiation" (*seu actio hypostatica*),[26] are reducible to judgments. And the understanding therefore or substantiative power may be adequately defined as the faculty of judging; for it is a faculty of thinking or of discursive thought and thus a knowledge by means of conceptions; and conceptions as predicates of possible judgments refer to some representation or other of some object not yet determined. Thus the conception of "body" refers to something that by means of this conception can be known and judged of—to metal, for instance. But it is a conception only inasmuch as several other representations are comprehended under it by means of which representations it can be referred to existing objects. Did it not contain such representations under it, it would not be a conception, but a form, image, or feeling. The conception "body" therefore is the predicate of a possible judgment, for instance, "every metal is a body". Previously therefore to the consideration of the functions of the understanding relatively to its objects and purposes, it will be advisable to consider the judgments in their own character and relatively to the faculty or as far as the understanding itself is alone concerned.[27] It may well happen that the attainment of the one may discover, if not make a road to, the attainment of the other; and that from the forms more strictly subjective we may find the means of deducing the laws on the subject by which objectivity is judicially given and attributd. In other words, the laws under which alone objects are representable as *objects*.

25 Here then we end our retrospect and recommence our progress. We will first enumerate these judgments in a tabular form and annex the few explanations that may appear necessary or expedient.[28]

The judgments are characterised according to

1
Quantity
Universal
Particular
Single

2
Quality
Affirmative
Negative
Limitless

3
Relation
Categorical
Hypothetical
Disjunctive

4
Modality
Problematic
Assertional
Apodictic

Remarks

26. One use of this table is that it gives us an opportunity of pointing out certain differences between common logic, or the canons of the understanding, and the transcendental logic, or the analysis of the faculty itself.

27. First. In common logic, which enquires into the use of the different judgments in connection with each other, the judgments according to quantity are divided into two, the universal, or what we affirm of all in common, being the same with the single. It is indifferent whether I speak of a subject as having no particulars included, an atom, for instance, or of all without occasion to particularise any of its parts either by exception or by attributing to one more than to another-as "the ocean" or "the world". It is indifferent as to the use, and of course as to the rules concerning the use of such judgments, whether I think of a thing, *or all,* as *one*. But if I am to speak of the judgment itself in each case in its own nature, in respect, namely, to its own quantity, it would be strange indeed to assert that I form the same judgment where I affirm of a number that it is one and of another that it is infinite. The rule in common logic depends on the principle that the one, or the single point, can have no circumference because it has no extension, while the infinite quantity can have no circumference inasmuch as it has no boundary. Hence the dictum *de judiciis singularibus* and *communibus eadem est ratio.*[29]

28. Secondly. In like manner, respecting the quality, the third species (though limitless) has no place in common logic, which knows only of affirmative and negative, the limitless being comprehended in the former. The reason may be easily understood. In common logic we abstract wholly from the matter or purport of the predicate which may perhaps be negative and consider only whether it be attributed to the subject or opposed to it, or denied with regard to it. But the analyst or transcendental logician contemplates the judgment likewise with respect to the value or purport of this logical affirmation by means of a really negative predicate, and thus, if possible,

to determine what advantage is obtained thereby with regard to out knowledge of the subject in general. An example will make this plain. "The soul is not mortal." Here a negative predicate is attributed affirmatively, and by means of this negative I have at least prevented an error; but still I have said no more than this—of the whole extent of possible beings, the mortal forms one division, and the not-mortal another, with the addition that the soul is one of that infinite number of things that remain after I have subtracted all that is mortal. The boundless sphere of the possible is so far therefore decreased that I have excluded from it one portion, the mortal. The remainder, however, still remains boundless, and many other portions might be supposed excluded without the least positive access to my knowledge of the soul or what it positively is, and without my judgment being in itself actually affirmative as well as *formally*.[30]

29. Compare with this the position, "the radius of a given circle is curveless". Here the predicate, though as in the former instance negative, is actually affirmative. I acquire a definite and positive knowledge of the line, viz. that it is straight. But in common logic, which respects only the forms of discourse, the two judgments fall under the same character, both are formally affirmative or affirmed of the subject, and with other than formal affirmation the common or formal logic has no concern; but in reference to the judgments themselves and the knowledge derived or derivable therefrom, that is, in transcendental logic, I need not say that it is far otherwise.

30. Thirdly. All relations of the though in our judgments are: A. The relation of the predicate to the subject. B. The relation of the antecedent to the consequent. And C. That of the division (or distribution) of the contents, and the numbers of the division or distribution to each other. In the first (A) there are two *conceptions*; in the second (B) two *judgments*; in the third (C) *several* judgments are contemplated relatively to each other. "The moral government of the world is marked by perfect justice." This is called a categorical relation, or a

relation categorically stated. "If a perfect justice obtain in the government of the world the impenitently and perseveringly wicked do not escape punishment." This is an hypothetical judgment or position, and as the former contained two *conceptions* in relation to each other, so the latter contains two *judgments* in similar relation, viz. "There exists a perfect justice", and secondly, "the perseveringly wicked are punished". Whether both or either of the positions are true, severally considered, remains undetermined. It is the *consequence* only which is thought of at the moment that we form this judgment.[31]

31. N.B. It is called hypothetical or suppositive (*not* in the popular use, as when we say, of a report, it is only a *supposition*; but) in reference to the primary sense of the word, namely, to put one thing under another, as its ground or basement. Hence this, being the relation of *the antecedent* to the *consequent*, or of *the ground* to that which it is made to support, is named hypothetical—from υπο, "under", and θεσιζ, "position".

32. Of the third species called the disjunctive judgment, the following is and instance: "The world exists either by blind chance, or by necessity in itself, or by a cause out of itself".[32]

33. In this judgment the number of the positions placed in relation to each other is indifferent. There may be two or three or several; but we may still more clearly distinguish it from the second and preceding judgment by the difference in the relation itself, which is not that of consequence to ground but in the first place that of exclusive opposition inasmuch as the one position excludes the other. But in the second place, and when all the positions are taken conjointly as a single judgment in the relation of community—a phrase which I have tried in vain to exchange for a more expressive one—it means, however, that the several positions taken collectively fill the whole sphere of our knowledge on the given point, inasmuch as the sphere of each part is a complement of the sphere of the other. But how, it may be asked, can the same positions be at the same time exclusive each of the other and yet supplemental each of the other? We reply that the first, that

is, the character of reciprocal exclusion, holds good in reference to the positive knowledge and the thing itself: thus chance excludes the position of an inward necessity, and an inward necessity that of an external cause. But the same positions are supplemental of each other in reference to the mind and to the possible knowledge or the sphere of possibility. All the knowledge I can acquire is contained within a determinate sphere consisting of three or more spheres. In which of the three it lies is not determined, but that in some one it does exist, and consequently my judgment would be defective if I had omitted either, though at the same time I understand that the knowledge can lie in one only, to the exclusion of the other.[33]

34(a). This third species is not properly a part of syllogistic logic, though it may at first sight appear to constitute a syllogism in exception or even opposition to the canon which in the first section of this work is laid down as universal—that of clusion, inclusion, and conclusion. Major."The world exists either by chance or inward necessity." [Conclusion.] "Therefore it exists by an outward cause." In this syllogism the minor is evidently an act of exclusion, and the consequence, instead of being concluded with the major, asserts an absolute identification with a part only of the major. But in fact the reasoning here is not properly logical, that is, discursive and consequently syllogical or syllogistic; as far as it is logical it is a repetition of single positions affirmative or negative; but as far as the consequence and connection of the positions are concerned, it is purely intuitive and mathematical.

34(b). Take two from three, and one remains. Nevertheless, the disjunctive judgment itself is formed discursively, hath its origin in the understanding, and belongs, therefore, to the analysis of the understanding, that is, transcendental logic, though it does not form the ground of any reasoning purely and exclusively logical. And herein we discover an important distinction between the common and transcendental logic: that the former abstracts from all materials of knowledge and considers the form only. The contents or real import it receives or is supposed to have received from other sources previously.[34] In other words, the common logic employs itself on conceptions already formed and concerns itself with them only as conceptions without reference either to the products of the sense or the affections of the sensibility out of which they were formed. On the other hand, the transcendental logic contemplates the formations of the conceptions and is enabled so to do by including the transcendental aesthetic, and hence, though equally with the common logic it abstracts from mixed intuitions and the affections of the sensibility; yet the pure intuitions and the intuitive constructions lie before it and within its sphere, and from these it is enabled to derive a proper and actual import and substance for its conceptions; and consequently is concerned with judgments that are not merely formal.

35 (a) Fourthly and lastly we are to speak of the modal judgments or judgments expressive of the mode of thinking. A species already by Aristotle accurately mentioned and distinguished[35] and only too prolixly treated of by all his commentators. The mode, say they, refers neither to the subject nor to the predicate, nor to the copula between both, but to the understanding itself; or the mode may be defined as that which expresses the value of the copula in reference to the way of thinking, or the way in which we think it. The judgments in the sentence above given, "The world exists, etc", are problematic, problematically stated. "The girdle of trees below the snowy region of Etna consists chiefly of oak".[36] this is an assertory judgment. "All the angles of every triangle are equal to two right angles": this is an apodictic or necessary judgment. The difference between this and the preceding is evident, but yet does not at all concern the use made of them in common logic; the apodictic being treated in the same manner as the assertory and consequently holding no place in its catalogue.[37]

35(b). When these remarks have been thoroughly considered, the student will do well to revise[38] the table of the judgments and experimentally to convince himself that in it all the functions of his understanding are contained-in other words, that he can form no judgment which, taken in and for itself abstractedly from the matter judged of, or the matter of the judgment characterised either by its quantity, its quality, or relation, or mode, which is not in respect to the first either universal, or particular, or single; in respect to the second, either affirmative, or negative, or interminable; in respect to the third, either categorical, or hypothetic, or disjunctive; and in respect to the last, either problematic, assertory, or apodictic. We may then proceed to the forms of the understanding in relation to the object as far as these forms pre-exist in the mind itself as the conditions under which alone phenomena can *become* objects of the understanding. We suppose the student to know that the accusative case is the same with, and in many grammars called, the "objective", and in one of the oldest, the "predicamental", and that the Greek words answering to predicamental or object predicamental and objective are κατηγορια and κατηγορικοζ, that is, "category" and "categorical". And lastly, that this word as expressing the fundamental conceptions of the understanding was introduced by Aristotle, and has been continued by all logicians from the time of that great father and founder of logic to the present day, and the differences, important as they are, between the views of the Peripatetic logic and ours do not necessitate and therefore do not appear to me to warrant a change in the name.

Footnotes

1. There is no such previous discussion; C seems to be referring to the material that appears later, on pp 254ff, especially the table on p 256. Cf *Cdr* V 95 (106-7).

2. Cf WW's "we murder to dissect", in *The Tables Turned* line 28: *WPW* IV 57.

3. Kant does not claim to have noticed it first. For his mentions of trichotomy see C d r V 110 (116) and *Critik der Urtheilskraft* Einleitung $ ix n.

4. Cf above p 232 nn 2,3.

5. The reference has been left incomplete, but it could well be to the material that begins on p 71 line 4.

6. Cf BM MS Egerton 2801 f 121 for C's sympathetic view of Pythagoras' "numerical symbols". Cf *CN* III 4436: " The more I reflect, the more important do both the Pythagorean or arithmetical, and the Platonic or harmonical Schemes of Nature present themselves to my mind."

7. Story untraced. Could the philosopher have been Davy and the metaphysician Beddoes? C himself used the phrase "visible & tangible Ideas" in a letter to Josiah Wedgwood in Feb 1801: *CL* II 699.

8. Marcus Herz (1747-1803), Kant's friend and correspondent. Author of *Betrachtungen aus der spekulativen Weltweisheit* (Königsberg 1771) and other works.

9. De *mundi sensibilis*§ 1: *VS* II 439-40. "hence it is clear, from what cause many reject the notion of the continuous and the infinite.They take, namely, the words irrepresentable and impossible in one and the same meaning; and, according to the forms of sensuous evidence, the notion of the continuous and the infinite is doubtless impossible. I am not now pleading the cause of these laws, which not a few schools have thought proper to explode, especially the former (the law of continuity). But it is of the highest importance to admonish the reader, that those, who adopt so perverted a mode of reasoning, are under a grievous error. Whatever opposes the formal principles of the understanding and the reason is confessedly impossible; but not therefore that, which is therefore not amenable to the forms of *sensuous* evidence, because it is exclusively an object of pure intellect. For this noncoincidence of the sensuous and the intellectual (the nature of which I shall presently lay open)proves nothing more, but that the mind cannot always adequately represent in the concrete, and transform into distinct images, abstract notions derived from the pure intellect.But this contradiction, which is in itself merely subjective (i.e. an incapacity in the nature of man), too often passes for an incongruity or impossibility in the object (i.e. the notions themselves), and seduces the incautious to mistake the limitations of the human faculties for the limits of things, as they really exist." C's tr in BL ch 12 (1907) I 190n, where he quotes the same passage. In

Apr 1818 he recommended the essay to a Mr Pryce (*CL* IV 851). Part of the same passage is quoted in BM MS Egerton 2801 f 159.

10. The missing passage is probably an example of the transcriber's eye slipping from "rationis" to "rationis". The underlining follows *BL* closely.
11. "And by way of controlling error".
12. *Ennead* 3.8.4. Cf above, p 74 and n 1.
13. Shakespeare *Hamlet* I ii 150. Cf *SM* (*CC*) 69.
14. Cf the distinction made in *BL* ch 10 (1907) I 109.
15. Paragraph 20 up to this point is from *C d r V* 92-3 (105).
16. Claudian *Panegyricus de sexto consulatu Honorii Augusti* line 633. Tr Maurice Platnaure (LCL 1922) II 121: "wheeling and counter-wheeling with ordered skill". More literally: "there is a running about in various circles in disciplined ranks"—C linking "discursive" with *discurritur*.
17. "From the innermost part".
18. "A constitution arises whenver one [is formed] from many(= *consequent* unity) and whenever many are in one(= antecedent unity)."
19. *Religious Musings* lines 130-1 (var): *PW* (EHC) I 114. Comparison with the original is instructive: "But 'tis God/ Diffused through all, that doth make all one whole...".
20. "Whatever exists in the consequent, really of apparently, exists eminently in its antecedent."
21. Cf Kant's definition: *C d r V* 93 (105).
22. Stanley e.g. discusses Anaxagoras and his "homoiomora" p 63. See also Tennemann I 308-11.
23. Public interest in craniological theories was revived by George Combe (1788-1858) in his *Elements of Phrenology* (1824). The 2nd ed was attacked by Francis jeffrey in *Ed* Rev Sept 1825 and the controversy was joined by Sir William Hamilton in addresses to the Royal Society of Edinburgh in 1826 and 1827.
24. Source untraced. C uses it in *CN* III 4058 and 4418. "He who distinguishes well teaches well" Said to be a Scholastic maxim.

25. For Brewster's kaleidoscope, see above, p 163 and n 1. The geometric lathe was an automatic engraving machine, one of a number of devices designed to put a stop to the counterfeiting of banknotes. The lathe and its development are described by its inventor in "Vindication of Claims to Certain Inventions and Improvements in the Graphic Art" The *American Journal of Science and Arts* XLIV (1843) Appendix to No.1 (between 216-17 in some copies) 1-12. Spencer states that the machine was known in London in 1820 (11).

26. "Or under-standing action". See above, p 239.

27. Paragraph 24(b) and the final sentence of paragraph 24(a) are from *C d r V* 93-4 (105-6).

28. The following table is from *C d r V* 95 (107). Cf *Prolegomena* § 21 (1783) 86.

29. "For singular and general judgments the reasoning is the same". Paragraph 27 is based on *C d r V* 96 (107).

30. Paragraph 28 is based on *C d r V* 97-8 (108).

31. Paragraph 30 is based on *C d r V* 98-9 (108-9).

32. Paragraph 32 is excerpted from *C d r V* 99 (109).

33. Paragraph 33 is based on *C d r V* 99 (109).

34. Cf the definition in *C d r V* 102 (111).

35. *Prior Analytics* 1.2; Aristotle treats of them further at 1.3, 8-22 (25a-b, 29b-40b) and *On Interpretation* XII-XIII (21a-23a). See Kneale 81-96.

36. C remarked of Mt Etna in 1804: "The fertility at its feet was dimly visible". *CN* II 2202.

37. Paragraph 35(a) is based on *C d r V* 99-101 (109-10).

38. In the sense of "review".

Chapter-5

Constructing a Logical Calculus

Chapter 5

5.1 Introduction

The object of this book is to show how logic can be used for testing what is often called the 'validity', and I shall call the correctness, of arguments (on any subject matter). In Chapter 6 I shall examine a condition, whose fulfilment by any argument is enough to prove the argument correct, though its non-fulfilment is not enough to prove the argument incorrect. The four logical calculi described in Chapters 7 to 10 provide a basis for discovering, in many important cases, whether this condition is fulfilled, and Chapter 11 gives some examples of the calculi at work. The condition can be stated quite succinctly once we have adequate technical language at our disposal. It is an argument is correct if it is an instance in some *logical language* of a *sequent* that is *derivable* in some *system* that is sound in that language. The task facing the reader in Chapters 5 and 6 is to gain understanding of the technical expressions in this statement and of the reasons for thinking that it is true. I have split that task into two parts:Chapter 5 will explain the words italicised above (and, naturally, some others, by the way); Chapter 6 will argue for the the truth of the statement as well as explaining the words 'correct', 'instance', 'sound' and some others, especially the key word 'valid'. The effect of this split is to make Chapter 5 an outline account of the nature of a logical calculus, without reference to its possible usefulness. Historically of course things were the other way round: logic grew and grows largely as an instrument for use—in testing arguments among other things. But there is no point in repeating the historical order in a survey, and it seems sensible to put 'What is it?'before 'What is it for?'

In the sense which I employ in this book 'logic' is synonymous with 'symbolic logic', 'formal logic' and 'mathematical logic'. It is called symbolic because it uses symbols, i.e. written marks that are not words; formal either because it can be studied in abstract (the sense used in 'formal semantics', p. 97. 'formal system', p.15) or because it deals with forms or patterns of argument or because its operations are rule-bound; and mathematical either because it is commonl invoked in the quest for foundations of mathematics or because it is a part of mathematics. Logic has grown mightily since Kant rashly described it as 'to all appearance a closed and completed body of doctrine'(KANT *CPR* B viii, cf. KANT *L* pp.10-1[1]), and the changes of the last hundred years or so have been in two directions. First, Aristotle's syllogistic, which was virtually all that Kant knew, has been shown to cover only a part of the subject, and that not the most fundamental. Among the ancients it was not Aristotle but the Stoic logicians, till recently unremembered and unhonoured, who first explored what the Kneales have rightly called 'primary logic' (W. & M. KNEALE pp. 175-6), now systematised in the *propositional calculus*. Syllogistic itself, though perfectly respectable, has turned out to be less useful in most ways than its modern counterpart the *predicate calculus*, which contains but goes beyond the propositional calculus. *Modal logic* was started by Aristotle but again owes most to modern development. So the first change brought about during the last century has been new foundations—almost a new subject, though partly anticipated by the Stoics. The second change is in the higher reaches where logic coalesces with parts of advanced mathematics. For the system which Kant knew was not only deficient but also elementary, a system of truths and rules which any intelligent person could understand and manipulate.Things are very different today, when work at the frontiers of the subject has become formidably complex and abstract.

This book is concerned only with elementary logic, with the new foundations laid by Frege, Peano, Russell, Lewis and others. There are many good treatments in print of this part of the subject, differing in various ways: in symbolism (unfortunately), in technical terminology, in arrangement and emphasis, and in doctrine. When the student has got past the stage of reliance on a single textbook—and in logic that ought to happen quite early—he faces the problem of assessing these differences in order to decide which of them, if any, matter: for divergent language may conceal the same opinions or different but compatible opinions, and it is only sometimes that real disagreement lurks. A part of my purpose is to bring some of these disagreements into the open and to take sides on them. In airing controversies I shall refer especially to five recent books which, though diverse in other ways, are like one another and the present book in being written from a fairly non-mathematical standpoint: they are QUINE *Mof L*, HUGHES & LONDEY, MATES, LEMMON *BL*, and MASSEY. In my choice of terminology and notation I have tried to avoid gratuitous innovation, but I do introduce some technical words that are not used, or are not given the same sense, by any of these authors.

A logical calculus consists of a logical language plus derivation rules. I begin by considering the vocabulary of logical languages.

5.2 Schematic letters

The sentences 'John came' and 'John went' share a pattern,'John-'; likewise the sentences 'John came' and 'Mary came' share the pattern'—came'. For reasons which will be explained in a moment, logicians write these patterns with letters rather than gaps: 'John *f*', '*a* came'; and letter-filled sentence patterns are called sentence-schemata, or **schemata** for short (QUINE *MofL* p.29, HUGHES & LONDEY pp.1-2). A schema becomes a sentence when its gaps are filled, its letters replaced, by words ('substituted' for the letters, QUINE *MofL* ch. 26). Letters in this role are called schematic letters. Right from the beginning logicians have used schematic letters or a similar device, as in the following modern versions of ancient sets of schemata:

everything that *f*, *g*; everything that *g*, *h*; so everything that *f*, *h*.

if *p* then *q*; so if not *q* then not *p*.

The advantage of writing schemata with letters rather than gaps is twofold. First, it allows the convention to be adopted that repetition of the same letter, either in a single sentence-schema or, if the context so indicates, between one sentence-schema and another, demands replacement by the same word or phrase. This convention is familiar from algebra where, for example, the value of x can be calculated from x + x = 2 but not from x + y = 2; if gaps were left in place of the letters 'x' and 'y' these two equations could not even be distinguished. Replacement conforming to this convention is called uniform. It is important to notice that uniformity, while demanding the same replacement for the same letter, also permits, without demanding, the same replacement for different letters. For example either of the sentences 'John loves John' and 'John loves Mary' may replace the schema '*a* loves *b*' (or '*b* loves *a*'); only the former may replace the schema '*a* loves *a*' (or '*b* loves *b*').

The second advantage of letters over gaps is the possibility of restricting each letter to replacement by words or phrases of a single grammatical category. The logical languages to be studied in this book have an extremely simple grammar. For the purpose of classifying schematic letters they recognise only three categories: sentences, subjects, and predicates. I shall discuss the problems of recognising these categories in 9.2 and 9.3, but here is a preliminary outline. Sentences must be indicative, and the word will henceforward be short for 'indicative sentence' ('statement' QUINE *MofL* p.1, 'declarative sentence' MATES p.5). Subjects must be singular and definite, excluding phrases that begin with 'a', 'some', 'every', 'no' and the like (QUINE *MofL* p.211 and MASSEY p. 225 call them 'singular terms', others 'referring expressions'). Grammatical objects can be subjects in this logical sense, as in 'Everyone loves Mary'. **Predicates** are what is left over when one or more subjects are removed from a sentence, and they are called one-place (unary, monadic), two-place (binary, dyadic) etc. according to the number of subjects, the same or different, needed to restore them into sentences. I shall write predicates with gaps to show the number and disposition of their places; so henceforward '—came', for example, will be a predicate, i.e. part of various sentences, not a schema, i.e. pattern of various sentences. (Other ways of writing predicates are as in '(1) came' or 'ξ came'.) Properly speaking the predicate in a sentence such as 'John is tall' is '—is tall', not '—tall'. But sometimes it makes for easier reading to treat 'is' in the manner of traditional logic as a copula between subject and predicate, not part of either (see p.213). Notice that by the usage I adopt subjects and predicates are expressions rather than things or properties or relations indicated by expressions. Notice too that predicates can be extracted mechanically once the other two categories are recognised. But recognition of the other two is not mechanical, because they are defined by role, not form. For example 'belief that God is dead' and 'belief in God is dead' end with the same three words in the same order, but only in the former do those words function as a sentence (cf. GEACH *LM* p.110). Or again the initial words in 'poison Napoleon', 'poison ivy' and 'poison kills' are the same, or at least have the same shape; yet only in the last does the initial word function as a subject.

I shall appropriate schematic letters to these three categories as follows. '*p*', '*q*','*r*', supplemented as necessary (upper case in MATES and LEMMON) will be replaceable by sentences and will be called propositional letters ('sentential letters' MATES p. 45, 'sentence letters' QUINE *MofL* p.121 'propositional variables' HUGHES & LONDEY p.2, LEMMON *BL* p. 7, 'sentential variables' MASSEY p.12). '*a*', '*b*', '*c*', supplemented as necessary, will be replaceable by subjects and will be called **subject letters** ('individual constants' MATES p.45). '*f*', '*g*', '*h*', supplemented as necessary (upper case except in HUGHES & LONDEY) will be replaceable by predicates and will be called **predicate letters** ('predicate variables' HUGHES & LONDEY p. 168, MASSEY p. 230). QUINE, HUGHES &

LONDEY and MASSEY have no subject letters. LEMMON has them but uses different letters (‘*m*’,‘*n*’,‘*o*’) and a misleading title (proper name’, LEMMON BL p. 93); nothing in this book corresponds to Lemmon’s ‘arbitrary names’ (LEMMON BL p. 107).

Let us say that a sentence or other string of words fits a schema when it results from the schema through uniform replacement of words or phrases by letters appropriate to their grammatical categories. The conventions about grammatical categories ensure that every sentence fits many schemata. For example ‘John came’ fits ‘a came’, ‘John *f*’ and ‘*p*’, and that is only a selection because we have a large; perhaps infinite, supply of subject, predicate, and propositional letters.

5.3 Variables

In the sentence

Charles praised Rex to his mother

‘his’ is used for backward linkage, but the linkage is ambiguous. One way of resolving the ambiguity in favour of ‘Charles’ is to repeat that name in place of ‘his’. But in

(A) Everyone praised Rex to his mother

linkage with ‘everyone’ cannot be elicited by repeating that word in place of ‘his’, because the meaning of

Everyone praised Rex to everyone’s mother

differs from both the possible meanings of (A). English idiom has many devices for resolving linkage-ambiguities of this general kind, e.g. the contrasts between ‘him’ and ‘himself’, or ‘the former’ and ‘the latter’ (see JESPERSEN pp. 220-1 QUINE W & O pp. 134-7).Logic adds another device, index-letters as in

Everyone x praised Rex to x’s mother
Everyone x is such that x praised Rex to x’s mother
For everyone x,x praised Rex to x’s mother

The last two of these sentences are closest to the standard

logical notation. They break up into two parts, a prefix 'everyone *x* is such that' or 'for everyone *x*', and what is called an **open sentence** '*x* praised Rex to *x*'s mother'. An open sentence is similar to a relative clause, completable into a full sentence by backward linkage to a suitable prefix. On their own open sentences are incomplete, and share that feature with schemata. But schemata are distinct from open sentences because their letters have different roles: in the one case as hooks for backward linkage, in the other marking gaps for filling by words. Linkage letters, or index,-letters, are called variables.(It is best to ignore the etymology of this word, and its associations with mathematics; it is also best to ignore the fact that some authors, as we have seen, apply the word to schematic letters as well, blurring their difference of role.)

When an open sentence is fully linked up to prefixes, its variables are said to be **bound**; and any unlinked variable is said to be free. So the difference of role amounts to : schematic letters are replaceable, variables are bindable. Some logicians (e.g. QUINE *MofL* p.121) use 'sentence' as a generic term, distinguishing complete sentences as 'closed'; but in my usage 'closed sentence' will be pleonastic, and open sentences will not count as sentences. An expression such as '*x* loves *a*', containing both free variables and schematic letters, is an open schema (QUINE *MofL* p.123); so in my usage 'closed schema' will likewise be pleonastic. An open sentence in which the varible 'x' and no other is free is an open sentence in '*x*'; and similarly for other variables and groups of them. A sentence which results from linking an open sentence in any variables to prefixes, one in each of those variables, is called a closure of the open sentence. Kinds of closure are distinguished by the meanings of the prefixes: e.g. 'For every *x*, for every *y*, *x* loves *y*' is a universal closure of '*x* loves *y*'; and 'For every *x*. for some *y*; *x* loves *y*' is a mixed closure of '*x* loves *y*'.

The role of variables is conventionally assigned to the letters '*x*', '*y*', '*z*', supplemented as necessary.

5.4 Dummy letters

Schematic letters have a role but no meanings. They are not like code-signs, which abbreviate or stand for words and phrases. Since a schema such as '*a* is tall' is a pattern shared by 'John is tall', 'Mary is tall' and so on, its '*a*' does not abbreviate 'John' or 'Mary' nor yet 'John or Mary or...' or 'John and Mary and ....' The letter is written not as proxy or substitute for some subject but to mark a gap open to any subject, and replacing it by a word is a contribution towards making a complete sentence where before was only a pattern, not towards recasting or translating an already complete sentence.

But not all logical calculi use schematic letters: an alternative is what I shall call dummy letters. Whereas the role of a schematic letter is to be capable of replacement by meaningful words or phrases, the role of a dummy letter is to be capable of having a meaning assigned to it, different on different occasions of use. So dummy letters are a kind of abbreviation, with the peculiarity that their meanings are left quite unfixed, except for restriction to a grammatical category. The logician might stipulate: 'You may use "*F*" to be synonymous with "is tall" or "loves Mary" or "loves" or any other predicate you choose'. In this role '*F*' is a predicate, albeit with unfixed meaning; whereas '*f*' in the schematic role' which I called predicate letter, is not a predicate. Likewise 'John *f*' is a schema, but 'John F', in the new role, would be a sentence, though of unfixed meaning.

These dummy letters are an alternative to schematic letters. No calculus needs both. So it is common to find the very same range of letters allotted the different roles by different authors; in MASSEY, for example, '*p*', '*q*', '*r*', '*F*', '*G*', '*H*' are all dummy, but in QUINE the same letters are all schematic. I shall choose the schematic interpretation, for reasons to be explained in 2.5, but I shall occasionally use upper case letters in the dummy role although these will not be part of the vocabulary of any of the calculi in the book. The word 'dummy' is from MASSEY p. 237; we must ignore the fact that QUINE once uses it to explain 'schematic' (MofL p.29).

5.5 Connectives

Aristotle's logic already contained schematic letters. The major innovation of modern logic, as regards vocabulary, is to replace words like 'if', 'all', 'is the same as' by further symbols, usually not letters (FREGE BS p.1) introduced on the analogy of '+' etc. in mathematics: e.g. '&' for 'and', '=' for 'is the same as'. These are connectives, otherwise called operators (HUGHES &LONDEY p.9) or logical constants (MATES p.45),constants because they are unlike the various kinds of letter so far described in having fixed meanings within each calculus (in fact their meanings are also fairly uniform between calculi, and between authors). If the meanings of the connectives are fixed by means of synonyms in English or some other language, as virtually happens in HUGHES & LONDEY (p.20), the value of having them lies only in brevity. More commonly, translations into another language give only a rough and preliminary guide to their meaning(e.g. LEMMON BL p. 7), which is later fixed by other means. Then those other means are so chosen as to make it possible to devise systematic logical procedures-especially the procedures for proving validity to be discussed in Chapter 7-which would not be possible with words.

Connectives that attach to two expressions, as 'and' does to two sentences or 'is the same as' to two subjects, are called binary; those that attach to a single expression, as 'it is not the case that' does to a sentence, are called **unary**.

5.6 Formulae

My survey of the symbols used in logic is now complete. Aside from punctuation marks, which will be described in Chapter7, the vocabulary of a logical calculus comprises: schematic letters (or dummy letters), connectives, and, for some calculi, variables.

Symbols of these three kinds may be combined with words of English or any other language to make sentences such as 'John came & Mary came', schemata such as 'a came & Mary came', open sentences such as 'John came & x came', and open schemata such as 'a came & x came'. But the logician is particularly interested in expressions which, while like these examples in containing symbols from the logical vocabulary, are unlike them in containing nothing else; such purely symbolic expressions I shall call formulae (LEMMON *BL* p.44). 1.2 already provided means of constructing formulae from the logical vocabulary sketched: e.g. 'p' which is replaceable by any sentence and so functions on its own as a sentence-schema. Similarly the process of replacing subjects and predicates within a sentence might obviously be continued to the point at which no words remain: from 'John came' we would construct first 'John f' and then the purely symbolic expressions 'fa' or 'fx', which are formulae (in logic the predicate letters conventionally come first). Connectives extend the possibilities, allowing such schemata as 'p and q' to be transformed into the purely symbolic schema 'p & q' which is a formula.

5.7 Sequents

It is possible to develop logic just in terms of formulae—in this book they would be formulae interpreted as schemata fitted by sentences. But since we shall be concerned from Chapter 6 onwards with arguments, and arguments are expressed in sets of sentences, it is not surprising that a good deal of naturalness is gained by operating not with single formulae but with certain sets of formulae. We shall find that these are sets in which it matters which formula is last, although the non-last formulae, if there are any, may come in any order. Sets (or classes-I use the two words synonymously) in which order matters are called **ordered sets**, or n-tuples, or sequences. We can represent the jumble among non-last formulae by lumping them together into a set (possibly infinite, possibly empty) in which order does not matter, and then we can represent the special position of the last formulae by forming a two-membered ordered set (an ordered pair or couple) whose first member is the unordered set and whose second member is the last formula. Such a pair, consisting of a set (possibly infinite, possibly empty) of formulae followed by a formula, I call a **sequent**. (This definition is in the spirit of LEMMON *BL* p. 12. Others would define a sequent as two sets of formulae in an order, or as itself a formula of a special kind-see p. 84. It is for the sake of conformity to MATES, and others, that I permit the initial set of formulae in a sequent to be infinite, though the methods of this book will apply, for simplicity, only to finite sequents.) One may be tempted to think of the members of a sequent as a premiss set and a conclusion, but the temptation ought to be resisted since, as we shall see in the next section, systematic logic characterises formulae and sequents in a purely abstract way.

The initial sets of formulae in two sequents sometimes need to be joined by the operation called 'union', i.e. pooled (QUINE *MofL* p. 108, LEMMON *BL* p.11). The union of two sets is the set of things belonging to one or both of them; e.g. the union of the set '*p*', '*q*' with the set '*q*', '*r*' is the set '*p*', '*q*', '*r*'.

5.8 The role of formation rules

A vocabulary does not make a language. We need also to know how the items in it may be combined into complex expressions (syntax)and what the items mean (semantics). Some of this work has been hinted at already, but we must now turn to a more systematic treatment, beginning with syntax. Syntax in logic has four peculiarities: it is laid down or stipulated, not discovered (for the logical language is being invented); the stipulation takes the form of explicit and exceptionless rules, called formation rules; only formulae and sequents are admitted, so that permissible complex expressions contain no words; and no reference is made at the syntactical stage to the roles of permitted formulae and sequents (e.g. as schemata). Instead they are abstractly described as **well-formed formulae** ('wffs' for short, LEMMON BL p.44, HUGHES & LONDEY p. 47, MASSEY p.13; MATES just uses 'formula', p.45) and **well-formed sequents**.

Different formulae and sequents may be well-formed in different calculi; no formula or sequent can be so described absolutely. For example I shall use the expression 'QC-formula' as short for 'formula that is well-formed according to the formation rules of the calculus to be called QC'; and likewise 'QC-Sequent'.

A preliminary example, for formulae, will help to show how sets of formation rules are constructed and at the same time to bring out distinctions within them. In QC each propositional letter '*p*', '*q*' etc. will be a well-formed formula on its own, as will be the result of putting a finite number of subject letters '*a*', '*b*' etc. the same or different, after a single predicate letter '*f*', '*g*' etc. This admits as well-formed e.g. '*p*', '*fa*', '*hccbca*', but not (at least so far) '*a*', '*Fa*; '*af*, '*pap*','&&', '?'. Notice three things. The method bypasses separate listing of a vocabulary: admissible symbols are just those that appear in the well-formed formulae. Secondly, predicate letters must precede subject letters (and variables); this convention could be relaxed by further formation rules, but will not be. Thirdly, the rules are abstract as forecast in the last section. They do not assert (or deny) that the letters admitted are to function as schematic letters, or the well-formed formulae as schemata. This is in spite of the fact that it is convenient to use expressions like 'propositional letter' as labels for particular groups of letters; when such labels appear in formation rules they should not, in this book, be taken to prejudge the question of role.

Continuing the example, the QC formation rules will next bring in certain connectives (as they may still be called, similarly without prejudice as to role). This leads to a complication. To take the typical case of '&', we shall want to rule not only that '&' makes a well-formed formula when inserted between two propositional letters, the same or different, as in '*p* & *q*', but also that '&' may join formulae that are themselves complex and, if necessary, bracketed, as in '*fb* & *fa*'. '(*hba* & *r*) & *r*'. Yet not every complex formula may enter into a combination, just as not every letter might: what is common to the two cases is that the combined items must themselves be well-formed formulae. So the formation rule for '&' will be: '&' between any two QC-formulae makes a QC-formula. Or putting it in an explicitly hypothetical way: if any two formulae, the same or defferent, are QC- formulae, so also is the result of inserting '&' between them (strictly we should add 'and enclosing the whole in brackets',See 3.5).

Such hypothetical or conditional licences are a normal feature of formation rules. Characteristically a set of such rules licenses formulae in three stages: there are initial or categorical rules (basis clauses) laying down that formulae meeting certain specifications are licensed (these are called 'atomic'formulae); subsequent or hypothetical rules (induction clauses) laying down that if one or more formulae are licensed so also is a given related formula; and finally an **extremal** rule (LEMMON *BL* p. 46) laying down that no formula is licensed except under the preceding rules (and the definitions, see 3.3), i.e. that the set of licensed formulae is the smallest set satisfying the other rules-in technical language the set of well-formed formulae is the 'closure' of the set of atomic formulae under the relations of '&'-insertion etc. specified in the hypothetical rules. A set of rules of this type is said to give a **recursive** or inductive **definition** of well-formedness (HUGHES & LONDEY p.49), 'definition' in the sense 'specification', 'recursive' because no fromula can be licensed by its subsequent clauses unless some formula is licensed by its initial clauses: all the licences run back, as it were, to the categorical licences.

The formation rule for sequents will be: a sequent is well-formed in a calculus if and only if its component formulae are finite in number and all well-formed in that calculus.

5.9 The role of interpretation rules

Semantics follows syntax, and like that it is laid down, in logic, by means of explicit and exceptionless rules. The rules assign roles to all admitted symbols, but meanings to only some of them (the connectives). For that reason I prefer the broader title 'interpretation rules' in place of 'semantic rules'.

The role of variables is as in 1.3. The other letters may, as we have seen, be interpreted either as dummies or as schematic. If they are dummy letters, they are generally interpreted by means of truth-conditions for sentences, i.e. rules laying down the conditions under which and expression is a true or false sentence (see pp. 86-8). Roughly the rules are: any propositional letter is a true or false sentence; any predicate letter follwed by a single subject letter is a true or false sentence according as the thing referred to by the subject letter has or lacks the property attributed by the predicate letter; and the same with complications for predicate letters followed by more than one subject letter. Such clauses stop short of assigning meanings to the letters, but indicate the limits within which we are free to assign them meanings on each occasion of use. If, on the other hand, the letters are to be interpreted schematically, as schemata or parts of schemata rather than of sentences, the interpretation cannot use truth-conditions, which are rules for constructing true or false sentences. Instead the rule for the propositional letters is simply that they are replaceable by sentences, and the truth-condition for the predicate-leading construction applies not to '*fa*' etc.—which are to be schemata—but to strings of ordinary words fitting'*fa*' etc., strings which the new construction artificially adds as sentences to natural languages, much as variables and open sentences were added in 1.3.

In the case of connectives assignment of role is simply assignment of meaning. This too is managed by means of truth-conditions, now hypothetical, e.g.: if two sentences are both true, so is the result of inserting '&' between them, and if not. not. Which sentences these hypothetical rules are to apply to well depend on the interpretation of the letters. If they are dummies, truth-conditions for connectives are generally made to apply only to symbolic sentences, i.e. to formulae such as '*P*', '*FA*' (so MATES, MASSEY). Then the truth-conditions as a whole give a recursive specification of true and false formulae, the letter-clauses being categorical, the connective-clauses hypothetical. This neat restriction of the connectives to formulae is not possible on the schematic view, by which if you want to put '&' into a sentence rather than a schema you must, in general, combine it with words. Schemata are not true or false; so if formulae are interpreted as schemata the truth-conditions for the connectives must apply to something other than formulae, viz. to sentences of a natural language enriched by those connectives.

5.10 The role of derivation rules

When rules of formation and interpretation are combined, the construction of a language is complete. A *calculus* adds further rules for passing from one formula or sequent to another. These can be presented in various ways, and are variously labelled derivation rules (LEMMON *BL* p. 8), transformation rules (HUGHES & LONDEY p. 96), or rules for deduction (QUINE *MofL* ch. 37) or inference (MATES ch.7) My presentation will make them, like formation rules, entirely abstract: just as formation rules sort formulae and sequents into two lots, the well-formed and the rest, so derivation rules will sort them—or in practice those of them that are well-formed-into two lots, the derivable and the rest. Derivable formulae and sequents, like well-formed ones,are so only relative to a calculus; and e.g.'QC-derivable' will mean 'derivable according to the derivation rules of the calculus QC'. Derivable formulae are often called theorems.

Derivation rules are always associated with methods of proving derivability; usually indeed, and in this book, they are presented as rules for constructing such proofs. I shall show in Chapters 6 and 11 how proofs of derivability form a part of one of the procedures that the book aims to provide: procedures for testing the correctness of arguments. But the procedures have other parts,as Chapter 6 will explain; logicians oversimplify when they describe derivation as deducing or inferring (see 5.1).

Most authors give derivation rules just for sequents or just for formulae. There is no need for both sorts in the same calculus. But I shall include both sorts, as alternative ways of developing each calculus.

5.11 Languages, systems, calculi

Formation rules plus interpretation rules make a logical language ('symbolic language' HUGHES & LONDEY pp. 47-8, 'formal language' LEMMON *BL* p. 42, 'artificial language' MATES p. 14, LEMMON *BL* p. 42, 'formalised language' FREGE *BS* p.3). Logical languages differ from natural languages in being invented, and symbolic. Some have no further important difference (e.g. the language of set theory, see pp.253-5); but most, including the four examined in this book, also contain symbols which are interpreted either as having unfixed meanings (dummy letters) or as having no meanings at all (schematic letters). These are languages only in an attenuated sense of the word, for few truths can be conveyed by them without supplementary explanation: even if the interpretation rules make provision for sentences as opposed to schemata, the meanings of the sentences are not in general fixed by the rules. For the same reason few sentences of a natural language can be translated into one of these logical languages, in any normal sense of 'translate'.

Words can however be translated into connectives. So it is possible to construct sentences with fixed meanings in which some words remain and others have been replaced by connectives, as in 'John came & Mary came'. Such mixed languages, e.g. English plus connectives interpreted as in QC, will be central in the devising of procedures for testing arguments. I shall say, for example, that any language enriched by the QC interpretation rules for connectives is a QC-incorporating language. A QC-incorporating language is not necessarily a logical language, in the sense of symbolic formation rules plus interpretation rules, for it may be a natural language to which connectives have been added with their QC meanings. If you like, the logical language of QC itself can be thought of as a schema for all QC-incorporating languages (cf. MASSEY p. 27).

Rules of interpretation and derivation need have no connection with one another. In particular it is possible to include the former without the latter, as in a logical language, or conversely. Derivation rules do, however, presuppose formation rules, specifying derivable formulae or sequents as a subset of well-formed ones.The combination of rules of formation and derivation without rules of interpretation is sometimes called a logic,otherwise a logistic system or formal system (HUGHES & LONDEY p.93), names which I shall usually abbreviate to 'system' (having no need for wider uses of that word). Because of its lack of interpretation rules a system is wholly abstract: it assigns no meaning or role to any of its symbols. Quine has has emphasised that the notion of truth is what ties logic to the world (QUINE POF P.35); in systems truth is not on the cast list.

Systems are of various kinds. In some the derivation rules specify certain formulae as derivable *from* certain sets of formulae, and these are called natural deduction systems. Others, called axiomatic, specify certain formulae, instead or additionally, as derivable absolutely, i.e. as theorems. Others again deal with derivable sequents. The systems in this book will be of two kinds: sequent systems, in which sequents alone are derivable (these are at least very similar to natural deduction systems), and formula systems, in which formulae alone are derivable (absolutely).

Any system can be put together with any logical language which shares the same formation rules. The result is a calculus. Thus a calculus turns out to be no more and no less than the combination of three sets of rules, one from each of the three types discussed in the previous three sections. A useful calculus is another matter: to be useful its formation rules must be appropriate to the other two sets, and those sets must be related at least by the relation of sondness, which I shall introduce in 6.12.

Interpretation rules are often, not quite aptly, called 'semantic'. This usage is probably responsible for a tendency to contrast logical languages as 'semantic' with systems as 'syntactic'. But the contrast is unfortunate too, since syntax is part of the study of language and systems are not languages by any stretch. The general study and comparison of systems is sometimes called proof theory, of logical languages model theory.

I.12 Classification of calculi

Calculi are classified by the connectives they contain. Here are the connectives used in this book, together with suggested ways of 'pronouncing' them (falling back, in many cases, on the name of the symbol) and a rough indication of the meanings they will be given by the interpretation rules.

Symbol	*Suggested pronunciation*	*Approximate meaning*
~	'tilde' or 'not'	not
&	'ampersand' or 'and'	and
v	'wedge' or 'vel'	or
⊃	'horseshoe' or 'hook'	if
≡	'if and only if'	if and only if
∀	'ay'	for everything
∃	'ee'	for something
=	'equals'	is the same as
□	'box' or 'necessarily'	necessarily
◊	'diamond' or 'possibly'	possibly

The first five connectives in the list are truth-functional (see p.I04) and any calculus whose connectives are confined to this group is a version of the propositional or sentential calculus, or calculus of truth-functions. The next two,'∀' and , '∃' are called quantifiers; when joined to variables they form examples of the prefixes discussed in 5.3. A calculus containing truth-functional connectives plus these quantifiers is a version of the predicate or functional calculus, and when, as in 5.3, the variables bound by quantifiers must occupy places suitable for subject letters the calculus is a first order, or lower, predicate calculus. By adding '=' we get a version of the lower predicate calculus with identity. The last two connectives in the list are called modal. They may be added to any of the preceding groups to give, respectively, modal propositional calculi, modal predicate calculi, and modal predicate calculi with identity. Some authors reserve the word 'connective' for the first and last groups, excluding quantifiers and '='.

In this book four calculi will be treated: PC is a propositional calculus and QC a lower predicate calculus with identity ('Q' for 'quantifier'), S5 is a modal propositional calculus (so called because it is the fifth in a series constructed by LEWIS & LANGFORD p.501), and QS5 is a modal lower predicate calculus with identity. Since these four are not the only specimens of their kinds the question arises how to tell when some calculus, e.g. in another book, is identical with one of them. What criteria of identity are we to adopt for calculi? I propose the following. (i) The rules of two versions may differ and yet have the same effect. That is, one may find two sets of rules, each comprising rules of formation, derivation and interpretation, according to which the same formulae are well-formed, the same formulae and sequents are derivable, and the symbols have the same interpretations. These will count as versions of the same calculus. (ii) It may be that the well-formed formulae of one version, though differing from those of another, 'match' them in the sense that each set results from the other by uniform substitutions of one symbol for another, e.g. '*P*' for '*p*' and '—' for '~ ', or by similar operations. If such matching runs right through the versions, applying also to interpretations and to the sets of derivable formulae or sequents, it is reasonable to treat the differences as merely notational. Versions so related will count as versions of the same calculus. (When there is partial but not exact matching it is a good deal harder to decide whether the differences between calculi are *partly* notational; but this book ignores the many cases where that problem arises, for which see HAACK ch. I.) (iii) Two versions may differ in that one interprets letters as schematic, the other as dummy. This difference is unimportant in practice and I shall not allow it to count against identity. (iv) One version may give derivation rules for formulae, another for sequents. Two such versions will be counted the same calculus when (given that their formation and interpretation rules have the same effect) a formula is derivable in one of them if and only if the sequent containing just that formula, once, is derivable in the other (see 8.2). (v) Two versions of the same predicate calculus may have different policies over free variables (p.83) or over vacuous quantification (p.72).

5.I3 Metalogical notation

Logic studies arguments and to that end studies sentences, formulae, sequents, symbols. These are its subject matter. It also *uses* arguments in order to prove results about the subject matter. Chapter 6 will be an example of such an argument, leading to the conclusion stated at the beginning of I.I; and 7.4 will argue to the conclusion that any formula derivable in one of the four calculi is valid in that calculus. Such conclusions about the subject matter are often called metatheorems, to distinguish them from 'theorems' in the sense of derivable formulae; metatheorems are not formulae but statements about formulae (or about sentences, sequents etc.) . Theorems and other formulae are expressed in a logical language; but meta-theorems are expressed, partly or wholly, in a natural language such as English. The logical languages referred to in meta-theorems are called object languages (objects of study) and the language such as English in which the metatheorems are expressed is called the metalanguage of the study.

Even at an elementary level a metalanguage is going to need technical terms. If it is English, it will be a use of English in which words like 'formula', 'instance', 'definition' are given special senses. This chapter has begun the task of elucidating such senses. The technical words might be said to constitute a metalogical vocabulary, vocabulary used not in the logical language but in talk about it. As a logician advances to more abstruse questions about his calculi, so he needs more such vocabulary. Quite soon, also, he will find that even technical English is excessively cumbersome. He will feel the need to abbreviate, and to write schematically: in other words he will feel the need for metalogical symbols. There is a danger, clearly, that the introduction of such symbols may deceive a reader (and writer) into thinking that they are part of the logical subject matter, so confusing logical with metalogical symbolism. In an elementary book such as this it might be possible to avoid the danger by doing without metalogical symbols altogether. But even at the level of this book a total ban on them would be awkward, and perhaps ridiculous. I shall not attempt it. The rest of this section accordingly introduces the metalogical notation I shall use.

First, metalogical abbreviations.(i)'PC','QC','S5' and 'QS5' will be names of different calculi.(ii)'$=_{def}$'will be short for 'is short for'.(iii)For referring to sequents it is useful to employ a small part of the symbolism of set theory. '{Romulus, Remus}'means the set whose only members are Romulus and Remus'.'< Romulus,Remus>' means 'the ordered set whose only members are Romulus and Remus in that order'.Since sequents are ordered sets whose second member is a formula and whose first member is a set of formulae,the sequent whose last formula is '*p*&*q*'and whose other formulae are '*p*' and '*q*' will be referred to as

(B) <{'*p*','*q*'},'*p*&*q*'>

'Λ' is a symbol for the empty set; so the sequent whose last and only formula is '*p*&*q*' will be referred to as '<Λ, '*p*& *q*'>' ' '. ' is the symbol for union;so '{'*p*','*q*'} {'*r*','*p*'}'means 'the union of {'*p*','*q*'} with {'*r*', '*p*'}(this is the set {'*p*,'*q*'}). For more one the symbolism of set theory see pp.2 53-5.(iv) Lemmon's notation for (B) is '*p*, *q* '⊢' *p* & *q*'⊢' interpretable as the conjunction'therefor' (LEMMON BL pp.11,48) Although this is simpler, I reject it as much too easy to confuse with "*p*', '*q*',⊢'*p* & *q*", whose standared meaning is

(C) <{'*p*','*q*'},'*p* & *q*'> is derivable

so that '⊢' abbreviates the verb 'is derivable' (LEBLANC p.31). In this book '⊢' will have the latter, metalogical, meaning, but to avoid confussion with Lemmon's usage I shall write the symbolic version of (C)as

⊢<{'*p*', *q*'},'*p* & *q*'>

Similarly '⊢' '*a* = *a*" will mean 'the formula '*a* = *a*' is derivable"⊢ 'called the **turnstile**.

Secondly, metalogical varibales.Rules,in this book ,are universal statements, and rules about formulae or sequents state truths about all formulae or sequents of a certain class. The same goes for metatheorems, inferred from the rules. It is no good writing, for example, 'if "*p*"is a well formed formula, so is " □*p*" ' when one wishes to convey at the same time that if '*q*' is well-formed formule, so is '□*q*', and that if '=*xC*', is a well-formed formulae, so is '□ = *xC*', and so on. The right formulation is obviously ' "□" followed by any well-formed formula is a well-formed formula'. Sometimes, though not in this simple case, such metalogical universality is most neatly conveyed by variables, as in 'Every thing '*x* is such that, if *x* is a well-formed formula, so is "□" followed by '*x*'. But there are two reasons for not using the variables '*x*' '*y*' '*z*' in formulating rules and metatheorems. First, those variables belong to the logical notation so that it can be confusing to employ them metalogically as well. Secondly, it is convenient to have metalogical variables whose *range* is restricted to particular kinds of thing, one set for formulae, one for subject letters, one for set of formulae,and so on. I shall use Greek and (mostly) boldface letters for this purpose, as follows:

'α', 'β', 'α_1', 'α_2' etc. for subject letters
'ν', 'μ', 'ν_1', 'ν_2' etc. for (logical) variables
(LEMMON *BL* has '*v*')

'π', 'ϙ' (the obsolete Greek Koppa), 'ρ', 'π_1', 'π_2' etc. for formulae (LEMMON BL and MASSEY have '*A*', '*B*', '*C*', MATES 'ϕ', 'ψ', 'χ', ", HUGHES & LONDEY 'X', 'Y', 'Z')

'σ', 'τ' for sentences
'ϕ', 'ψ' for stencils
'1' for logical languages
'*n*' for non-negative integers

Less commonly I shall use

'δ' for predicate letters
'Γ', 'Δ', 'E' for sets of formulae
'd' for domains
'v', 'v_1' for valuations
'w', 'w_1' for worlds

It is unimportant whether these metalogical letters are thought of as variables or schematic letters. For example in the formulation 'If π is well formed, so is "□" followed by π' it makes no difference whether we understand an elided prefix 'for all formulae π'or supply the gloss "The following states a truth whatever formula is referred to by a subject put uniformly for "π" in it'. But notice that in the latter case the subjects put for 'π' must be quoted formulae as in if "*p*" is well-formed so is "□" followed by "*p*".

Thirdly, quasi-quotation. It is tempting to abbreviate the specimen rule about '□'still further, into 'if π is well-formed, so is □π'. But strictly this is inaccurate.What we want is is something that generalise If "*p*" is well-formed, so is "□*p*", and so on; but because 'π' is for replacement by quoted formulae the suggested abbreviation genaralises If "*p*"is well-formed, so is "□*p*", and so on. So it is worth introducing a metalogical notation specially farmed to abbreviate such phrases as' "□" followed by *π*'. This is Quine's device of quasi-quotation or **corners**, according to which '□*π*' is short for '"□" followed by *π*', '(*π* &ϙ)' is short for ' "("followed *π* followed by "&" followed by ϙ followed by ")" ', and so on (see MASSEY pp.16-7). The interpretation of an expression enclosed in corners depends on the reader'sability to recognise any metalogical variables it may contain :if there are none,the corners do the same work as ordinary quotation marks,and if the expression consists wholly of metalogical letters the corners may be omitted without danger.Actually,many logicians omit corners altogether (so in effect MATES and LEMMON *BL and* HUGHES & LONDAY tacitly.) I shall give in to this temptation when no ambiguity results, sacrificing accuracy to simplicity

5.14 Definitions

Three meanings of the word 'definition' ofton get confussed in logicians parlance. One is the sense in which you define a classs by specifying conditions for membership of it.In this sense any adequate set of logical rules constitutes a definition'as we have seen that formation rules define recursively the class of well-formed formula.

In a second sense a definition explains,or is intended to explainthe *meaning* of some word or phrase or symbol. I shallo-ftean use the world 'when'to introducesuch definitions informally; e.g 'a binary relation is reflexive ...when..:p .23. formation and derivation rules can be regarded as definitons in this sense too, since they do in a way explain what is meant by the technical terms 'well-formed' and 'derivable'e.g 'is a QC-formula' means 'is member of the smallest set such that ...'with suitable completion and any preexisting associations between well-formedness and intelligibility, or between derivation and inference,can be ignored once the rules have been stated, and need to be ingnored if the rules comprise an abstractsystsm. But interpretation rules although their semantic component helps to define in the first sense the class of truth-in-a-language, by on means define the word 'true' in the second sense. Their purpose being to contribure towards defining, explaining the meaning of, certan logical symbols such as '&', they require that the word 'true', which they call in aid, should already be understood. They cannot work the other way round, defining a special meaning of 'true' in terms of the connectives, because the connectives are so far unintelligible (DUMMENTT p. 460). In this second sense,then the interpretation rules define not 'true' but the connectives.

Thirdly, a definition may introduce one expression as an alternative, usually a shorter alternative, for another. This is the sense in which definitions are a way of eliminating redundant terminology,of extracting from a notation a primitive part which alone is theoretically necessary and for which the rest is more than convenient shorthand. For example the following rules will be *eliminative* definitions of the connectives ◊ and'⊃':

'◊' $=_{def}$ '~□~'

for all well-formed formulae π and ϙ, (π ⊃ ϙ)⌝

$=_{def}$ ⌜~(π & ~ϙ)⌝.

The former of these examples is an 'explicit'definition licensing replacement of '◊' by other symbols,or conversely; the lattr is a 'contextual' definition ('dcfinition in use') licensing replacement of a type of expression ('context') containing '⊃' by a type of expresion not containingit, and conversely. Definitions eliminating some type of symbol-containing expression will not do their work of eliminating the symbol completely unless all permitted expressions containing the symbol either are or can be rewritten as expressionsof that type. Eliminative definitions may be definitions in the second sense too, for they may explain the meaning of the eliminated expressions. But plainly this requires a further condition:in the above examples we must already know the meanings of '~', '□' and '&'. Perhaps it is misleading to call eliminative definitions by that name unless the further condition is met; but logicians do use the name even in uninterpreted systems when it is not met, and their usage will be followed in this book. I shall call such elim -inative rules as the above symbolic definitions, and I shall make them an adjunct to formation rules. That part of the vocabulary of a calculus which is not introduced by symbolic definition is called primitive.

5.15. Some properties of relations

Here are some definitions for future use. A binary relation holds or fails to hold from something *x* to something *y* (*x* and *y* need not be distinct): e.g. the relation expressed in the two-place predicate '—is taller than.......'. A **ternary relation** similarly holds or fails to hold between three things, again not necessarily distinct: e.g. the relation expressed in the three-place predicate '—loves.... more than,,, does'. A binary relation is **reflexive**, or 'totally reflexive', when for all *x* it holds from *x* to x; **irreflexive** when for *no* *x* does it hold from *x* to *x*; transitive when for all *x*, *y* and *z*, if it holds from *x* to *y* and from *y* to *z*, it holds from *x* to *z*; intransitive when for all *x*, *y* and *z*, if it holds from *x* to *y* and from *y* to *z*, it does *not* hold from *x* to *z*; **symmetrical** when for all *x* and *y*, if it holds from *x* to *y*, it holds from *y* to *x*; and **asymmetrical** when for all *x* and *y*, it it holds from *x* to *y*, it does not hold from *y* to *x*. A binary relation such as hating, which holds from some but not all things to themselves,is neither refexive nor irreflexive. Likewise many binary relations are neither transitive nor intransitive, and many are neither symmetrical nor asymmetrical. See LEMMON *BL* pp. 179-87, QUINE *Mof* L p. 159, HUGHES & LONDEY p. 272-4, MASSEY pp. 37-8.

Chapter-6

Using a Logical Calculus

Chapter 6

6.1 Introduction

There are many possible reasons for studying logic. Russell, for example, was struck by "the importance of logical reform for the philosophy of mathematics" (RUSELL *MPD* p. 65); his 'logicist' programme aimed at reducing "the primitive apparatus of the mathematician... to such purely logical terms *as or, not, all* and *some*"(ib. p. 7 1). Electrical circuits, as in computers, have structural analogies with the propositional calculus. Linguists increasingly look to logical languages for illumination of the far greater complexities in natural languages. And logic can, like any other subject, be studied and advanced purely for its own sake. Finally, and perhaps most obviously, modern developments make it profitable to revive the ancient and mediaeval ambition of using logic to test and display the correctness and incorrectness of arguments.

I am concerned in this book only with the last of these uses. It is of special, and growing, interest to philosophers, partly because the study of argument is one of the departments of philosophy and partly because even in other departments philosophers find that their arguments are often so subtle and abstruse as to need all the technical help that can be got towards elucidation and criticism. But there are two reasons why it would be a mistake to think that the application of logical techniques to the criticism of arguments should be of interest to professional philosophers alone. First, in this application logic seems to bring diminishing returns; it is the elementary parts of the subject that most conspicuously increase one's mastery of philosophical material. So even the novice or amateur student of philosophy ought to be introduced to the subject. Secondly, it is reasonable to expect that these elementary parts will help anyone who wants to think clearly on any topic: logic is a universal tool, and not very hard to apply profitably.

Arguments, then, are the subject matter. But logic deals with only one of the desirable features of an argument, correctness, and with only one kind of correctness, the deductive kind. The next two sections will isolate these features.

6.2 Truth and correctness

An argument consists of a conclusion drawn from one or more premisses (later I shall, for technical convenience, change 'one or more' to 'none or one or more'). If the conclusion comes last it is characteristically introduced by a 'so' or a 'therefore'; if first, the premisses may be introduced by a 'because' or a 'for'; and if in the middle, both kinds of particle may be used. In some arguments there are also intermediate conclusions, drawn from certain of the premisses and themselves used as premisses for drawing futher conclusions. But when we find more than one final conclusion, not so used, then I shall say that we have more than one argument, perhaps sharing premisses. The words 'premiss' and 'conclusion' (unqualified) will hencefoward exclude intermediate conclusions. Arguments with an infinite number of premisses are possible, but not important outside mathematics and not considered in this book. Nor is it going to be possible by the methods of this book to test arguments containing a premiss or conclusion that is neither true nor false.

Arguments are appraised as correct or incorrect. In place of 'correct'(MASSEY p.42) many other words are in fairly common use, especially 'valid' and 'sound'. But these latter alternatives are dangerously ambiguous. 'Valid' often has the more restricted sense I shall give to 'deductively correct'; 'sound' sometimes means 'correct and having true premisses' (MASSEY p.42). More important, the words 'valid' and 'sound' are often assigned technical meanings within logic itself, the one for a property of sequents and formulae and the other for a property of systems and calculi. Many students get deeply confused in the initial stages if the technical meanings are allowed to coexist with the non-technical, and especially if validity is allowed to be a property of both arguments and sequents. I shall reserve 'valid' and 'sound' for the technical meanings, which will be introduced in 6.7 and 6.12.

Although arguments are not themselves true or false, their premisses and conclusions may be, and for our purposes must be. Yet the correctness of an argument does not consist in its having true premisses, or a true conclusion, or both. Many incorrect arguments have true premisses and a true conclusion, e.g. this from LEMMON *BL* p.2:

(A) Napoleon was French; all Frenchmen are Europeans; so Hitler was Austrian.

Conversely, many correct arguments have some or all false premisses, with or without falsity in the conclusion, e.g. this from the same page of LEMMON *BL*:

(B) Napoleon was German; all Germans are Europeans; so Napoleon was European.

The correctness of an argument is thus independent of its having true premisses. However, there is some connection between correctness and truth: no correct argument combines all true premisses with an untrue conclusion—in Lemmon's words "from truths only truths follow" (*BL* p.2.). Let us speak of this combination of all true premisses with an untrue conclusion as the offending combination. Then avoidance of the offending combination is necessary for correctness. But it is not sufficient. The ways of avoiding the offending combination might be classified into these three: all true premisses with a true conclusion, some or all untrue premisses with a true conclusion, and some or all untrue premisses with an untrue conclusion. Though each of these three ways is exemplified by many correct arguments, each is also exemplified by many incorrect ones. Example (A) combines true premisses with a true conclusion and yet is incorrect; and it is easy to construct other examples on that model which are likewise incorrect while combining truth and untruth in one of the two remaining ways. The reason why this is easy is that the various combinations make no demand on the *relevance* of conclusion to premisses. In (A) itself the conclusion, though true, is irrelevant to the premisses; and so it might be with the other two non-offending combinations. In fact anyone who held that avoidance of the offending combination suffices to make an argument correct would be committed to the absurd view that every argument with at least some untrue premisses is correct, whatever its conclusion, and to the equally absurd view that every argument with a true conclusion is correct, whatever its premisses.

Correctness, therefore, is not just a matter of combining truth with untruth in certain ways. In 6.4 I shall try to show that for one kind of correctness the right account does involve the concept of truth, afforced by that of necessity. But this requires that we first isolate the intended kind of correctness from other kinds.

6.3 Deductive correctness

Aristotle, in introducing his syllogistic logic, defined a syllogism as an argument "in which, certain things being premissed, something else follow of necessity from their being so" (ARISTOTLE *An. Pr.* I 24 ᵇ I 8-20). If we allow 'things' to cover the singular case, and ignore 'else', this will nearly serve as a definition of 'correct argument': but not quite, because of the words 'of necessity'. Many, perhaps most, of the arguments we employ lack the feature that their conclusions follow of necessity from their premisses. Yet we rarely count that lack as a bar to correctness. For example I argue correctly if from the premiss that your grandfather's great-uncle carried a standard at the battle of Waterloo I conclude that he is not alive today, even though the conclusion does not follow of necessity from that premiss alone. Following of necessity defines, then, one kind of correctness which is not the only kind.

This special kind has many names. When it is present in an argument one may say that the conclusion of the argument 'follows logically from' (QUINE *MofL* p.39, HUGHES & LONDEY p.4), or 'is deducible from', or'is a consequence of' (MATES p.2)the premisses, or that the premisses 'entail' the conclusion (LEMMON *BL* p.I), or that the argument is 'deductive', or 'deductively correct'. Accordingly it is a metalogical principle that

6.3(I) An argument is correct if (but not only if) it is deductively correct, i.e. its premisses entail its conclusion.

The next task is to examine the standards, or criteria, of deductive correctness. Other standards, e.g. inductive, do not come within the purview of logic as understood in this book.

6.4 Criterion of deductive correctness

What are the conditions under which premisses entail conclusions? What makes an argument deductively correct? Consider this specimen argument:

(C) Today is Monday; so tomorrow will be Tuesday.

(C) is, I shall contend, deductively correct just on condition that, i.e. if and only if, it should not have been Monday today without being Tuesday tomorrow. Before explaining and defending this contention it will be useful to generalise it over all arguments. There are broadly two ways of doing so, one bringing out the requirement of a necessary *connection* or relation between the premisses and conclusion of any deductively correct argument, the other pointing to a necessary *truth* which must lie behind the argument as what is sometimes called its 'principle'. Corresponding to these two ways of stating, in general terms, the conditions under which any argument is deductively correct—the criterion of deductive correctness, as I shall henceforth call it—there have grown up in logic two methods of testing arguments, one of which, using sequents, seeks to discover whether the argument has a valid form, while the other, using formulae, seeks to discover whether the principle of the argument is a formal, otherwise called logical, truth. In this and the next eight sections I shall confine attention to the first method, deferring the other to 6.13.

Generalising then in terms of the connection between premisses and conclusion we get: an argument is deductively correct if an only if its premisses could not all have been true without its conclusion being true. Two things are worth remarking in the language of this formulation. First, it imports the words 'premiss', 'conclusion', and 'true' which were not used in stating the conditions for the deductive correctness of (C) itself. The importation of such words, dubbed 'semantic ascent' by Quine (QUINE *PofL* pp. I0-3),is a method of obtaining the generality we are looking for. Secondly the words 'could not' are carried over from the statement about (C).

I use 'could not' as short for 'could not logically', invoking the notion of logical impossibility. This must be explained, if it can satisfactorily be explained at all, either (a) by contrast with other kinds of impossibility or (b) in terms of self-contradiction. (a) Logical impossibility contrasts both with human incapacity or lack of opportunity (it is logically though not humanly possible for me to swim the Atlantic, or dine nightly with the Queen) and with physical impossibility (it is logically though not physically possible for a cobweb to cut cheese). These latter impossibilities are, we may say, relative to or contingent on things being as they are-contingent on the desires, wit and strength of men, the constitution of material bodies, and so on. By contrast logical impossibilities are impossible absolutely, no matter what. (b) It is also frequently and plausibly held that it is logically impossible for something to be the case if and only if anyone who says that it is the case contradicts himself, and hence that it is logically impossible for certain premisses to be true and a certain conclusion not true if and only if anyone who says that the former are true and the latter not true contradicts himself. There is some difficulty however in saving this account from being at once too wide and too narrow.On the one hand a certain kind of contradiction, sometimes called pragmatic inconsistency or logical oddity, infects sayings like 'I believe that it is raining,but it isn't'; yet there is nothing impossible about my believing that it is raining when it isn't, and there is likely to be no correctness at all, let alone deductive correctness, in the argument 'I believe that it is raining; so it is raining'. The logician needs to understand self-contradiction so as to exclude these cases. On the other hand there are logical imposibilities, such as the impossibility that root two is rational and in general the impossibility of the denials of mathematical truths, which are not very obviously self-contradictory. The weaker suggestion that the denial of a mathematical truth entails a self-contradiction without itself being one will not suffice to explain logical impossibility if the latter is in turn being used, as here suggested, to explain entailment.

Necessity, like impossibility, is to be understood in this book as logical, i.e. absolute. What is so-and-so of necessity is so-and-so and could not have been otherwise; it would have been so no matter what, whatever the facts;to anticipate language which will be introduced in 6.10, it is so in all 'worlds'. Anything true of necessity is called a necessary truth.

The suggested criterion of deductive correctness fastens on the combination mentioned on p.26, the offending combination of true premisses with an untrue conclusion. But instead of claiming, absurdly, that a correct argument is any argument in which that combination is not present, the criterion claims that a deductively correct argument is any argument in which that combination could not have been present, i.e. in which the *offending, combination is avoided of necessity*. So the 'could not have been' is vital. Were it replaced by 'are not' the criterion would collapse into what was rejected in 6.2; we should have the absurd consequences that every argument with some or all untrue premisses, and every argument with a true conclusion, is deductively correct.

As it is, the criterion faces a challenge. Just as the premisses of some arguments are not all true, i.e. are jointly untrue, so that premisses of some arguments could not all have been true, i.e. are jointly impossible. But if they could not all have been true, then *a fortiori* they could not all have been true without the conclusion being true, and so, by the criterion, the argument is deductively correct. That is to say, it is a consequence of the criterion that any argument with jointly impossible premisses is deductively correct no matter what its conclusion may be: every conclusion will be entailed by jointly impossible premisses. Furthermore any premisses are jointly impossible if one or more of their number is impossible on its own. So since, for example.'Root two is rational'is not merely false but impossible, it will entail 'The Rhine is longer than the Rhone', 'The Rhone is longer than the Rhine', 'Root two is irrational', and so on indefinitely. There is a parallel consequence for conclusions. If the conclusion of an argument is a necessary truth, then it could not have been untrue. So *a fortiori* the premisses could not all have been truc without the conclusion being true. So, by the criterion, the argument will be deductively correct. That is to say, it is a consequence of the criterion that any argument whose conclusion is a necessary truth is deductively correct no matter what its premisses may be: any premisses will entail a necessary truth. Since, for example. 'Root two is irrational' is not merely true but a necessary truth, it will be entailed by 'The Rhine is longer than the Rhone', 'The Rhone is longer than the Rhine', 'Root two is rational', and so on indefinitely.

These two consequences of the criterion are paradoxical, in the original sense of going against unreflecting opinion. They are paradoxical especially because they yield examples—not so readily as in 6.2, but readily enough—of deductively correct arguments in which premisses and conclusion are irrelevant to one another. But are the paradoxes false? This question divides logicians. Most agree that the condition 'avoids the offending combination of necessity', like the weaker 'avoids the offending combination', is required for deductive correctness. But some insist that it is still not strong enough; for it lets in such arguments as 'The Rhine is longer than the Rhone. therfore root two is irrational', which they wish to exclude. Although various attempts have been made to devise other conditions which exclude these cases, the price of excluding them is surprisingly high. Here is a specimen argument from a pair of jointly impossible premisses to an irrelevant and arbitrarily chosen conclusion. The premisses are at the top, the conclusion at the bottom, and the horizontal lines represent 'therefore':

(D) Eugene is married — Eugene is bachelor

Eugene is married or grass is pink — Eugene is not married

grass is pink

If this argument is deductively correct, then so, surely, will be any argument from a set of jointly impossible premisses to any conclusion whatever. Yet how can this one fail to be deductively correct? It resolves into the simple arguments (let us call them inferences) 'Eugene is married; so Eugene is married or grass is pink', 'Eugene is a bachelor; so Eugene is not married',and 'Eugene is married or grass is pink; Eugene is not married; so grass is pink'. Anyone who challenges the argument must either reject one of these inferences as deductively incorrect or reject the principle that an argument which resolves into deductively correct inferences is itself deductively correct (technically that the set of things entailed by a given set is 'closed under entailment', i.e. entails only its own members, i.e. entails only things entailed by the given set).Inferences of these types have in fact been challenged, as has the principle of resolution (or transitivity of entailment as it is sometimes loosely called) but it seems to me as it has seemed to others that they are acceptable and consequently that we have to admit the deductive correctness of (D). Similar reasoning will confirm that a necessary truth is entailed by any premisses whatever. I conclude that the criterion of deductive correctness is, although paradoxical, acceptable as stated. (In agreement with this is e.g. BENNETT; in dissent e.g. ANDERSON.)

Notice that the paradoxes concern entailment, not proof. A conclusion entailed by jointly impossible premisses cannot be proved from them, because the premisses of a proof must be true. A set of premisses entailing a necessary truth as conclusion may, even if true, fail to prove that conclusion, because proofs must avoid begging the question.

The criterion of deductive correctness can be reformulated in various ways. In place of 'The premisses and conclusion avoid the offending combination of necessity' we may say 'The premisses **materially imply** the conclusion of necessity', where material implication is the relation which holds between premisses and conclusion when it is not the case that all the former are true and the latter untrue. In place of 'materially imply of necessity' **we** may say '**strictly imply**', so that the criterion asserts that entailment is strict implication. For this reason the paradoxical consequences of the criterion are often known as the paradoxes of strict implication.

The criterion can now be set down as another metalogical principle:

6.4(I) An argument is deductively correct if and only if its premisses strictly imply its conclusion, i.e. of necessity it is not the case that its premisses are all true and its conclusion untrue.

6.5 Form: Sentences versus schemata

The criterion of deductive correctness does not yet bring us to the point at which logical techniques can be applied to the testing of arguments. In order to apply them we need a new property which is technical not only in the sense of being explained in technical language (such as 'strictly implies')but also in the sense that it introduces the special concepts of symbolic logic, e.g. schemata, formulae, sequents: and this is the property of having a valid form. I shall explicate the property in the next seven sections: form in this one, having a form in 6.6, and validity in 6.7-II. The aim is to provide an explication under which it will be true to say that every argument having a valid form deductively correct, but this will not be achieved until 6.II. Many logic books give little space to these matters, sometimes only a few lines.

Suppose we take it that the following argument (E)—a trivial specimen for the sake of brevity—has (Es) for its form, or rather for one of its forms:

(E) John is tall and John is handsome; so John is tall

(Es) *p* and *q*; so *p*.

How are the letters in (Es) to be interpreted? We could rewrite them upper case as dummy letters, so that (Es) would simply restate (E) in a partly symoblic language; or we can take them as schematic letters, so that (Es) gives the pattern of (E).On the former interpretation the two components of (Es) would be sentences which the sentences of (E) translate; on the latter they are sentence-schemata which the sentences of (E) fit. It is clear how the schematic interpretation elucidates the idea of form: not only (E) but infinitely many other arguments can be arranged into sentences which fit the schemata of (Es) according to the conventions for fitting explained in 6.2, and what those arguments have in common is a form or pattern. However if we are to exhibit this relationship among arguments throgh the other interpretation it is not enough to say that (Es) recasts (E) in symbolic language; we must add that (Es) is available for recasting the other arguments too. (E) has (Es) for its form, on the dummy interpretation, because the meaning of each of its component English sentences is the same as one among *many* admissible meanings of the dummy letters 'P' and 'Q'.

It can now be made explicit what a form (argument form) is according to each interpretaion. In the one case it is a set of sentences in which at least one word or phrase is replaced by a schematic letter (I shall call such a set an inference-schema, HUGHES & LONDEY p.3); having it will then be something like fitting it. In the other case it is a set of sentences in which at least one word or phrase is replaced by a dummy letter, i.e. a letter with unfixed meaning; having it will then be something like being synonymous with one of its admissible meanings. Forms are to contain nothing corresponding to intermediate conclusions.

Both these explications of 'form' need to be backed up by interpretation rules for symbols, in the one case rules about grammatical categories and uniformity of replacement determining which sentences fit a given schema, in the other by rules determining the admissible meanings of dummy letters and hence the admissible translations of sentence containing them into English. and other natural languages. But it is probable that the rules could be framed so as to achieve an exact match between the two interpretations, and once a match is obtained there is no longer any practical difference between them, so that forms can be understood indifferently as sets of schemata or sets of semi-symbolic sentences. I follow the former course (with QUINE *MofL* p.29 and HUGHES & LONDEY pp. I-2, against MATES p. 69ff. and MASSEY p. 25),because the prescription to interpret symbols as open to various interpretations(meanings) seems mildly more confusing than the prescription to interpret them as schematic, and also mildly less natural as a way of explicating the concept of form.

Corresponding to this ambiguity in the meaning of 'form' is an ambiguity in the meaning of the verb 'formalise'. When a student of logic is asked to formalise and argument in a symbolism, it may be unclear whether he is meant to undrstand what he is doing as translating into a set of symbolic sentences or as exhibiting a pattern in a set of sentence-schemata.

6.6 Form: Sentences versus propositions

The elucidation of 'having a form'depends not only on the question examined in the last section, whether forms are to be construed as containing schematic letters or dummy letters, but also on the question to which I now turn, whether the arguments that have them are to be construed as sets of sentences or sets of propositios expressed in sentences. If a form consisted of semi-symbolic sentences, to have it might be either to be a set of sentences, e.g. in English, which translate it (so MATES and MASSEY) or to be expressible in such a set: here the difference amounts to that between (a) being synonymous with, and (b) being expressible in, a form. But if a form is, as I take it to be, an inference-schema, to have it may be either to be a set of sentences which fit it (so QUINE) or to be expressible in such a set (so HUGHES &LONDEY). I propose to use the words **'instantiates'** and **'is an instance of'** as short for 'is expressible in a set of sentences fitting the successive schemata of' an inference-schema. So the second difference amounts to that between (c) fitting and (d) instantiating a form. The question for this section therefore, given the indentification of forms with inferenc-schemata, becomes the question whether to identify having (a form) with fitting or instantiating.

It will turn out that this question depends on another which is the main subject of the section; namely what is the arithmetic, or criterion of identity, of arguments, i.e. under what conditions should we say that one and the same argument recurs and on what conditions that there occur two different arguments? It is uncontentious that the same argument recurs just when the same conclusion is drawn from the same premisses (hence adding or subtracting premisses produces a different argument). But this at once raises the further question 'When do we have the same premiss or conclusion?'. One suggestion can be discarded right away: that the indentity of a premiss or conclusion depends on its authorship and time of utterance. A reason why this won't do is that we want to be able to say such things as that the same argument was used by Descartes and Locke, or that one of Locke's conclusions was a premiss in an argument of Hume's. To secure communication at all it must be possible for one person to say the very same thing as another; for if people could not in that way express agreement, they could not express disagreement either. Admittedly it is possible with things said, as in general with the products of action, to define a kind whose indentity does depend on authorship and time of utterance: these are technically called sentence-tokens. But for the purpose of logical appraisal it is essential that we should be able to abstract from such tokens and collect them into groups. It is such abstractions that are counted when two utterances are counted as, for example, utterances of the same premiss.

But what should be the principle of collection or abstraction? There is no end to the variety of answers that could be given to this question, but if we have regard both to the locgician's convenience and to the layman's predispositions two possibilities stand out as most attractive: we could rule that utterances are utterances of the same premiss (and similarly for conclusions and mixed cases) (a) if and only if they consist of the same words in the same order, or (b) if and only if they say the same things about the same things. To convey 'same words in the same order' we can conveniently appropriate the grammarian's word 'sentence', since it will be near enough true that every utterance of a premiss or conclusion is expressed in what is grammatically a sentence. Of course there remains the sense in which different utterances require different sentences, for they require different sentence-tokens; but these may still be tokens of the same sentence-type, and it is in the sense 'sentence-type' that I shall hencefoward speak of sentences. Accordingly, we can formulate the first of the two proposed prinicples of collection as:

> The same premiss or conclusion recurs if and only if the same sentence is reused.

For the second principle I shall employ the word 'proposition', ruling that two utterances are utterances of the same proposition if and only if each is used to say the same thing about the same things. Some authors prefer 'statement'to 'proposition' in this role (LEMMON SSP), on the grounds that there are logicians who give the arithmetic of propositions in terms of meaning-the-same rather than saying-the-same (I shall come back to this) and other logicians who mysteriously hold that porposition *are* meaning (MATES p. II); but even though philisophical usage of "proposition" has been, as one might expect, very diverse over the centuries, it is the word most favourd in current logical writing for expressing the second principle of collection. (The usage of "statement" is hardly less diverse; in QUINE *MofL* it means "indicative sentence"). Given this terminology the second principle of collection can be formulated as:

> The same premiss of conclusion recurs if and only the same proposition is re-expressed.

Before adjudicating between these principle of collection it is necessery to elucidate "saying the same thing about the same things" the propos criterion of identity for propositions. I do not attempt a full account of the nature of propositions, but confine myself mainly to negative points, (i) I the case of singular propositions the criterion anounts to "attributing the same property to the same thing, of attributing the same relation to the same set of thing in the same order". (ii) The criterion is intended of, course, to have the consequence that sameness of proposition and sameness of sentence do not coincide. For example the single sentence "Hamlet is sad" will express different propositions according to the reference (play or character) of its subject and the meaning ('saddening or' saddened) of its predicate; and the different sentences "I am sad" and "You are sad' will express the same proposition if "sad" is univocal and the second is addressed to the current other of the first. (iii) Propositions are to be taken as true of false absolutely, and so in particular eternally. If someone says 'I am unmarried' on Monday and Wednesday, and gets married on the intervening Tuesday, he is not to count as having attributed the same property to himself on the two occasions of utterance, nor therefore as having expressed the same proposition twice. Rather the first utterance truly attributed, say, the property of being unmarried at 2.0 p.m. on 2nd June A.D 1975 and the second falsely attributed the different property of being unmarried at 10.15 a.m. on 4th

June A.D. 1975.So sameness of propositions entails sameness as regards truth or falsity.(iv) But obviusly the converse entailment does not hold. (v) Similarly same ness of proposition entails but is not entailed by sameness for truth-conditions. Every necessarily true or necessarly false propositions is true or false on the same conditions, namely on all conditions and yet there are different necesarily true propositins, and different necessarily false ones. In this respect may criterion differs from that in LEWIS p. 46. (vi) Sameness of proposition neither entails nor is entailed by sameness of meaning. Two sentences may have the same meaning and yet express different propositions, e.g. because they are used with different references ('I am sad' and 'Je suis triste' said by different people), and two sentences may differ in meaning and yet express the same proposition ('I am sad' and 'You are sad' said about the same person). In this respect my criterion differs from that in LEMMON SSP. (vii) Sameness of proposition neither entails nor is entailed by samenss of cognitive value (informative potential). There is perhaps no end to the information that a sentence could convey, so that all sentences have, in a way, the same cognitive value. But if we discount special circumstances (tone of voice, prearranged codes, and so on) we can still find sentences with the same informative potential which express defferent propositions, e.g. 'A puppy is a young dog' and '"Puppy" means "young dog" '. The former sentence cannot tell a hearer anything, special circumstances aside, if he already understands it. But it can tell him something if he doesn't, namely what 'puppy' means (cf. CARNAP p. 63); and that is just what the latter sentence serves to tell him explicitly. On the other hand the propositions expressed by these sentences are different—in the one case a necessary truth about puppies, in the other a contingent truth about the English word 'puppy'. Conversely, two sentences may express the same proposition and yet convey information on different conditions. For example 'The Lord Protector had warts' will need recasting into other words if it is to get its message across to someone who does not know who the Lord Protector was, or does not understand English; and I shall argue in 10.6 that 'The morning star is the evening star' and 'The morning star is the morning star' can express the same proposition even though the latter entirely lacks informative potential. In this respect my criterion differs from that suggested in QUINE *PofL* p.3. (viii) Some, e.g. CHISHOLM, identify propositions with objects of belief. This raises a problem. A man might, for example. (a) believe that's Hertogenbosch is near the Maas while at the same time believing that Bois le Duc is not near the Meuse, through ignorance of the identities concerned. Does he believe and disbelieve (believe false) the same proposition? There is nothing contradictory about that supposition, but a contrdiction would follow if we supposed, slightly differently, that a man might (b) believe that's Hertogenbosch is near the Maas while at the same time *not* believing that Bois le Duc is near the Meuse, and if we treated this as a case of believing and not believing the same proposition. There are three ways out. We might conclude that case (b) cannot occur, but only case (a); or that case (b) can occur, but the propositions expressed by ''sHertogenbosch is near the Maas' and 'Bois le Duc is near the Meuse' are different, even when those sentences are used to attribute the same relation to the same two things; or that case (b) can occur, and the two sentences do express the same proposition, but believing that 'sHertogenbosch is near the Maas is not a matter of believing that proposition, or any proposition. I reject the second solution, leaving a choice between the other two (see also pp. 209-12).

We may now seek to adjudicate between the two principles of collection. A layman would, I submit, be likely to favour the second one. He would be likely to say, for example, that the same argument is presented twice in

(E) John is tall and John is handsome; so John is tall
(F) John is tall and handsome; so John is tall

and therefore that the same premiss recurs in (E) and (F) though in partially different words. This suggests that we should indentify premisses and conclusions as propositions Yet the layman's predispositions, even if I am right about them, ought not to weigh with a logician if he finds that they do not serve his theoretical purposes. Here a certain tension becomes apparent. The logician needs the premisses and conclusions he discusses to he capable of truth and falsity (and that will be assumed in defining 'valid', as it was for the criterion of deductive correctness) but be also needs them, like the arguments they compose, to have forms. It is more natural to think of form as a property of sentences, but also more natural to think of truth and falsity as properties of propositions. I shall try to show that this tension can be relaxed in either direction: either we can treat premisses and conclusions as sentences which fit schemata, and accept slight complications in the concept of truth; or (the way I shall take) we can treat premisses and conclusions as propositions which are straightforwardly true or false, and link them to schemata by the slightly more complicated relation of instantiating.

First as to form. It is clear that the inferenc-schema (Es), which was '*p* and *q*; so *p*', is fitted by the sentences used in (E) but not given the conventins f 1.2, by those used in (F). But the logician is looking for system and economy. He cannot be content to say that (F) has no relevant connection with (Es) and to devise some other schema, e.g. '*a* is *f* and *g*; so *a* is *f*', which is fitted by the sentences used in (F); on the contrary he will wish to say that (Es) has the same role to play in the logical appraisal of (F) as of (E) and that both (E) and (F) have (Es) among their forms. His means of achieving this result will depend on whether he agrees with our supposed layman that the same premiss recurs in (E) and (F). If he does agree, he can rule (as I shall) that an argument which has a certain form need not actually be expressed in sentences which fit the schema; it suffices that it should be possible, conformably with the rules of the language employed, to express it in words which fit the schema: that is, he will relax the requirement of fitting to one of instantiating. And since, as he will say, the very same argument as is expressed in the words of (F) could be expressed in the words of (E), and (E) does fit (Es), this relaxed requirement is satisfied by (F). Now suppose secondly that the logician regards premisses and conclusions as sentences, and hence does not agree that the same premiss recurs in (F) and (E), nor therefore that those are the same argument. He will achieve nothing by allowing that it suffices if (F) could be expressed in words fitting (Es), for on his view (F) could be expressed only in the words in which it is expressed, and they do not fit (Es). Instead he must say something to this effect: that it suffices if (F) is being used to say the same thing as could be said in some other argument which fits (Es). It may be that he will not use the words say the same thing as' (he may talk of recasting, paraphrasing or the like), but that is what he must mean if he is to achieve the desired economy in schemata by making as many arguments as possible—but not too many—have (Es) among their forms. In this way he, like the logician who favours the second principle of collection, can accommodate his predilection to the demands of logical theory.

As to truth, the logician requires that premisses and conclusions be in some cases true; so, if they are to be regarded as propositions, there must be true propositions, if as sentences true sentences. Some people have asserted that no sentences are true (or false), usually on the ground that no sentences are consumary true (or false). Many kinds of circumstance can change a sentence from true to false or conversely. For example the sentence 'Pillarboxes are green' can become true by a change in language (if 'green'acquires the meaning now given to 'red')or by a change in the context of utterance (if uttered after they have been painted green) or by a change in the frame of reference (if one is talking about Eire). These are facts. But they are not a good ground for denying that sentences are true or false (one might as well argue that chameleons are colourless); all they show is that the truth and falsity of sentences is relative. The relativity is admittedly a nuisance, and a reason for preferring to do logic in terms of propositions which are true or false absolutely. Nevertheless it is not a decisive nuisance, and we shall find that it is unavoidable anyhow in the definition of validity.

In reference to truth, therefore, as in reference to form, both of the two principles for collecting utterances allow logical appraisal to proceed. How then are we to adjudicate between them? In favour of propositions some, as we have seen, assert that sentences are not capable of truth or falsity; but that is a mistake. In favour of sentences some urge that because propositions are abstract (MATES p. II, they 'reflect no light') their existence is doubtful; but again we have seen that sentences, by which is means sentence-types, involve exactly parallel abstraction from sentence-takens (see COHEN, p. I 62). Nor can there be any force in the objection against propositions that the idea of saying the same thing about the same things, on which their arithmetic rests, is an unclear one. For I have shown that the application of logical techniques to testing the correctness of arguments must use that idea in any case, though not necessarily those words, on pain of an unmanageable proliferation of schemata. Faced with this indifference from the point of view of logical theory it seems reasonable if after all we allow weight to the layman's feeling that the identity of arguments, and hence of their premisses and conclusions, depends not on the words in which they are expressed but on what is expressed in them. I therefore propose to treat premisses and conclusions as propositions and not sentences, and to develop the apparatus of logic in terms of propositions (following LEMMON *BL* and HUGHES & LONDEY). The other way (favoured by QUINE *MofL*, MATES and MASSEY) is equally respectable, and would involve only fairly minor adjustments.

We are now in a position to answer the question with which this section began. Since arguments are not to be treated as sets of sentences they cannot be said to fit any inference-schema; since they are to be treated as sets of propositions expressible in sentences they can be said to instantiate inference-schemata, i.e. to be expressible in sentences fitting them.

I shall henceforward use the words **'truth'** and **'falsehood'** for 'true proposition' and 'false proposition' respectively. This makes the word 'truth' ambiguous, because it will continue to be used also as the name of the property of being true; for the property of being false I shall use 'falsity'. These properties are called truth-values.

6.7 Validity: languages

The technical sense of 'valid' now to be introduced brings together the key logical concepts of form and truth. Our overall aim is to define validity in such a way that having a valid form ensures deductive correctness.

A first shot at the definition is this: an inference-schema is valid when all its instances avoid the offending combination of true premisses with an untrue conclusion. In the present section and the three which follow it this definition will need to be refined, in various ways and for broadly three reasons. One reason is that validity so defined is *shared* avoidance of the offending combination, whereas deductive correctness was fond in 6.4 to require *necessary* avoidance. We shall need to investigate whether an argument whose avoidance of the offending combination is shared with all others of the same form is thereby certified as avoiding that combination of necessity; this will be the subject of 6.10. Another reason for refining the definition is to ensure that we can find valid forms; for it is practically useless to know that all instances of a valid form are correct if we cannot establish the validity of any forms. This will be the subject of the present section and 6.8. Thirdly, 6.9 will introduce reasons for a further refinement.

None of the refinements will relax the condition that all instances of a valid form avoid the offending combination. Because of this condition validity-claims can be destroyed—forms invalidated—by a single instance which has that combination. Such counterexamples are surprisingly easy to find. Their pervasiveness will provide a motive in this section for making validity relative to logical languages and applying it to sequents rather than inferenc-schemata containing words.

Consider the following arguments:

(G) Eugene is unmarried; so Eugene is not married.

(H) There are old men in London; so some men in London are old.

(I) All bishops are clergymen; so all redheaded bishops are redheaded clergymen.

(J) Homo est animal; Socrates est homo; ergo Socrates est animal.

These arguments are correct, and moreover each appears to have a valid form. For each is expressed and therefore expressible in sentences fitting, i.e. is an instance of, one of the following apparently valid inference-schemata:

(Gs) *a* is un- *f*; so *a* is not *f*.

(Hs) There are *g* *f*s in *a*; so some *f*s in *a* are *g*.

(Is) All *f*s are *g*s; so all *h* *f*s are *h* *g*s.

(Js) *f* est *g*; *a* est *f*; ergo *a* est *g*.

But none of the inference-schemata is in fact valid, for they are also instantiated (for example) by the following arguments with the offending combination of true premisses and an untrue conclusion. 'Paolo is un American; so Paolo is not American;, 'There are many men in London; so some men in London are many', 'All bishops are clergymen; so all retired bishops are retired clergymen', 'Homo est species; Socrates est homo; ergo Socrates est species'. Now admittedly the failure of the inference-schemata (Gs)-(Js) to be valid is not enough to show that (G)-(J) have no valid forms, since there might be other inference-schemata instantiated by (G)-(J) which are valid. The possibility of other schemata arises in two ways: first, for each sentence that can correctly be used to express a proposition, there is always more than one schema fitted by that sentence (e.g. all indicative sentences fit '*p*'); and secondly each proposition is expressible in more than one sentence (e.g. by translation into another language). The second possibility offers promise of vindicating the claim that (G)-(J) have some valid form. We might notice for example that (J) can also be expressed in the sentences (sticking to Latin) '*omnis* homo est animal; Socrates est homo; ergo Socrates est animal', which fits the inference-schema 'omnis *f* est *g*; *a* est *f*; ergo *a* est *g*'. The latter schema is not proved invalid by 'Omnis homo est species; Socrates est homo; ergo Socrates est species' because the premiss expressed in 'Omnis homo est species', unlike that expressed in 'Homo est species', is untrue and hence the latter argument does avoid the offending combination. Similarly the alternative schema 'There are *fs* in *a* each of which is *g*; so some *fs* in *a* are *g*' is also instantiated by (H), but is not invalidated by the new argument beginning 'there are men in London each of whom is many; so...',which again avoids the offending combination through the untruth of its premiss. In a parallel way alternative schemata might be devised for (G) and (I).

These and other such examples suggest a first step in refinement of the notion of a valid inference-schema. By bringing to out notice the fact that a single proposition, e.g. that man is an animal, can be expressed in sentences which fit different sentence-schemata constructed around '*f*' and '*g*', e.g. '*f* est *g*' and 'omnis f est *g*', they prompt us, as did (E) and (F) in 6.6, to try to reduce the variety of schemata treated by logic; and by setting the invalidity of (Js) which contains '*f* est *g*' against the apparent validity of the variant with 'omnis *f* est *g*' they give us a reason for preferring the latter. In this way the failure of (Gs)-(Js) to be valid brings a dividend. Yet it also points to a problem, for it reminds us that even a picked list of inference-schemata such as 'Omnis *f* est *g*;.......' *might* turn out to have instances with true premisses and untrue conclusions, and so not to be valid. Schemata (Gs)-(Js) were faulted by sets of sentences which, though capable of expressing arguments with true premisses and untrue conclusions, go against our intially simple expectations of the workings of adjectival phrases and of linguistic devices like 'un-'; sentences which exploit the unruliness—perhaps more strictly the idiomatic subtlety-of ordinary language. Such sentences shake our confidence, and make us wonder whether any ordinary-language schema can be trusted to be valid under the provisional definition and therefore whether any argument can be trusted to have a valid form.

Fear of such unruliness seems to have been felt from the beginning of logic. At any rate the modern response to it, substitution of formulae and sequents for ordinary-language schemata, is already adumbrated in Aristotle. Aristotle's logic covers propositions instantiating 'Omnis *f* est *g*', but in giving the schema for such propositions he used not the ordinary Greek corresponding to 'Omins *f* est *g*', nor of course to the more obviously vulnerable '*f* est *g*', but an overtly unordinary and unidiomatic formulation which may be translated 'The *g* belongs to all the *f*'. It is reasonable to guess that he chose such formulations because he judged that the unruliness of ordinary language is due to constant use, especially use by the stupid, the careless and the imaginative; abstruse and technical idioms are more likely to behave soberly. The same response can be found in modern logic. Instead of distinguishing. 'Man is an animal' from ' Man is a species' by pointing out that the former but not the latter instantiates 'Every *f* is a *g*', logicians some-times label the former an example of a class-inclusion proposition, the latter of a class-membership proposition. The labels permit the invalid (Js) to be replaced by the valid.

(Jt) the class of *f*s is included in the class of *gs*; *a* is a member of the class of *f*s; so *a* is a member of the class of *gs*.

The incorrect argument beginning 'Man is species' is an instance not of this valid schema but of the invalid schema beginning 'The class of *f*s is a member of the class of *g*s'.

Before showing how technical-language schemata like (Jt) go part of the way from being inference-schemata towards being sequents I should mention another response to the uneasiness produced by arguments like 'Paolo is unAmerican; so Paolo is not American' and the others mentioned. This is to protest that the arguments do not really invalidate schemata (Gs)-(Js) because their premisses and conclusions, although expressible in sentences fitting those schemata, are not *really* instances of those schemata. The relation between, for example, the sentence 'Paolo is unAmerican' and the schema '*a* is un-*f*' is said to be purely grammatical, not logical; the latter gives the grammatical form of the former, but not the real or logical form of the proposition expressed by it. Thus instead of casting round for an alternative inference-schema immune against 'Paolo is unAmerican; so Paolo is not American', e.g. the repetitious ordinary language schema '*a* is not *f*; so *a* is not *f*' or the respetitious techniocal-language schema '*a* is not *a* member of the class of *f*s; so *a* is not a member of the class of *f*s', the logician may stipulate that the original schema '*a* is un-*f*; so *a* is not *f*' should itself be understood in a restricted sense—the sense, presumably, of one of these repetitious alternatives. No doubt the proposition intended by the sentence 'Paolo is unAmerican' is genuinely expressible in that sentence; but it is stipulated that the sentence fits the original schema '*a* is un-*f*' only in a mechanical, 'grammatical', way, ignoring the proposition it is intended to express. Hence the sentences used in 'Paolo is unAmerican; so Paolo is not American', and similarly in the other allegedly invalidating arguments, are seen as misleading, though grammatically proper, expressions of the propositions intended in those arguments, for they wrongly suggest that the arguments have schemata (Gs)-(Js) for their logical forms.

This second response to the unruliness of ordinary language, which may be associated with the name of RYLE, brings into the open a difficulty already implicit in the first response. If we are to say that (Gs) fails to exhibit the real, logical, form of the argument expressed in 'Paolo is unAmerican; so Paolo is not American' we must have some independent idea of the meaning we wish to stpulate as logicians for the construction in (Gs), i.e. for the prefix 'un-'. We are asked to use ordinary language in an admittedly restricted, even if still ordinary, way; so the restrictions ought to be indicated. It is no good simply saying that the meaning of 'un-' in logic is to be such as to exclude the 'unAmerican' example as an instance of (Gs), for that may not be enough to immunise (Gs) against other incorrect instances; nor can we make a complete inventory of excluded arguments, for they may be infinite. It becomes important therefore, if we are going to treat schemata as immune against certain types of apparent, 'grammatical', counterexample, to have in view an *interpretation* of the words and constructions in the inference schemata which supplements—or in this case constricts—ordinary usage. But if so, candour requires us to amend the definition of 'instance', and hence of 'valid', so as to make room for a reference to rules of interpretation.

I shall return to this point, but not before describing a third and final response to the unruliness of ordinary language, which goes one step further. The need to have rules of interpretation in view, revealed by the Rylean response, is as I have said already implicit in the first, Aristotelian, response. For a logician's use of technical expressions like 'belongs to all the' and 'is a member of the class of',though a use of special terminology rather than a special use of ordinary terminology, still may be ambiguous and may be obscure; it too ought to be backed by rules. One way of drawing attention to this requirement, and at the same time avoiding the often cumber some language of technical schemata like (Jt), is to replace the technical terminology by symbols—connectives. Carried to its limit such replacement will leave shcemata like (Jt) with nothing in them but connectives and schematic (or dummy) letters, plus punctuation and, if there are quantifiers, variables; that is to say, it will turn them into sets of formulae. So for example we might progress from the vulnerable (Js) via the 'Aristotelian' (Jt) and the restricted 'Rylean' interpretation of (Js) to the set of formulae.

(Jf) {‘∀x(*fx* ⊃ *gx*)’, ‘*fa*’,‘*ga*’}

But now we have gone too far, for we have dropped the word ‘so’ which indicated in the inference schemata which component was to indicated in the inference schemata which component was to be matched to the conclusions of its instances. The method of logic is to replace this indicator by a requirement of order. In an argument the premisses and conclusion can come in any order whatever, although when the conclusion is marked with a ‘so’ or ‘therefore’ it is more perspicuous to put it at the end, and that convention has been adopted in the examples. We shall exploit the convention. A sequent, as was explained in 6.7, is an ordered pair whose first member is a set of formulae and whose second member is a formulae; so we can change (Jf) from an unordered set formulae to the sequent:

(*Jq*) <{‘*Ax* (*fx* ⊃ *gx*)’, ‘*fa*’}, ‘*ga*’>

and rule that an argument instantiates that sequent when it is expressible in a set of sentences which, when ordered with the conclusion sentence *last*, fit the successive formulae in the sequent.

When sequents, rather than (other) inference-schemata, become the things instantiated by arguments, validity becomes a property of sequents. Moreover the definition of ‘instance’, and so of ‘valid’, must now be made relative to interpretation, because sequents consist of formulae, formulae may contain connectives, and the meanings of connectives need to be specified through rules of interpretation, as in a logical language.Using ‘I’ as a metalogical variable ranging over logical languages, we can say that for any 1 a sequent is valid in 1, 1-valid for short, when all its instances in 1 avoid the offending combination; where an instance in 1, 1-instance for short, of a sequent is an argument expressible *in some* 1-*incorporating language* in a set of sentence which, when ordered with the conclusion sentence last, fit the successive formulae of the sequent.Because a logical language combines meaning-rules for connectives with conventions for fitting words to schematic letters, the new metalogical notation has the extra advantage of making room for a reference to those conventions too: we replace 'fit' in the definition by'1-fit', i.e.'fit *according to the conventions of*.

6.8 Validity: contexts

By making validity relative to a logical language we protect validity claims against certain sorts of counterexample. But other sorts remain which are pervasive enough to call for further refinement of the technical apparatus. These further counterexamples are generated by wrong usage and by equivocation.

An instance of an inference shcema is an argument expressible in a set of sentences fitting that schema, and an 1-instance of a sequent is an argument expressible in some 1-incorporating language in a suitably ordered set of sentences 1-fitting that sequent. But expressibility is vague. When we come to pin it down it seems natural to say, first, that what is expressible in a given sentence, or set of sentences, varies with the occasion of the sentences use and secondly that for each occasion of use it depends partly on the speaker's intention and partly perhaps on the hearer's understanding. For example any argument is expressible in a single word, or a gesture, on an occasion when that method has been prearanged as a code, or even conceivably when it has not but the utterer merely intends his performance so to be understood.Restriction to an 1-incorporating language limits the medium but not the uses that can be made of it; for an utterer can intend to express some argument (or proposition), and even be undersood as expressing it, though he violates the conventional or explicit meaning—rules of the language he employs. Such violation is wrong usage, and if we are to avoid fatuous counterexamples to a sequent's validity we must stipulate, what has so far been tacitly assumed, that an—1instance is an argument expressible in an 1-incorporating language *without wrong usage*.

Even right usage does not ban ambiguity. To be sure the

logical languages themselves are unambiguous, but the languages they enrich, such as English, contain many ambiguous expressions and constructions.For example there is no wrong usage involved in employment of the sentences

(K) Jonathan is one of the team's pitchers; every pitcher is a jug; so Jonathan is one of the team's jugs

to express an argument with true premisses and an untrue conclusion; for every pitcher is a jug in one accredited sense of 'pitcher'. Yet such examples had better not be allowed to invalidate sequents. An 1-instance must therefore be an argument expressible in an 1-incorporating language *without ambiguity*.

But this further restriction is still not enough, if ambiguity is just multiplicity of sence or meaning . Consider the sentences in

(L) It's well-formed and derivable; so it's well-formed.

In a use of (L) the 'it's might refer to different things (tone of voice, or pointing, could indicate this) and different supplementations could be intended for the occurrences of 'well-formed' (e.g. well-formed in the propositional calculus, well-formed in the predicate calculus. The difference of reference is certainly not a difference of meaning, or 'it' would have as many meanings as there are things; and the difference of supplementation is not necessarily, nor I think rightly, regarded as a difference of meaning ('well-formed formula' has neither, not both, the meanings 'PC-formula' and 'QC-formula)'. Yet here again it would be ridiculous to count (L) as invalidating the sequent <{'p&q'},'*p*'>. To cover this kind of case as well as straightforward ambiguity I introduce the word 'equivocal', stipulating that an 1-instance is an argument expressible in an 1-incorporating language without wrong *or equivocal* usage. It turns out to be adequate for logical purposes to define an equivocal use of a sentence or set of sentences as a use in which (a) two occurrences of the same subject have different references of (b) two occurrences of the same predicated have different meanings or implied supplementation or (c) two occurrences of the same sentence have different content, i.e. express different propositions.

Occasions of use I shall call **contexts; and** an **1-context** (for any 1) will be a context of ritht and unequivocal usage of some 1-incorporating language. I now change the definition of '1-instance' and '1-valid' so that an 1-instance of a sequent becomes an argument expresible *in some* I—*context* in a suitably ordered set of sentences 1—fitting the sequent, and an 1—valid sequent becomes a sequent all of whose 1-instances in this new sense avoid the offending combination. The same redefinition of '1-valid' could have been reached by first introducing a kind of validity that is relative to context : a sequent would be (let us say) 1-valid$_1$ in a context when all arguments expressible in *that* context in some 1-incorporating language in a suitably ordered set of sentences 1-fitting the sequent avoid the offending combination. A sequent 1-valid under the redefinition if and only if it is 1-valid$_1$ in every context of right and unequivocal usage.

There is a method by which reference to context might have been avoided: restriction to 'eternal' sentences, and adoption of a narrow criterion of identity for 'languages'. The restriction would stipulate that in order for a set of sentences to fit a sequent they must be eternal in ths sense 'not capable of expressing different propositions in different contexts of right usage': so they must contain no ambiguous words or constructions, no incomplete predicates like 'well-formed', and no expressions with variable reference like 'it', now 'John'. The criterion of identity would stipulate that all contexts are contexts of right usage in the language employed: violation of a meaning-rule simply creates a new 'language'. Reference to contexts would then become otiose in the definition of validity, and of instance. If sequents were interpreted as themselves sets of sentences—the dummy interpretation—these two stipulations could easily be built in : logical languages, as opposed to the natural languages enriched by them, are identified anyhow by the meanings of their connectives, and symbolic sentences, as opposed to verbal sentences fitting formulae, will be eternal provided that the ad hoc meanings of their component letters are suitably limited. But the stipulations are more irksome under the schematic interpretation, and I shall not follow those authors, e.g. Quine, who adopt them.

6.9 Validity : domains

In the last two sections reference to languages and contexts has been introduced into the definitions of 'instance' and 'valid' in order to reduce the risk that no inference schema or sequent would be valid and no argument have a valid form. Reference to domains has different motives. Partly, many logicians have argued that the interpretation rules of the predicate calculus cannot be precisely stated without it, and partly its purpose is to simplify proofs that an argument has a valid form.

The problem about interpretation starts from the logical paradoxes, of which Russell's will serve as a specimen. Russell reasoned like this. Some properties of men belong to them as a class, not individually : for example Cicero is not numerous, but the class of men is numerous. Conversely Cicero is a man, but the class of men is not; it is not among its own members. This latter is the commonest situation, but some classes, e.g. the class of classes with members, do seem to be members of themselves; certainly there are classes with members, and this seems to show that the class of them has members, and so itself satisfies the condition for membership of it. Suppose we set aside such self membered classes and 'form' the class of all those classes that are not self-membered. This class will have among its members the class of men, which is not self-membered, and many others. Will it have itself among its members? The paradox is that the condition for its being a member of itself is precisely that it should not be: it is if and only if it isn't. Russell's reaction was to construct a set-theoretic language in which the predicate 'is not a member of itself' did not make sense. A more modest reaction is to say that the predicate does not always make sense : in particular when we 'form' a class whose condition of membership is given by that predicate—the class of non-self-membered classes—it does not make sense to apply the predicate to that class. And in general we cannot assume that a predicate makes sense whatever it is applied to; so that if we try to specify its sense in the usual logical way be means of truth-conditions, the truth-conditions are liable to leave some, admittedly recherché, cases in which the truth-value of a senence applying, the predicate is indeterminate, and cannot be assigned one way or the other without contradiction.

If this is right, it affects the interpretation rules of the predicate calculus in the following way. Those rules need to lay down truth-conditions for the predicate leading construction schematised in such formulae as '*fa*', '*gcb*' etc. The construction is meant to be available for every predicate in every language, or, on the dummy letter account, for every ad hoc meaning of '*F*, '*G*', etc. But Russell's paradox seems to show that it is not possible to lay down truth-conditions for every predicate which will give a determinate answer to the question what things the predicate is true of i.e. what things it can be applied to so as to yield a truth, unless the range of things under consideration is limited in some way-perhaps to all things that are not classes or to all classes of a certain kind. These limitations will also affect the interpretation rule for '∀', the universal quantifier. We want to say, schematically, that '$\forall x f x$' is true on condition that '*f*' is true of everything, but for some replacements (or translations) of '*f*' it will be impossible to maintain consistently either that the condition is fulfilled or that it is not. A sentence such a 'Everything either is or is not self-membered' may fail to make sense even though its component predicate makes sense.

The standard response to this difficulty is to conclude that each piece of discourse in which all the propositions are of determinate truth-value must have an implicit subject matter, a class of things which the discourse is about. Classes in this role are called **domains** or universes of discourse. (LEMMON *BL* p. Io4, MATES p. 55, QUINE *MofL* p. 97, HUGHES & LONDEY pp. I9I, MASSEL, p 232). Nothing prevents a domain from being disparate, e.g. men-and-numbers; nothing I have said prevents it being, on some occasions of discourse, universal (though there are in fact difficulties in set theory, originally due to Cantor, about the existence of a class comprising everything, see pp. 252-3). Equipped with this notion we can rewrite the set of interpretation rules of the predicated calculus as a collection of sets of rules, one for each possible domain. Let us say that a property or relation is defined over a domain when it makes sense to attribute the property or relation to each member or ordered set of members of the domain. Then relative to a given domain a sentence fitting (translating) '*fa*', for example, will be true or false only if the subject fitting (translating) '*a*' in it has for its reference a member of the domain and the predicate fitting (translating) '*f*' in it attributes a property defined over the domain; the sentence being true if that property holds of that member, false otherwise. And relative to a given domain a sentence fitting (translating) '$\forall xfx$' will be true or false if and only if similarly the predicate fitting (translating) '*f*' in it is defined over the domain—true if the predicate attributes a property which holds of every member of the domain, false otherwise. In effect '$\forall$' is to be interpreted not as 'everything' but as 'everything under discussion'.

But Russell's paradox is not the only motive for framing truth-conditions with reference to domains. Actually it is a contentious motive, since one might avoid the contradiction threatened by 'the class of non-self-membered classes is a non-self-membered class', and by the parallel sentences which other paradoxes generate, if one concluded not that their predicates lack sense but that their subjects lack reference : there simply are no such things to be 'formed' as the class of non-self-membered classes, exactly as there is no barber to be found who shaves all and only those who do not shave themselves (see QUINE *Paradox* p.4). Let us turn then to the other motive, simplification of proofs that an argument has a valid form.

To prove that an argument has a valid form one would begin, of course, with the argument and seek a valid sequent of which it is an instance. Let us for a moment reverse that procedure, starting from the following sequent which is valid in the predicate calculus (QC-valid)

(Mq) <{'∀*x*(*fx* & *hx* ⊃ *gx*)', '*fa* & *ha*'}, '*ga*'>

If we now try to construct a QC-instance of (Mq), the QC interpretation rules for '∀', '&', '⊃' and the predicate-leading construction will permit such cases as the following:

> For any *x*, if *x* is happy and *x* is a person, *x* is honest; John is happy and John is a person; so John is honest.
>
> For any *x*, if *x* is derivable and *x* is a formula, *x* is well-formed; '*p* ⊃ *p*' is derivable and '*p* ⊃ *p*' is a formula; so '*p* ⊃ *p*' is well-formed.

Since the identity of arguments does not depend on the words in which they are expressed, and since instances are arguments, it follows that any paraphrase of the above words into more elegant English will still express an instance of (Mq) provided that it still expresses the same argument. Here are paraphrases:

> If anyone is happy, he is honest; John is a happy person; so he is honest.
>
> If any formula is derivable, it is well-formed; '*p* ⊃ *p*' is a derivable formula; so it is well-formed.

So far it is certain that we still have QC-instances of (Mq). But what happens if 'person' and 'formula' are elided from the second premisses? The elisions are not entirely neutral, since happy things do not have to be persons nor derivable things formulae (they might be sequents). Nevertheless I think it is reasonable to understand what results as still expressing the same arguments (the same premisses and conclusions), and therefore as still expressing QC-instances of (Mq). But now that the components corresponding to '*ha*' have disappeared from the specimen arguments, the question arises whether we cannot simplify the squent they instantiate from (Mq) to (Jq), which was

(Jq) <{'∀*x*(*fx* ⊃ *gx*)', '*fa*'}, '*ga*'>

There is no doubt that (Jq), like (Mq), is QC-valid. The question at issue is whether the arguments variously expressed above are QC-instances of it. It would be useful if we could count them so, since (Jq) is shorter than (Mq) and so easier to prove valid. The trouble is that (Jq) contains nothing answering to 'one' and 'formula' in 'anyone' and 'any formula', and it can hardly be right usage to express the specimen arguments in yet further truncated sentences which omit those indications of subject matter.

There are several ways in which to construct sequents at least approximating to the brevity of (Jq) and still insantiated by the specimen arguments. One way would be to replace 'person' and 'formula' by dummy or schematic letters, somehow attached to the quantifier as in '∀*xP* (*fx* ⊃ *gx*)' or '$\forall x_n$ (*fx* ⊃ *gx*)' or even '∀*h* (*f* ⊃ *g*)'. Another deivce, called many sorted logic, is to reserve different sets of variables for different sorts of things, as 'π' is reserved for formulae in the metalogical notation of this book; e.g. if 'π' were put into the logical language we could permit '∀*x* (*f*π ⊃ *g*π)' for 'if any formula is *f* it is *g*'. These devices have the disadvantage of calling for parallel restrictions on the admissible replacements of subject letters. The regular method (HUGHES & LONDEY pp. I9I-2, LAMBERT & VAN FRAASSEN p. 83) is to leave the logical notation as it stands and appeal once more to domains in defence of the claim that the specimen arguements are instances of (Jq) itself. First we perform the further truncation of 'anyone' and 'any formula' into 'anything'. Then we reason that although it does not absolutely accord with right usage to express the specimen arguments in these new words, nevertheless it does so accord relative to the assumption that the subject matter of discourse is, respectively, persons and formulae (this licence is restricted in modal contexts). This being so, the two arguments are each expressible relative to some domain in sentences QC—fitting the shorter sequent (Jq), and we can change the definition of 1-instances, once more so that that fact is enough to make them I-instances of (Jq) : an 1-instance of a sequent, we shall now say, is an argument expressible in some 1-context and *relative to some domain* in a suitably ordered set of sentences 1-fitting the sequent. An 1-valid sequent then becomes a sequent all of whose 1-instances in this further revised sense avoid the offending combination. Again the redefinition of '1-valid' could have been reached by another way: count a sequent 1-valid$_2$ in a domain when all argument expressible in an 1-context relative to *that* domain in a suitably ordered set of sentences 1-fitting the sequent avoid the offending combination. A sequent is l-valid under the further redefinition if and only if it is l-valid$_2$ in every domain.

One further point about domains needs to be made. They are classes, but they have to be classes with members; or alternatively, instead of writing 'relative to some domain' in the revised definition of l-instance', we must write 'relative to some non-empty domain'. In the view of many authors the reason for this is a technical one: without the qualification certain sequents that are otherwise QC-valid in the new sense would cease to be so, through not being QC-valid$_2$ in the empty domain (MASSEY pp. 259-6I). But the technical difficulty does not arise for the interpretation rules of the present book, according to which every sequent containing subject letters or quantifiers is QC-valid$_2$, vacuously, in the empty domain. A better reason is that the restriction to non-empty domains "is really no restriction at all"(W. & M. KNEALE p. 707), since no one can assume that his discourse has no subject matter. If follows from this that a proposition or argument is expressible relative to some domain if and only if it is expressible relative to some non-empty domain.If we explicate 'domain', therefore, as meaning 'doamain of *discourse*', in the manner of the previous paragraph, 'non-empty' becomes redundant; the explication ensures that domains are non-empty classes.

6.10 Validity : worlds

The first shot at defining validity brought out 'has a valid form' as meaning 'is an instance of an inference schema all of whose instances avoid the offending combination'. In the last three sections this has been relativised to logical languages, applied to sequents, and generalised over (non-empty) domains and contexts of right and unequivocal usage. It remains to be investigated whether the property of having a valid form, so refined, carries with it the property of deductive correctness.

We must not be lulled here by the word 'valid'. I have noted that in one customary sense 'valid' just means 'deductively correct'; but in the technical sense under examination in these sections it does not mean that, and cannot because it is applied to forms of argument (sequents or inference schemata) rather than arguements themselves. Nor can we simply assume that valid forms validate, (SMULLYANp. 3. i.e) that what *has* a valid form in the technical sense *is* valid in the customary sense (students of logic need to be wary of other words with a similarly dual-role, e.g. 'implies', 'logical truth', 'consequence;)

To be valid under the provisional definition is to be truthpreserving, i.e. to be had by no argument leading from true premisses to an untrue conclusion. So if one sticks to arguments having a valid form under that definition one will 'never be led astray'(PRIOR *FL* P. 15.) in the sense of passing from truths to untruths. But we are looking for a test of correctness, and 6.2 has shown that it is possible to meet the condition of never passing from truth to untruth without always—or-ever—arguing correctly, since the condition is met by anyone who argues from jointly unture premisses, whatever his conclusions. It is even possible to meet the condition and also avoid untrue premisses without arguing correctly, since it is met by anyone who argues to true conclusions, whatever his premisses.

It might seem then that the property of having a valid form, thus defined, provides no more assurance of correctness than does the property of avoiding the offending combination. But this is not fair. An argument which has a valid form, thus defined, not only avoids the offending combination but also *shares* avoidance of it with all other arguments of the same form. Shared avoidance is still different from what I argued in 6.4 to be the criterion of deductive correctness, necessary avoidance. On the other hand some logicians prefer to substitute shared avoidance as a better criterion, and their case must now be examined.

Quine, a notable champion of this alternative, would object to the criterion of deductive correctness defended in 6.4 on the ground that the notion of necessity (strict implication) which it invokes is unclear and ought in large part "to be dispensed with in serious science"(QUINE *PofL* p. 10). The right procedure "from the point of view of logical theory" is to "analyse" the deductive correctness of an argument into two circumstances: the argument has a certain form, and no argument of that form combines true premisses with an untrue conclusion (QUINE *MofL* p. 39). Thus the criterion becomes shared avoidance of the offending combination.

Two doubts may be raised about Quine's proposal: is notion of necessity really so obscure as to be unfit for serious science and, even if it is, are we justified in substituting shared avoidance as the criterion of deductive correctness? As to the unclarity of necessity and the concepts related to it—analyticity, logical possibility, strict implication-I do not intend to contribute to the debate that has surrounded this topic since the publication of Quine's article 2 *Dogmas* in 1951, beyond merely sketching what seem to be the major arguments on each side and indicating my response to them. It is said on the one side that the boundaries between the necessary and the non-necessary are intolerably hazy, and that necessity can be explicated only in terms of a circle of related concepts with no way of breaking out of the circle. It is said on the other side that the haziness must not be exaggerated—most truths can be classified without dispute as necessary or not necessary—and that explanation in a circle can still be efficacious (MATESP.9); moreover there is no difficulty about understanding the notion of self-contradiction or inconsistency and 'It is necessary that' might be glossed 'It is self-contradictory that not'(see STRAWSON *ILT* Ch-1). Secondly, as to the proposal that necessity and the other concepts in its family ought to be dispensed with in the criterion of deductive correctness, it is not obvious that they are dispensable even if unclear. A single argument which avoids the offending combination may still be incorrect: how is it protected against this risk by sharing that avoidance with other arguments of the same form? Where is the safety in numbers? It is as though someone, noticing that he cannot assure a catch of fish by buying a fishing rod, were to seek the assurance by joining a fishing club all of whose members have rods (cf. LEMMON *BL* p. 81 "this condition at least").

For these reasons we must keep the criterion of deductive correctness defended in 6.4. It might still be true that shared avoidance brings necessary avoidance in its train, and so satisfies that criterion i.e. that there is, in this logical case, safety in numbers. So it might still be true that every argument having a valid form,under our provisional definition of 'valid', is deductively correct according to the criterion of 6.4. To some this seems 'intuitively acceptable (I LUGHES & CRESSWELL pp. 10, 28-9, SUPPES pp. 21-2)', but to me it seems to need proof, which I am unable to supply.

The alternative is to set up a stronger definition of 'valid form', and an particular of '1-valid sequent'. I do so by means of the notion of possible facts, i.e. what might have been the case. A true proposition is true given the actual facts, but many true propositions would not have been true given other possible facts. Combinations of truth-value can likewise be made relative to possible facts. For example the argument 'Something is black; so something is white' combines a premiss would (still) have been true had there currently been no white things, with a conclusion which would in that case have been untrue. So even though it avoids the offending combination given the actual facts, it would not have done so had things been appropriately otherwise. Sets of possible facts are conventionally distinguished as possible worlds, or just worlds. In these terms the new and stronger definition of 'valid' will stipulate that a form is valid (a sequent l-valid) only when all arguments having it (all its l-instances) avoid the offending combination in every world, i.e. would avoid it whatever the facts, i.e. avoid it of necessity (cf p. 29). As before the definition could have been reached in a more roundabout way: count a sequent l-valid_3 in a world when all l-instances of it avoid the offending combination in *that* world. A sequent is l-valid under the stronger definition if and only if it is l-valid_3 in every world.

The difference between this and the provisional definition of 'valid form' is a difference between the strict and the material. In the one case a form is valid when the premisses of all arguments having it strictly imply their conclusions; in the other case it is valid when they materially imply their conclusions. Some logicians offer both definitions of 'valid' side by side (HUGHES & LONDEY pp. 4, 17, LAMBERT &VAN FRAASSEN pp. 8, 85) or both definitions of 'has a valid form' side by side (MATES p. 16). But this is unsatisfactory without a proof, which they do not supply, that the definitions in each pair come to the same thing, i.e. that shared material implication brings strict implication in its train.

6.11 The definition of 'valid sequent'

Here are the results of the last four sections.

6.11(I) An l-instance of a sequent (for any logical language 1) is an argument expressible in some context of right and unequivocal usage of some 1-incorporating language,relative to some domain, in a set of sentences which, when ordered with the conclusion sentence last, fit by the conventions of l the successive formulae of the sequent.

More briefly: an l-instance of a sequent is an argument

expressible in some l-context and domain in a set of sentences l-fitting the sequent.

6.11 (2) An l-valid sequent (for any logical language 1) is a sequent all of whose l-instances avoid the offending combination of necessity, i.e. are arguments whose premisses strictly imply their conclusions.

A clarificaiton is needed at this point. 'Inference-schema' was defined on p. 33 with an eye only to arguments of the normal type having at least one premiss; hence inference-schemataweare assi,ed tp cpmtyaom at ;east two sentence-schemata. But some sequents pair the empty set of formulae with a formula, so containing only one formula. To make sure that not all one-formula sequents are valid we have to provide them with instances, and therefore we have to admit the possibility of arguments without premisses. The simplest way is to identify such 'arguments with their conclusions, thus treating all propositions as premissless arguments. Then a one-formula sequent will be valid, i.e. each of its l-instances will of necessity avoid combining true premisses with an untrue conclusion, if and only if each of its l-instances of necessity avoids being untrue, i.e. is a necessary truth.

6.11 (3) 'has a valid form' is to be given the technical sense 'is, for some logical language l, an l-instance of an l-valid sequent'.

With these definitions we can establish a further metalogical principle, to add to 6.3 (I) and 6.4. (I). Take any argument which has a valid form. by 6.11 (3) it is an l-instance, for some l, of some l-valid sequent. By 6.11 (2) the premisses of every l-instance, for that l, of that sequent strictly imply the instance's conclusion. So the argument's premisses strictly imply its conclusion. So:

6.11 (4) The premisses of an argument strictly imply its conclusion if it has a valid form, i.e. if for at least one logical language l it is an l-instance of at least one l-valid sequent.

6.12 Proof

If we know that some argument is an l-instance, for some l, of an l-valid sequent, metalogical principle 6.11 (4) permits the inference that its premisses strictly imply its conclusion. Then metalogical principle 6.4(I) permits the further inference that it is deductively correct. Finally by metalogical principle 6.3 (I) we can conclude that is is correct. The point of using this chain of inferences is that there exist logical techniques for proving, in some cases, that an argument is an l-instance for some l of an l-valid sequent. The proofs are of course metalogical, because they prove that an *argument* has a certain property.

Metalogical proofs ought to be as rigorous as possible, but they do not differ from other rigorous proofs except in being metalogical, i.e. having a logical subject matter. It will be as well at this stage, therefore, to say something general about the concept of proof. A proof is generally an argument, but it is more than a correct, even deductively correct, argument, for that might have a false conclusion. It is also more than a correct arguement with true premisses, because then one could prove any true conclusion by deducing it, for example, from itself or from the conjunction of itself with any other true premisses: but clearly '*p*; *q*; so *p*' is not the schema of any proof, whether metalogical or otherwise (this faults HUGHES & LONDEY p.44). The remaining necessary condition for proof by argument can be stated in Aristotle's way: the premisses of a probative argument, and the principles of inference by which its conclusion is drawn from them, must be more evident than the conclusion (An. *Post. I* 2.71^{b}21). The hearer must be 'carried along' from premisses which he is initially willing to accept as true (once he understands them), by inferences which he is willing to accept a correct, to a conclusion which he is not initially willing to accept as true. This shows that proving can be treated as a relative matter: what proves a conclusion to one audience may not do so to another. But the advancement of knowledge, and especially the writing of books, depends on the fact that the relation of being-more-evident-than is to some extent a natural one, so that some arguments are 'naturally probative' in a sense which rather uneasily straddles the difference between 'Everyone who understands them finds their conclusions relatively non-evident' and 'Everyone who unde-rstands them ought to find their conclusions relatively non-evident'.An argument which fails as a proof because it asserts its conclusion among its premisses is said to the **beg to question**. This is not so clear a definition as its seems, because asserting shades into 'implying' and yet the premisses of a good proof must, of course, imply its conclusion in some sense, e.g. 'entail' (see MILL, II iii 2). So the label 'begging the question' comes to be used in a general way to describe any argument which fails to meet the condition of relative evidentness. The concepts of proof, evidentness, and begging the question are epistemological, rather than logical. But though logic, as I understand the word, does not study proofs, it uses them.

Begging the question is often called a fallacy, but it is not a fallacy in the sense 'incorrect argument'. Indeed its clearest cases, instances if '*p*; *q*; so *p*', are patently correct. This point was noticed by PETER OF SPAIN (7.54); see HAMBLIN p.33.

Metalogical proofs have a recurrent pattern. Typically they seek to show that all entities of a certain class or classes—e.g. well-formed formulae, or sentences, or l-contexts—have a certain feature if certain conditions are met, or if and only if they are met. A proof which aims at such a result will start off by making assumptions of two kinds. First, it will 'take' or 'select' an arbitrary member of each of the classes concerned: 'Let π be σ formula and o a sentence fitting it' or some such. Secondly it will'suppose' or 'hypothesise' that the conditions are met. Then it will proceed, using results previously arrived at, to deduce that the desired feature does hold of the chosen member. If the conclusion is to contain 'if and only if, this process must next be repeated in the reverse direction. Finally the conclusion is formed by putting each supposition into an 'if' clause and generalising over all members of the classes concerned. We shall see how this pattern is reproduced in some predicate calculus sequent-derivations.

If the metalogical principles 6.3 (I), 6.4 (I) and 6.11 (4) are to be used as I have suggested in proofs of correctness, then three conditions must be met. First, the correctness of the metalogical arguments from these principles to the conclusion that a given argument is correct must be relatively evident. It is important to notice this fact, which shows that although logic seeks to prove correctness it depends on prior acceptance that certain kinds of argument (in this case among the instances of predicate calculus sequents) are correct; of. LAMBERT & VAN FRAASSEN p. I70. Secondly, the metalogical principles must themselves be proved; I have attempted to do so in the present chapter. Thirdly, there must exist ways of proving what waṣ hypothesised in the first sentence of this section, that certain arguments are 1-instances for certain 1s of certain 1-valid sequents.This last requirement in turn breaks down into two stages: finding a sequent of which the argument is an 1-instance for same 1;and proving that the sequent is 1-valid for that 1.

The second stage, proof of validity, can be direct or indirect. In some logical languages, notably the propositional calculus, there are quite simple direct methods for proving a valid sequent valid-and in fact for proving an invalid sequent invalid. Two of these will be discussed and others mentioned in 7.2. Direct methods can be used in other calculi too, but it is generally more convenient to proceed indirectly through the notion of derivability. An indication of this is the name 'proof theory' for the study of logistic systems, which deal with derivability. Logistic systems include, indeed in this book will be constituted by, methods of proving the derivability of all their derivable sequents (and formulae).

Proof theory might be studied for its own sake, but it will not serve the purposes of this book unless some connection can be established between derivability and validity. A derivable;

sequent is derival relative to rules of derivatin; a valid sequent is valid relative to a kabguage, i.e. rules of interpretation. What we need therefore is a further technical concept linking the two kinds of rules, and this is the concept of the soundness of a system in a language (see MATES p. I39, MASSEY p.280). A sequent system is called sound with respect to a language 1, 1-sound for short, when every sequent derivable in it is 1-valid. Given this definition it is easy to deduce a further metalogical principle:

6.12(I) An argument has a valid form if for at least one logical language 1 it is an 1-instance of at least one sequent which is derivable in at least one 1-sound sequent system.

A proof of correctness which goes through 6.12 (I) as well as 6.3 (I) 6.4 (I) and 6.11 (4) needs three starting points instead of two. It must establish that the argument under scrutiny is an l-instance of some sequent, that the sequent is derivable in some sequent system and that the system is l-sound, i.e. all its derivable sequents are l-valid. This last property cannot be assumed. Although a calculus is defined as a system sharing formation rules with a logical language, and so must contain sets of derivation and interpretation rules, these two latter sets are stated quite independently of one another and might fail to 'match'. Indeed given a derivable sequent it is always going to be possible, obviously, to invent some interpretation of its symbols under which it turns out not to be valid. A calculus is called 'argument sound' when the sequents derivable in it are all valid in it. So for each calculus we shall need a proof of argument soundness.

6.13 Alternative route

In 5.11 I noted the existence of formula systsms, in which derivability is a property of formulae rather than sequents. If one were to use forumla systems for proving the correctness of correct arguments, at least principle 6.12 (I) would have to be replaced. In practice it is normal to replace 6.4 (I) and 6.11

(4) also, proceeding by an alternative route which must now be briefly traced.

We need to go back to the criterion of deductive correctness, and to describe the second of the two ways I distinguished in 6.4 of generalising the assertion that the argument expressed in 'Today is Monday; so tomorrow will be Tuesday' is deductively correct if and only if it could not have been Monday today without being Tuesday tomorrow. The new generalisation yields: an argument is deductively correct if and only if the conjunction of its premisses with the negation (denial, contradictory) of its conclusion could not hav e been true, i.e. if and only if the negation of that conjunction is a necessary truth. Technical abbreviation now re-enters. The negation of the conjunction of an argument's premisses with the negation of its conclusion may be called the material conditional corresponding to the argument. Hence the criterion of deductive correctness can now be put in the form:

6.13(I) An argument is deductively correct if and only if its corresponding material conditional is a necessary truth.

In this formulation there is no longer talk of one thing's materially implying another; just of a single material conditional's being true.

The status of negations and conjunctions, and hence of material conditionals, is as much in need of clarification as was that of premisses and conclusions. According to QUINE (*Mof L* pp. 1, 5, 12) and MATES (p.7 and, speaking of logical languages,p.49) these things are sentences, and Quine and Mates make the extra stipulation that one sentence is to count as, for example, the negation of another only if it is formed from that other by the addition of some negative expression or connective or connective (thus no two sentences are, in their usage, negations of each other). But since the reasons which favour doing logic in terms of propositions rather than sentences carry over from the sequent route to the formula route, I shall construe negations, conjunctions, and conditionals as propositions (so LEMMON *BL* pp. 7, 19, HUGHES & LONDEY p. 20).

As the word 'conditional' suggests, it is possible, and in the Quine—Mates usage necessary, to frame conditionals by means of some word or connective answering to 'if'. For example the material conditional expressed in 'It is not the case that both today is Monday and tomorrow will not be Tuesday' can be expressed less clumsily in'If today is Monday, tomorrow will be Tuesday'. For this reason the conjunction of the premisses of an argument is known as the antecedent of the corresponding material conditional and its conclusion as the consequent (arguements, which may be correct or incorrect, have premisses and conclusions; conditionals, which as propositions may be true or false, have antecedents and consequents). But the 'if' idiom carries dangers familiar to students of logic, both because not all 'if' sentences express conditional propositions, e.g, 'If the song is set too high, transpose it', and because in the case of those that do express conditional propositions it is often unclear whether the conditional is 'material' or not (QUINE *Mof L* pp. 19-23 and see 9.5).

I next define the notion of a formal truth, or, as it is more usually called, **logical truth**. This is analogous to 'argument having a valid form' and runs into analogous difficulties. Should a logical truth fit a schema or translate a symbolic sentence? Is it to be a sentence or a proposition? Is it to be an instance relative to some logical language and in some context and domain? In the end we emerge with these three definitions corresponding to 6.11 (I)-(3):

6.13(2) An l-instance of a formula is a proposition expressible in some context of right and unequivocal usage of some l-incorporating language, relative to some domain, in a sentence which fits the formula by the l conventions.

6.13(3) An l-valid formula is a formula all of whose l-instances are necessary truths.

6.13(4) 'is a logical truth' is to be given the technical sense 'is, for some logical language l, an l-instance of an l-valid formula'.

By reasoning parallel to p. 59 it follows that

6.13(5) The material conditional corresponding to an argument is a necessary truth if it is a logical truth, i.e. is for at least one logical language l an l-instance of at least one l-valid formula.

As with sequent systmes, a formula system is sound with respect to a logical language l, l-sound for short, when all formulae derivable in it are l-valid. A calculus is called 'statement sound' when all formulae derivable in it are valid in it. Hence as in 6.12 (I).

6.13(6) The material conditional corresponding to an argument is a logical truth if for at least one logical language l it is an l-instance of at least one formula which is derivable in at least one l-sound formula system.

6.3(I), 6.13 (1) 6.13 (5) and 6.13 (6) combine to provide the alternative route from proof of derivability in a formula system to proof of correctness.

6.14 The power of logic

How much help can logic give in the enterprise of testing arguments? If the methods of this book are to apply, the premisses of a tested argument must be finite in number (p.25) and, together with the conclusion, all true or false. But there are three more general and serious limitations.

(i) In order or be useful (e.g. in a proof) an argument must normally have true premisses as well as being correct. We have seen in 6.2 that these properties are independent of one another. But the truth of premisses cannot be tested by logical means, save in the exceptional case where they are logical truths or logical falsehoods.

(ii) A test of correctness will be a metalogical proof, proving an argument correct or incorrect as the case may be. But proofs of incorrectness fall outside the main methods of this book, because they do not involve the concept of validity. The reason is that whereas every l-instance of an l-valid sequent is correct, not every l-instance of an l-invalid sequent is incorrect. On the contrary, *every* correct argument instantiates *some* invalid sequent: e.g. every one-premiss arguement, correct or incorrect, PC-instantiates the PC-invalid sequent <{'p'}, '*q*'>. Hence proofs of invalidity, though available, afford no more than a challenge, showing that a sequent which might have been thought to certify some argument as correct fails to do so because it is actually invalid in some calculus. There always remain the possibilities that the sequent is valid in some other calculs, or that the argument instantiates some other sequent which is valid in some calculus (LAMBERT & VAN FRAASSEN p. 51), or that the argument is deductively correct though not in virtue of its form, or correct though not deductively correct. Logic can indeed assist in proofs of incorrectness, by another method that will be described later. But the main method, through validity, is only a method of proving correctness.

(iii) Even when confined to proofs of correctness the main method not 'effective', in the sense of prescribing a step by step procedure which if duly applied is bound to lead in a finite number of stages to an affirmative answer to the question 'is such and such an argument correct?' whenever an affirmative answer is the right one. This may be surprising to those who are aware of logic's reputation as a mechanical science, in which insight and ingenuity are thought to be supplanted by mere (even if complex) computation. But the fact is that computations take us only part of the way. Logic breaks up proofs of correctness into two main stages (see QUINE *W & O* p. 159 on this "division of labor"): finding, for a given argument, some sequent of which it is an l-instance in some l; and proving that the sequent is l-valid. The proving can sometimes be managed by computation—though the indirect methods that I shall stress in this bbook, of proving validity through derivability in some sound system, call for ingenuity as well. But the finding is not at present reducible to rule. Arguments are normally presented in a set of sentences of some natural language. Transformation from these sentences into an instantiated sequent or formula, which I shall call formalising, involves replacing some words by schematic letters and translating others into connectives. Linguists aspire tomechanise translation; but translation between English and the logical languages of this book is not mechanical (MATES p. 69).

Even if it could be made so—perhaps for other logical languages it is doubtful whether the remaining tasks of the formaliser, notably certifying right and unequivocal usage, could ever be mechanised.

The range of arguments that can be proved correct by the methods of logic depends, of course, on the richness of the logical calculi available. The four calculi covered in this book, and particularly the first two of them which almost are logic in the eyes of many contemporary philsophers, constitute a powerful tool for proving correctness. On the other hand it is easy to devise arguments which are at least apparently correct, and apparently correct in virtue of their form, but which probably do not instantiate valid sequents of any of the calculi in this book. Here are some examples:

(P) The man in the brown hat is a spy; so some spy wears a brown hat.

(Q) You are required to reserve a seat if you travel on the 10.50; so you are permitted to travel on the 10.50 only if you reserve a seat.

(R) What is past is inevitable; so whatever is possible will come to be (the Master Argument of Diodorus; see PRIOR PPF pp. 32-3).

(S) John believes that Napoleon won the battle of—Waterloo; so if he believes that Napoleon was an Englishman, he believes that an Englishman won the battle of Waterloo.

Work has been done or is in progress on calculi which comprehend these arguments. (P) belongs to the theory of—definite descriptions (see QUINE M of L pp. 227-30, LEMMON BL ppl. 166-7), (Q) to deontic logic, (R) to tense logic, (S) to intentional logic, the logic of 'propositional attitude' verbs like 'believe'. But such developments are outside the scope of this book.

Finally, a word of perhaps needless caution. In approaching the question 'Is such and such an argument correct?' through the question 'Does it (its corresponding material conditional) instantiate in such and such a language a sequent (formula) which is derivable in some system which is sound in that language?' the logician increases the number of errors and confusions into which it is possible to fall. He also makes it easier, sometimes much easier, for thinkers to avoid error and confusion-once they have mastered the skills involved. Often, especially when an argument in known to be difficult or disputed, the benefits of symbolism are worth the price. But it cannot always be so. This is a matter for judgment in each particular case.

Chapter-7

Formation Rules and Definitions

Chapter 7

7.I Syntax refined

In the grammar of a language the part called syntax deals with two sorts of question: what combinations of words are premitted(baiscally,how to construct a grammatical sentence) and how combination determines the meaninig of phrases and sentences from the meanings of words. These questions overlap because of the still current practice of stating the former kind of rules, composition rules, in terms of parts of speech or grammatical categories,which classify words and phrases according to the way in which they contribute to the meanings of sentences. Hence instructions for testing whether some string of English words,e.g.'Pigs fly', is a grammatical sentence will, when they are given in the currently standard manner, be useful only to someone who knows that'pigs' is a noun and'fly' can be a verb, which is just the knowledge that bridges the gap between understanding the meaning of those words, e.g. from a dictionary, and understanding the meanings of the sentence formed from them. On the other hand standard composition rules plus the information in a dictionary are not enough to reveal the meaning of every English sentence.For example the meaning of 'People eat frogs'depends on which noun is subject, which object; and'subject' and 'object', unlike 'noun' and 'verb', do not figure in composition rules because they do not name parts of speech. Here the two aspects of syntax, rules for telling whether a sentence is grammatical and rules for inferring sentence-meaning from word-meaning,fail to coincide.

In current linguistic theory it is customary to lable questions about meaning as falling under 'semantics', and to contrast semantics with syntax. In view of what has been said the contrast is a blurred one, but it could be sharpened by restricting the application of the lable 'syntax' in two ways: questions about the dependence of sentence-meaning on word-meaning would have to be banished from syntax into the 'semantics of constructions', and composition rules would have to be stated in a meaning-neutral way, i.e. in terms of a description and classification of elementary expressions which makes no reference to their shared or different roles in contributing to the meanings of sentences. The kind of syntax which emerges from this refining process is what logicians call a system of formation rules.Logical formation rules take, or specify, a set of elementary expressions divide them in some meaning-neutral way into classes, and state in terms of this classification how to make compounds(strings) out of the elements.

It may be asked why logic insists on such a refined notion of syntax, especially since the refinement is ignored in the syntax of natural languages on which logical formation rules are often assumed to be modelled.The reason is that logic is tied as closely to mathematics as to linguistics. From an linital interest in patterns common to different inference, i.e. in inference-schemata,the logician has come to discern common to different inference-schemata and patterns shared with things which are not inference-schemata at all.As in mathematics,this leads to independent study of the secondary patterns without regard to what they are patterns of—to the study, for exemple, of relations among formulae without regard to the fact that they are relations among elements of inference-schemata.An expression representing a patterns which is shared by inference-schemata among other things is an expression which can be interpreted as an inference-schemata.Hence any decision to leave open the question what some pattern is a pattern of carries with it the decision to leave such representative expressions uninterpreted. If formation rules are to come at this abstract, uninterpreted, stage, they must either avoid words like 'word', 'noun', 'sentence', 'schematic letter', 'subject letter', 'sentence-schema', or, if they use any of them (as I shall), they must use them without prejudice to interpretation.

7.2 Formulating the rules

The rule I adopt are set out in Appendix Two.

The formation rules of the propositional calculus can be stated like this:[FL] every propositional letter is a well-formed; formulas [F~] the result of writing '~' followed by a well-formed formula is a well-formed formula; and[F&] the result of writing '('followed by a well-formed formula followed by '&'followed by a well-formed formula followed by')' is a well-formed formula. This set of rules constitutes a recursive definition of well-formedness in the sense explained in 5.8, except that it contains so far no extremal clause.The first rual in the set is categorical; if stated as above it must be accompanied by a specification of what are to count as propositional letter,viz. the infinite series beginning'*p*','*q*','*r*','p_1','q_1','r_1','p_2'. The other two rules are hypothetical and could be put in the form 'If such-and-such is (are) well-formed, so also is such-and-such'.Already in this simple case it is going to be convenient to introduce metalogical symbolism,as forecast in 5.13. If we use 'PC-formula'as short for 'formula that is well-formed in the propositional calculus' and ' ', ' ♀ ' as metalogical variables ranging over formula the hypothetical rules can be reformulated as: for any and ♀ , if and ♀ are PC-formulae,so also are ~ and (& ♀). Here '~ & ' and'(& ♀)' are lazy shorthand for ~ and '(& ♀) which in turn mean 'the result of writing "~" followed by ' and'the result of writing "**", than than"&", than ♀ than")". So we are not to suppose that ~ *is* aPC-formula: in fact it is not, since is not in the series of propositional letters. Rather the '~ '-rule licenses as PC-formulae such formulae as ~*p*', '~*q*', '~~*p*', '~(*p*&*q*)', '~(*q*&*p*)' , '~(*q*&*p*) ' '~(~*p*&*p*) and so on. This set is obviouslyinfinite, and wolud be so even if there were not an infinite supply of proposotional letters. Notice too that 'for any and ♀ ' means 'for any and ♀ not necessarily distinct': so we have also such PC-formulae as '(*p*&*q*)','((~*r* &~*p*) & (~*r* &~*r*))'.

In the predicate calculus with identity all the foregoing kind of formulae are well-formed,and more. We now need to add a list of predicate letters, viz.the infinite series beginning'*f*','*g*','h','f_1' and a list of subject letters,viz.the infinite series beginning '*a*', '*b*', '*c*', 'a_1'. Two new categorical rules state that:[FP] any predicate letter followed by one or more subject letters, the same or different,is a well-formed formula;and [F=] '='between two subject letters, the same or different,is a well-formed formula.These rules license respectively such formulae as '*fa*','*gbbcb*',and '*b=b*','*c=a*'.Notice that'=' thus becomes alogical symbol,unlike '*def*' which is metalogical. The predicate calulus also adds a list of varibles,viz.the infinite series beginning '*x*', '*y*', '*z*', '*f*', and a hypothetical rule f '∀.The statement of this rule is more difficult because a well-formed formula starting,for example with '∀γ' will need to be followed by formulae containing the variable '*y*'(e.g.'*fy*','& *p*,) and nothing said so far licenses formulae contaring variabale as well-formed.In fact the rules I adopt do not permit free,i.e. unquantified, occurrences of a variable in any well-formed formula. So the construction of a well-formed formula beginning '∀' has to proceed in two stages.First,taking a well-formed formulae containing a subject letters, e.g.'*fc*', '(*gaa* & *p*)', we transform it into something that is not well-formed by substituting a variable for at least one occurrence of the subject letter in it' as in'*fy*','(*gay* & *p*)';secondly we prefix '∀' followed by the chosen variable, as in '∀*γfy*', '∀γ (*gay* & *p*)',. The mutilation of one well-formed formula thus makes it suitable for grafting into another.This process involves at its first stage the operation of *substituting* some one variable for occurrences of some one subject letter. Although in the presentcase substitution is a simple affair, the correct statement of substitution rules can become very tricky elsewhere; I shall return to the subject in 6.6.

The rule for '∀' sketched above would prmit construction of such formulae as '*∀x∀xfxx*' and '∀z~ (∀zgzz & *p*)' in which it is not claer which of two quantifiers 'binds'which occurrences of a variable.There are two ways of dealing with this uncertainty.We could wait for the interpretation rules to indicate when a quantifier is forestalled by another in its attempt to bind a variable, and when in particular it is forestalled in all its attempts and so become 'vacuous' (HUGHES & LONDEY p.295; this is the method of MASSEY p.239,MATESp45). Or we could emend the formation rule so as to forbid all such uncertainties, and forbid vacuous quantification.Ishall follow Lemmon in adopting the latter course,by ruling that the well-formed formula into which a variable is substituted for a subjet letter may not already contain that variable (LEMMON *BL* p.142).Although this emendation is effective in preventing such uncertainties,it is an underdiscriminating instrument for the purpose;it is not so sweeping as to ban '(∀*xfx* & ∀*xgx*)', for example,which is constructed by the '&'-rule from two perfectly well formed formulae '∀*xfx'* and '∀*xgx*' but it does ban—or rather fail to license-such barely ambiguous groupings as '∀*x (fx* & ∀*xgx*)' which would have to be constructed by substitutin '*x*' into a well-formed formulae already containg 'x' such as ('(*fa* & ∀*xgx*)',)

We can think of the construction of ' ∀'-formulae in another way which will be useful later on. Instead of starting form a well-formed formula,e.g.'(*gaa* & *p*)',and deleting occurrences of a subject letter in it so as substitute occurrences of a variable,we are to start from a formula in which there are already gaps.Such formulae with one or more gaps in I call **stencils** (MATES p.178).In a peripheral passage of it will be necessary to mark these gaps by numerals, which may be repeated, so yieding stencils such as'(*ga*① & *p*)','(*g* ② ① &*p*)','(*g* ① ① & *p*)', but the rules in Appendix Two require only the numeral ① or blanks as in' (*g—a* ,& *p)',* '(*g*— —& *p*',. (This definition of 'stencil' differs from Mates's in not stipulating any particular kind of filling for the gaps nor that a filled up stencil necessarily becomes a well-formed formulae.Quine's passing use of the words, *MofL* p.146 is different, referring to mutilated sentence,not mutilated formulae; the stencils we are concerned with will get interpreted as what Quine calls predicate-schemata, MofLlp.150)

The '∀'-rule restated in terms of stencils will say that if a stencil becomes a well-formed formula by having its gaps filled uniformly by a subject letter,it also becomes a well-formed formulae by having its gaps filled uniformly by a variable and then having '∀' followed by the variable prefixed to the whole;i.e.[F∀] if the result of inserting a subject letter once into each gap in a stencil is well-formed,so also is the result of inserting a variable(not already present) once into each gap in it and prefixing '∀' followed by that variable.

As before these predicate calculus rules can be shortened by metalogical notation.I use 'QC-formula, for'formula that is well-formed in predicate calculus with identity', 'α', 'β', as metealogical variables ranging over subject letters 'ν' as a metalogical variable ranging over variables, and 'ϕ', ' ψ', as metalogical variables ranging over stencils. Once more '$\forall\nu$' is a lazy way of writing '∀v', i. e. 'the result of writing '∀' followed by υ'; and 'α = β' similarly. But '$\phi\alpha$'will have a special meaning, not'the result of writing ϕ followed by a' but 'the result of inserting a once into each gap in ϕ'; similary for 'ϕv', 'ϕβ' etc.The formulation of F= and F∀ now becomes: for any α and β, $a = \beta$ is a QC-formula; and for any a, υ, and ϕ not already containing υ, if ϕa is a QC-formula; so also is ∀vϕv.

The formation rules for the modal calculi S_5 and QS_5 are obtained by adding,to PC and QC respectively, a rule licesing as well-formed any well-formed formula preceded by '□'; for example '□P', '□~q', '□□p', '□(~q & □r)' become well-formed in S_5 and additionally such formulae as '□∀xfx', '□fa' and thence '∀x□fx' become well-formed in QS_5 . The symbolic formulation of the rule is: [F□] for any π, if π is an S_5-(QS_5-) formula so also is □π.

Although in an obvious sense QS_5 is an extension of both S_5 and QC, which in turn are extensions of PC, it is worth noticing that the extensions to each class of well-formed formulae cannot be made by simply tacking on new formation rules to the old;or rather that only suffices if we reinterpret 'well-formed' in the old rules as now meaning well-formed according to the new ones. This because we want to count for example,'(*fa* & *p*)' as a QC-formula and '(—*r* & *p*)' as an S_5-formula. Only an '&'-rule will license them as well-formed, but the original '&'-rule permitted '&'only between PC-formulae, so excluding both 'fa'and—as component.A full statement of the QC formation rules must include adaptations of the PC rules, in which'QC-formula' is written for'PC-formula' throughout; and similarly in the other cases.

Formulae that are licensed as well-formed by one of the categorical rules of a calculus are called **atomic formulae** of that calculus.The atomic formulae of PC and S_5 are the propositional letters; of QC and QS_5 those plus formulae consisting of predicate letters followed by subject letters,and also formulae such as '*a*=*a*','*b*=*c*',.

A sequent is well-formed in a calculus if and if its component formulae are infinite number and all well-formed in that calculus.For example any finit sequent of S_5 formulae is an S_5 sequent.

7.3 Symbolic definitions

A recursive definitions,i.e.specification of well-formed formulae will need to end,as we saw in 5.8,with an extremal rule to the effect that the set of well-formed formulae is the smallest set satisfying the other rules,so that everything left unlicensed by those rules is denied a licence.But there are many formulae left unlicensed by the rules stated in 7.2 which nevertheless appear in most presentations of four calculi distinguished; there and these are formulae containing other connectives than '~', '&' '=', '∀', '□'. Any of three policies, apart from outright rejection, could be adopted for such connectives.We could supply them with their own formation rules; we could bring them in by eliminative definition;or we could keep them outside the logical notation itself but permit them as convenient shorthand in what are strictly will-formed formulae.

The advantage of avoiding the first course is to reduce the number of interpretation and derivation rules that will be needed at a later stage.For the other courses have the effect of saying that the connectives '~', '&' '=', '∀', '□' constitute, toge ther with letters and variable and punctuation,the whole of the primitive vocabulary of the four calculi.Any further symbols introduced by eliminative definition or by informal convention are to be seen as merely shorthand for the primitive notation,a concession to men's obtuseness in detecting the structure of long formulae (machines wouldn't want them).We might,it is true,positively welcome the opportunity of stating independent formation rules for a wider vocabulary of connectives; and this will happen especially if we are interested in comparing variant sets of iterpretation and derivation rules which agree over formulae containing '~', '&' '=', '∀', '□' but diverge elsewhere.Intuitionist logic can be presented as such a variant. But for the purposes of this book the vocabulary of 7.2 will suffice as primitive.

Given, then, that further connectives are worth admitting but do not need independent formation rules because their role is to serve as dispensable shorthand,it makes no practical difference whether we license formulae containing them as well-formed,or tolerate them as unlicensed convenicences. I shall do the former,so inserting symbolic definitions among the logical rules. There are five main definitions,one each for the connectives 'y', '⊃', '≡', '∃', '□'. The last which comes into play only in S_5 and QS_5 is very simple: | Def ◊] '◊' is short for '~□~'.The others are contextual definitions displaying not a primitive formula which abbreviates to the new symbol but a formula containing primitive connectives which abberviates to a formula containing the new symbol.If we take 'V' as an example '~(~ *p* & ~*q*)' is to abbreviate to '(*p* v *q*)', and the corresponding abbreviation is to be perimitted with any other well-formed formula (whether or not it is a propositional letter) in place of '*p*' and '*q*'. In metalogical notation this becomes: for any well-formed formulae π and ϙ , [Def ∪] (π ⊃ ϙ) is short for ~ (π & ~ ϙ). Similarly the definitions of '⊃' and '≡' are: for any well-formed formulae p and ϙ , [def É] (π ⊃ ϙ) is short for ~(p & ~ϙ); [Def ≐] (p ≡ ϙ) is short for ((p ⊃ ϙ) & (ϙ ⊃ π)). These belong to all four calculi. Finally in QC and QS_5 we have: [Def ∃] for any variable *υ*, ∃v, is short for ~ ∀ v ~.

The definitions are to be understood of course,as two-way licences to abbreviate and to expand.Their use does not have to involve the of any formula.For example the formulae '(*p* & ~ (~ *r* & ~ ∀*xfx*))' and '~ ~ (~ *r* & ~ ∀ *xfx*)' both contain '~ (~ *r*&~∀*xfx*)' as an embedded part; so Def ∨ licenses their abbreviation to '(*p* & (*r* ∨ ∀*xfx*))' and '~ (*r* ∨ ∀ *xfx*)'. .It is however required that the units which finish up attached to the new connective should be well-formed formulae(hence' for any well-formed π and ϙ in the formulations); we may not shorten '~ (~ (*p* & ~ *q*) & *r*)' to '((*p* ∨ *q*) & *r*)' by taking the will-formed ('p' as the first unit and the ill-formed'*q*')& *r*' as the second. this requirement makes a difficulty in any version of the predicate calculus which excludes free variable from well-formed formulae,since the definitions cannot be applied as we should want in order to shorten,for example,'∀*x* ~ (~ *fx* & ~ *p*)' into '∀*x* (*fx* ∨ *p*)' : '*fx*' is not well-formed.The way out of this difficulty that I shall take is to add a hypothetical definition rule: for any *α*, *ν*, *ϕ* and *ψ*, if *ϕα* is short for *ψα*, ∀*νϕν* is short for ∀*νψν* (and so ∃*νϕν* is short for ∃*νψν*).The extra convenience of having this hypothetical rule is not great; lemmon manages without it.

How do the definition ensure the well-formedness of formulae not primitive notation? Had we proceeded by way of extra formation rules instead of definitions,such formulae would have turned out well-formed under the extra rules. Had we adopted the third alternative of treating the definitions as informal conventions,the formulae would have remained ill-formed,though to aerated.As it is we have the following kind of situation: '~ (~ p & ~ q)' and '~ ~ ∀x ~ ~ □~ fx' are well-formed by the orignal formation rules; and '(p ∨ q)' and '~ ∃x◊fx' abbreviate them by the definitions. Is this enough to make the well-formed? The answer depends on whether we understand the definitions as producing new formulae or as rewriting the same formulae in different notation. If they rewrite the same formulae,no more needs to be said; for '~ (~p & ~ q)' is well-formed '(p ∨ q)' is that same formulae,and it therefore follows that '(p ∨ q)' is well-formed.But it is perhaps more natural to regard the criterion of identity for formulae as 'same symbols in the same order'(compare sentences), with the consequence that definitions produce different formulae. If so there seems to be need of an extra formation rule after all,to the effect that the definitions preserve well-formedness,i.e.never lead from a well-formed to an ill-formed.Its formulation could be:for any π and ♀ , if ♀ is short for π and π is well-formed,so also is ♀ (so MATES in the case of derivability,p.98).My own procedure will be a sort of compromise between these two:I shall understand the role of symbolic definitions in such a way that the operation of shortening or lengthening a formula by means of them produces a different formula,but preserves the logical properties of well-formedness and derivability; and this will include the provision that a sequent which results by definition from a derivable sequent is itself derivable. The compromise can be sufficiently indicated by referring to the definitions in the extremal formation and derivation rules,so that the former becomes:nothing is a well-formed formula except in consequence of the preceding formation rules and the symbolic definitions.

The vocabulary of a calculus is the set of all those symbols which are introduced by the formation rules and definitions of the calculus,i.e. which appear in its well-formed formulae and sequents. So we can speak of 'f' for example, as a QC or QS_5 letter, and '◊' as an S_5 or QS_5 connective.

3.4 Scope

The scope of an occurrence of a connective in a formula is shortest unbroken part of the formula encompassing that occurrence which is itself well-formed or would be if subject letters were substituted for variables in it—the shortest 'well-formed'part in a loose and inaccurate sense which covers formulae like'*fx*   *fx*' that have been mutilated ready for grafting to quantifiers.Consider,for example,the formula ' y(□ □*p*   *gy*)'. The occurrence of' ' in it occurs in various unbroken parts of it, ' ', ' *y*', ' *y*(', ' *y* (□' and so on.None of these is well-formed except the whole formula (which is to count as a part of itself for purpose of determining scope).

The first occurrence of '□' occurs in even more parts,some extemding leftwards from,it as'□', '(□', 'y(□' etc,some rightwards,as '□□', '□□p' etc, some in both directions . The shortest of these which is well- formed is'□□p'. Similarly the scope of the second occurrence of '□' is '□p', and the scope of ' ' is '(□□p   *gy*)' which although not itself well formed ,becomes so when a subject leter is substituted for *y*' in it. In the case of an occurrence of a primitive connective the rule means that the scope of the occurrence in a well-formed formula is that part of the formula to ecerge, in the process of formation, at the moment when the occurrence was introduced:and in the case of an occurrence of a non-primitive connective it is that part of the formula to emerge at the first moment at which the occurrence could have been introduced by the connectives definition .

Obviously connectives do not have a scope in every formula; for example ' ' 'has no scope in ' (p'. But every occurrence of a connective in a well-formed formula does have a scope .

A connective which has for its scope the whole of some formula is called the **main connective** of that formula (LEMMON *BL* pp.48, 66 QUINE M*of L* p.50). Every well-formed formula or well-formed part of one that contains a connective at all must contain a main connective ,and no such formula or part can contain more than one. In the following examples the main connectives are underlined ;

' *x* (*fx* v (*p* *p*))', '(*x* (*fx* *p*) *p*)', '(*xfx* (*p* *p*))'.

7.5 Indemnities

The formation rules of a calculus are framed with an eye to the elimination of syntactical ambiguity.This is the sort of ambiguity which makes it impossible to solve the equation 2*x* = 2–1–1 until we know whether to bracket the right-hand side as '(2–1 –1' or as '2 – (1–1)', and which makes it impossible to tell what is the antecedent of 'she ' in 'If you are kind to a girl's mother, she will be kind to you'An ambiguity similar to the second of these cases is present in such formulae as ' *x* *xfxx*', which **F** was framed so as to avoid licensing .An ambiguity similar to the first is present in '(*p* *q* *r*)', which will be short for '~ (*p* & ~ ~ (*q* & ~ *r*))' or '~ (~(*p* & ~ *q*) & ~ *r*)' according as its first or second ' ' is taken as main connective.

The ambiguity afflicting '(*p* *q* *r*)' is an ambiguity of scope. Such ambiguities are prevented in well-formed formulae by the requirement in the formation rule for '&' and the definitions of ' ', ' ', ' ', that the formula produced be surrounded by outer brackets. Brackets will always be present to distinguish , for example, '~ (*p* *q*)' or ' *x*(*fx* *p*)', in which '~' and ' ' are the main connectives, from '(~ *p* *q*)' or '(*xfx* *p*)', in which ' ' is. But the formation rules and definitions go further than avoidance of such scope ambiguity demands , resulting in certain amount of needless bracket-clutter. Here, as with primitive connectives, it would be possible to secure economies by extra formation rules or definitions; but in this case the extra rules would be quit complicated to state and work with . The universal practice among logicians is to close the formation rules , by an extremal rule, at the point at which I have closed them or earlier , and to introduce bracket-economies informally, as indemnities against breaking the extremal rule. By means of them we produce what are strictly ill-formed formulae, but formulae that can readily be 'thought back' in to a well-formed state,e.g. for the purpose of determining scope through the rules of the last section. Anyone who finds this process confusing does well to retain, for a time at least , all the brackets demanded by the formation rules and definitions.

I adopt four indemnities.(i) The pair of brackets enclosing the whole of any well- formed formula may be omitted (Lemmon BL P.46, HUGEES & LONDEY p.50, MATES P.51, MASSEY p.34). (ii) The binary connectives common to all four calculi are to have *dominance* in the order '≡', '⊃', 'v', '&', i.e. backwards through the order in which their definitions and formation rules were stated in 7.2 and 7.3 (cf. QUINE *MofL* p.25, MASSEY pp. 35, 60). What this means is that,for example, '$p \equiv q \supset r$' should be construed as '≡' joining 'p' to '$q \supset r$' so simpilfying '$p \equiv (q \supset r)$', and the bracketed part of '$(p \,\&\, q \supset r) \vee r$' should be construed as '⊃' joining '$p \,\&\, q$' to 'r', so that the whole simplifies '$((p \,\&\, q) \supset r) \vee r$'. Such formulae as '$((p \equiv q) \supset r)$' remain well-formed, of course, though not amenable to internal-bracket-economy.Like Lemmon (*BL* p. 46) I shall not in practice exploit the dominance of '*V*' over'&',which is not memorable. (iii) '$\sim a \equiv b$' may be written '$a \neq b$', and similary for other subject letters and variable(HUGHES &LONDEY p.295); also brackets may be added around such formulae as '$a = b$', '$a \neq b$' where this makes for clarity. (iv) '$((p \,\&\, q) \,\&\, r)$' and'$(p \,\&\, (q \,\&\, r))$' may alike be written '$(p \,\&\, q \,\&\, r)$',and similarly in the case of 'v' (but not in mixed cases, nor in runs of '⊃' or '≡'). This convention can be applied and then re-applied,to produce runs of more than two '&'s or 'v's; it can also be applied, of course, in cases where the component formulae are not just propositional letters (so an exact statement if it would use 'π' and 'ϙ '). Example of its use are '$r \,\&\, \exists x(fx \vee gx) \,\&\, \sim r$', '$p \vee p \vee (q \supset p) \vee \Box p$'. Unlike the first three indemnities this one does import scope- ambiguity, but the ambiguity is 'tolerable' (MASSEY p. 38) because of the fact that in the calculi of this book '&' and 'v' are *associative* (like '+' and '×' in arithmetic). What that means is that (a) for any well-formed formulae, π, ϙ and p, ((p & ϙ) & p) and (p & (ϙ v p)) can replace each other anywhere in a derivable or underivable formulae or sequent without its ceasing to be derivable or underivable as the case may be, and so can ((π v ϙ) v p) and (π v (ϙ v p)); and (b) the same goes for vaild and formulae and sequents.Given these four indemnities all but the last of the following are available as ways of simlifying the well-formed formula which comes first among them:

$(p \equiv ((\sim b = b \;\&\; (q \supset r)) \;\&\; r))$	QC-formula
$p \equiv ((\sim b = b \;\&\; (q \supset r)) \;\&\; r)$	omitting outer brackets
$p \equiv ((b \neq b \;\&\; (q \supset r)) \;\&\; r)$	abbreviating '~ b=b'
$p \equiv (b \neq b \;\&\; (q \supset r)) \;\&\; r$	' ≡' dominates '&'
$p \equiv b \neq b \;\&\; (q \supset r) \;\&\; r$	'&' associative
$p \equiv b \neq b \;\&\; q \supset r \;\&\; r$	wrong

The last formula is indemnified,but because '⊃' dominates'&'it simplifies the different QC-formula '$(p \equiv ((\sim b = b \;\&\; q) \supset (r \;\&\; r)))$'.

7.6 Other peoples's rules

There are eight main ways in which a set of formation rules covering the four calculi PC, QC, S_5, QS_5 may differ from those I adopt.

(I) It may use different symbols,e.g.'P' or 'A' for 'p', '→' for '⊃'. Some of there difference are listed in Appendix One.

(2) It may add extra connectives. For example the modal connctives 'O', 'Υ' '≡' (MASSEY pp.190,192) are definable as follows: for any well- formed π and ϙ ,π O ϙ is short for ◇ (π&ϙ),π Υ ϙ is short and is short for □ (π ⊃ ϙ), and π ≡)is short for □ (π ≡ ϙ).

(3) It may use a different set of primitive connectives. We have already seen in 7.3 that it is possible,and for some purpose

desirable,to enlarge the set of primitive connectives beyond '~', '&', '=', '∀', '□'. MASSEY adds '∨'and '∃', LEMMON *BL* '∨', '⊃', '∃', QUINE *Mof L* '∨', '⊃', '≡', '∃'. (None but MASSEY have modal connectives.) It is also possible to use an equally small but different set,replacing '~' and '&' by '~' and '∨' (HUGHES & LONDEY pp. 51-2) or by '~' and '⊃' (MATES pp. 98, 166), '∀' by '∃' (MATES p. 66), or '□' by '◇' (MASSEY p. 184). Each of these changes will of course affect the symbloic definitions. E.g. if '~' and '∨' are primitive but '&' is not, (π & ϙ) is read,for any well-formed π and ϙ) as short for ~ (~ π ∨ ~ ϙ); and if '~' and '⊃' are primitive but '&' is not, (π & ϙ) is read as short for ~ (π ⊃ ~ ϙ). Rules of interpretation must obviously be different too,since they have to be given for each primitive connective; and it turns out to be nacessary to change the rules of derivation if the same calculi are to be preserved. But all these change can be so managed that the same calculi are preserved,i:e.the resulting rules have exactly the same effect as before,in the sense explained on pp.17-18(this fact would be very laborious to prove comprehensively).It can be proved that if we stick to the connectives of the present book or notational variants for them,any choice of primitive connectives from among them must include '~') together with '&' or '∨' or '⊃' (puls,of course, '∀' or '∃', and □) if it is to be adequate for stating the four calculi.There are ways of economising still further in primitive notation (HUGHES & LONDEY pp. 54–5, LEMMON *BL* p. 74, QUINE *Mof L* p. 18, Massey pp. 49–51, 193–4), but they involve connectives with different interpretations from any that I use.

(4) Punctuation. Although brackets are currently the commonest punctuation marks in logic and are used as in 7.2 by LEMMON *BL*, HUGHES & LONDEY, MATES AND MASSEY, Two other devices are sometimes found: dots and order. One way of converting brackets into dots, which results in a system similar though not idential to that of QUINE *Mof Lpp.* is as follows. (a) Number brackets in pairs from the inside outwards, as in:

$(\forall x\ (fx \vee ((q \supset fx) \equiv p)) \supset (q \supset p))$
4 3 21 1 23 1 14

(b) Excise end brackets, thus:

$\forall x\ (fx \vee ((q \supset fx) \equiv p)) \supset (q \supset p)$
3 21 1 23 1

(c) If any two brackets adjoin, excise that with the lower number, thus:

$\forall x\ (fx \vee ((q \supset fx) \equiv p)) \supset (q \supset p)$
3 2 1 23 1

(d) Replace each remaining bracket by the same number of dots as its number, thus:

$\forall x \therefore fx \vee : q \supset fx\ . \equiv p \therefore \supset .\ q \supset p$

The alternative device of order makes punctuation superfluous by writing each binary connective in front on and not between the two formulae in its scope, thus:

$\supset \forall x \vee fx \equiv \supset q\ fxp \supset qp$

This is the method of the Polish notation given in Appendix One, in which the same formula would appear as:

$C\Pi x A\phi x E C q \phi x p C q p$

In Polish motation scope extends only to the right and the main connective always leads.

(5) There are quite important variations in the formation rule for atomic formulae with leading predicate letter. in QUINE *Mof L*, HUGHES & LONDEY (p. 296) and MASSEY (p. 239) the predicate letter must be followed by one or more variables, and subject letters are absent from the logical vocabulary.The corresponding rule in MATES (p. 45) permits both subject letters and variables, separately of mixed. In LEMMON, whom I have followed in this respect, variables can occur in well-formed formulae only when quantified i.e. bound. But Lemmon's rules differ from mine in another way, by admitting into atomic formulae not only '*a*', '*b*', '*c*' etc. which he calls arbitrary names but also '*m*', '*n*', '*o*' etc. which he calls proper names (LEMMON

BL pp. 139–40). Hence of the formulae '*fx*', '∀*xfx*', '*fa*', '*fm*' only the middle two are well-formed in this book, only the first two (ignoring fiffernces of notation) in QUINE *MofL*, HUGHES & LONDEY, and MASSEY, only the first three in MATWS, and only the last three in LEMMON *BL*.

The basic difference here is over the question whether to add to the well-formed formulae of 7.2 (which Mates calls 'sentences', p.45) a set of other well- formed formulae in which variables occur free. If we do admit formulae containing free variables as well-formed, the resulting calculi are likely (but not in MATES) to include derivable sequents such as <{'∀*xfx*'}, '*fx*'> which have no instances in the calculi since some of their component formulae are fitted only by open sentences, in which no premisses or conclusions are expressible. Similarly the derivable formulae are likely to include formulae fitted only by open sentences. The presence of these drone sequents and formulae does not matter so long as they have working coll-eagues like <{'∀*xfx*'}, '*fa*'> ; but it invites the speculation that we are intended to *identify* the role of free variables with that of subject letters; and in HUGES & LOBDEY and MASSEY, where subject letters are excluded and all admissible letters are described as kinds of variable (propositional, predicate, or individual), it becomes clear that no distinction is intended between the role of sechematic or dummy letters on the one hand and of free variables on the other. Massey, following the dummy interpretation is explicit: "Individual variables may function in either of two quite disparate ways. They may play the role of referring singular terms or they may function as pronouns, that is, as devices for cross-reference" (MASSEY p. 237, cf. HUGHES & LONDEY pp. 290–1). The first function is to belong to free variables, the second to bound. This approach has the advantage of economy in notation, but it is arguably confusing in assigning more than one role to the same letters and certainly complicating at the stage of interpretation and derivation rules. That is why I follow Mates in distinguishing variables from subject letters and LEMMON *BL* in banning free variables from well-formed formulae. But I do not understand, and shall not employ, Lemmon's distinction between "arbitrary names and "proper names".

(6) It is surprising and idiosyncratic feature of Hughes & Londey's book that even the most extensive of the many versions of the predicate calculus they discuss, the "Full Lower Predicate Calculus", does not include among its well-formed formulae all the well-formed formulae of the propositional calculus, and so is not an extension of the propositional calculus in the sense to be explained on p. 193. In fact it includes no such formulae, because it includes no propositional letters (HUGHES & LONDEY pp.294–6).

(7) A sequent is a set of formulae paired with a formula. It is therefore no more itself a formua than a argument, which could be regarded as a set of propositions paired with a proposition, is itself a proposition. Metalogical abbreviation permits the construction of (metalogical) formulae such as '< {'$\forall xfx$'}, '*fa*' >' to *refer* to sequents, but again the things so referred to are no more themselves formulae than the thing normally referred to by the word "Napoleon" is itself a word. However it would be possible to conceive sequents quite differently, as themselves a special kind of formulae (what lemmon calls 'sequent-expresions', *BL* p. 48). The following is a way of doing so: add to the logical notation, and allow commas as an extra mark of logical punctuation; then add to the formation rules the further rule for any n and any well-formed formulae $\pi_1, \ldots . \pi_n$, ♀ , **$\pi_1, \ldots \pi_n \rightarrow$ ♀) is a sequent; nothing else is a sequent. Specimen sequents ould be: '$p, q \rightarrow r$', '$\exists xfx, \exists xfx, \exists xfx \rightarrow p$', '$\rightarrow \Box\Diamond (p \vee {\sim} p)$'. The earliest sequent systems, due to GENTZEN (cf. LEBLANC, pp. 10, 30–1), were presented as applying to sequents so conceived; but my method requires fewer derivation rules.

(8) We saw in 7.2 that **F**$\forall$ can be stated either in terms of substituting into a formula or in terms of filling up a stencil. Just as the latter invites the introduction of metalogical stencil variables, so the former invites the introduction of a metalogical notation for subsituting, which usually looks like this (HUGHES

& LONDEY , p. 85, cf. MATES p. 50) : '$\pi(\nu/a)$' is short for 'the result of substituting ν for *a* throughout π'. F∀ cannot be stated exactly in this notation, because of the word 'throughout' in the above definition; but its effect can be captured by 'for any *a*, ν, and π, if π is well-formed and contains *a* but not *V*, $\forall\nu\pi(\nu/\alpha)$ is well-formed'.

As a further alternative we could adapt an idea of Lemmon's (*BL*p. 143) and define 'propositional function in υ_1, . . . υ_n' as short for 'formula containing each of υ_1, . . . υ_n free but not bound, which becomes well-formed when subject letters are substituted for υ_1, . . . υ_n' throughout. Propositioinal functions are thus formulae such as '(*gax* & *p*)' well formed except for occurrences of free variables which do not occur bound elsewhere in them—formulae ready mutilated for grafting to a quantifier. F∀ then becomes: for any π and *υ*, if π is a propositional function in *υ*, $\forall\upsilon\pi$ is well-formed. (On the schematic interpretation proposition functions so defined get interpreted as open schemata; on dummy interpretation as open sentences. For remarks on the history of the expression 'propositional function' see QUINE *MofL* pp. 123, 148).

Chapter-8

Interpretation Rules

Chapter 8

8.1 Formulating the rules for letters

Interpretation Rules for each calculus are in two parts, one interpreting, the letters one the connectives. In the propositional calculus the first part merely confirms the propositional (schematic) letters *p*, *q*, etc. in that title, which so far they have enjoyed only by courtesy and adopts the conventions of 1.2 for fitting sentences to letters. I shall write '**PC**' etc, bold- face to indicate that we are now dealing with the 'semantic' side od the calculi. So the iterpretation rules for the PC letters determine when an expression **PC**-fits one of them.

In the predicate calculus with indentity the same rules carry over and in addition the predicate letters, subject letters and variables are confirmed in their titles and the conventions of 1.2 adopted for fitting expressions to them. So '**QC**' fit replace-**PC** 'fit'.

S_5 has the same rules, at this stage, as **PC**; and $\mathbf{QS_5}$ as **QC**.

8.2 Formulating the rules for connectives

The second part of the interpretation rules—covering the predicate-leading construction as well as connectives, and also set out in Appendix Two—introduces the idea of a truth-condition, which must now be explicated. Truth-conditions belong primarily to sentences, and sun up the conditions contributing to a sentence's truth. The contributing conditions are of four kinds. (i) A sentence's truth normally depends on its (conventional) meaning of range of meanings, i.e. on te language to which it belongs or in which it is used (ii) Sentences also depend for their truth on the context of use, e.g. the speaker, the addressee, the time of utterance, and other such circumstances. For example 'You have read Chapter I' might be true of you but not of your father, in 1979 but not 1978, about Chapter I of this book but not of *Pride and Prejudice.* Among these circumstances are the sepaketr's intentions, especially whether to observe right usage and avoid equivocation (iii) The truth of some sentence depends on the frame of reference, i,e, domain. As we saw on p. 40 'All pillarboxes are green' would be true if used in talk about Eire rather than Britain. (iv) The truth of most sentences depends also on the facts—on which is actual among all the possible worlds. Sentences lacking this dependency, e.g. 'It's raining or not raining, in English, can be used to express necessary truths. Worlds, as I invoke them, are independent of laguages, contexts and domains: 'is true in world w' will mean can be used to express a proposition which would be true given w', not 'could, given w' be used to express a truth.'

Plainly no sentence is true under all conditions (see p.40) and when one says 'it is true' about some sentence without qualification one must assume certain elided conditions which would naturally be: right and unequivocal usage, the actual facts, and the context and domain within which the commenting, metalinguistic, sentence 'It is true' is uttered. Or again one might specify some of the relativities, eliding the rest, 'as in' It is true today 'or' It would be true if pigs could fly'. The latter will be my procedure in talking about the truth of sentences containing connectives.

We shall need eventually, to cross a bridge between the truth of sentences and the truth of propositions. The bridge is: a sentence is true in a language, context , domain and world if and only if it can be used, in that language and context and relative to that domain, to express a proposition which would be true given that world. This serves to explicate 'true sentence' in terms of 'true proposition' or. if you prefer, the other way round. 'Can be used' brings out the fact that sentences do not in general depend for their truth (at a time) on utterance (at that time), let alone on assertion; they can remain true, so to speak, throughout the night.

If we may assume that the first paragraph of this section covers the main conditions contributing to the truth of a sentence, then the conventional meaning of sentence determines a fairly full specification of the way in which its truth depends on the other conditions. But if truth-conditions are to be used as rules of interpretation, i.e. for revealing meaning, the converse must be assumed also: that some fairly full specification of the way in which a sentence's truth depends on the other conditions determines its conventional meaning. Workinng to that assumption, which will be examined in 8.4, we shall need to state truth-conditions for sentences in the form 'In a language, context, domain and world of certain kinds, the sentence is true if and only if....'where the 'certain kinds' are not too restrictive. An example would be:in any context of right German usage and utterance by some person at some time, any domain including hats, and any world in which pigs could fly, " Mein Hut ist grun" is true if and only if that person's hat would be green at that time if pigs could fly.

None of the connectives will be interpreted as sentences. How then can they have truth-conditions? The answer is that the meaning of each connective will be given by stating truth-conditions not for a single sentence but for the set of all sentences which embed the connective in a certain standard way; and these truth-conditions for sets of sentences are called, in a secondary sense, truth-conditions for the connectives. So the form of rule for a connective will be: in a language, context' domain and world of certain kinds, the result of affixing the connective in a certain way to certain categories of expression is true if and only if...', where 'is true' still means'is a true sentence'.

In the interpretation rules truth-conditions will be accompanied by falsity-conditions, which are not redundant because there might be conditions under which a sentence has both truth-values, or neither. Truth-conditions combine into rules of the form'In a language, context,domain and world of certain kinds, the result of affixing the connective in a certain way to certain categories of expression is true or false according as...or_', where the last six words mean 'true if and only if . . .', false if and only if—'. Henceforward I shall speak of these bipartite rules simply as truth-conditions.

A final preliminary. Sets of truth-conditions may be recursive, i.e. may include hypothetical clauses determining the truth-values of sentences in terms of semantic features (including truth-value) of other expressions (including sentences). Only the categorical clauses need to specify truth-values in terms of non-semantic features—e.g. the greenness of a hat rather than the truth of another sentence. But since the connectives, and also the predicate-leading construction, are to be introduced as enrichments of natural languages, these categorical clauses are not among the logical interpretation rules, all of which will be hypothetical.

We can now formulate the PC truth-conditions as follows: given (i) any language incorporating the logical lanaguage of the propositional calculus, (ii) any context of right and unequivocal usage, (iii) any domain, and (iv) any world, then [T ~] the result to prefixing '~' to any sentence is true or false in that language, context, domain, and world, according as the sentence itself is false or true in them; and [T&] the result of inserting '&' between any two sentences, the same or different, and enclosing the whole in brackets is true or false in them according as both sentences are true in them or at least one is false, and the other true or false, in them. This rigmarole had better be abbreviated. I shall compress conditions (i) and (ii) into 'in any PC-context' (see p.49).'is T' and 'is F' will be short for 'is a true sentence' and 'is a false sentence' respectively. 'σ' and 'τ' will be metalogical variables ranging over sentences; and '~' and '(π &τ)' will be lazy abbreviations, as in 8.2, for '~σ' and '(π ~τ)'. Then the rules become:for any σ and τ, in any PC-context, domain, and world,~σ is T or F according as σ is F or T; and (σ &τ) is T or F according as σ and τ are both T or one of them is F and the other F or T.

In the predicate calculus with identity T ~ and T& carry

over with 'QC-context' in place of 'PC-context'. Three new truth-conditions are added, to interpret '=', '∀-' and the predicate- leading construction. This last is intricate, mainly because it needs to be generalised over predicates with any number of places. For one-place predicates it runs: in any QC-context, domain and world, a predicate followed by a subject is T or F according as the subject refers in the context to a member of the domain and the predicate can be used in the context to attribute a property, defined over the domain(see p.52) , which would or would not hold of that member given that world. Notice that the first part of the condition applies to both T and F sentences of the construction; so that if a subject does not succeed, in some context of right and unequivocal usage of a QC- incorporating language, in referring to a member of some domain, or a predicate is not defined over the domain, any predicate-leading sentence containing one of them will be neither T nor F in that context and domain, This feature is to survive generalisation; shall comment on it in 8.6, as also on 'attributes a property which holds of'. For two-place predicates the rule is: in any QC-context, domain and world, a predicate followed by two subjects the same or different, in an order is T or F according as the subjects refer to members of the domain (perhaps the same member) and the predicate can be used to attribute a binary relation, defined over the domain which given that world would or would not hold between those members in that order. Two subjects which are the same' means two wccurrences of the same subject'. 'Perhaps the same member' takes care of the point that in a cotext of unequivocal usage occurrences of the same subject must, and occurrences of different subjects may, refer to the same member of the domain. A predicate-leading sentence could will be T in such a co-referring enter because some binary relations hold between a thing and itself for example being the same size as holds between Paris and itself or as we may alternatively say, holds of the ordered pair Paris, Paris>. Before generalising it will be useful to introduce the abbrevation 'is true of' for 'can be used to attribute a property/relation defined over the domain which holds of/between', and similarly 'is false of' for'... which does not hold of/between'. Notice that according to this abbreviation only predicates—linguistic expressions—are true or false of things, whereas properties and relations hold or fail to hold of or between things. Notice too that one-place predicates are true or false of things simply, two or-more place predicates are true or false of things in an order. For in an English context and domain the predicate'...is true of Paris and false of St. Tropze, and the predicate is worth of—' is true of Paris and St. Tropzes, in that order but not the reverse order. We can now generalize the rule with commonnuss over all predicates: [TP] for any positive n, in any QC-context, domain and world, an n-place predicate followed by n, the same or different, in an order is T or F according as the subjects each refer to a member of the domain and the predicate is true or false in that world of those members in that order.

The truth-condition for'=' is: [T=] in any QC-context,domain and world ,'=' between two subjects, the same or different, is T or F according as the subjects refer to members of the domain which in the same or different. Thus the truth of an '='sentence in a context requires the identity of the things referred to in that context by the subjects flanking '=', not the identity of those subjects (which are expressions). But where the subjects are identical, the sentence must be T on pain of equivocation.

The truth-condition for '∀' brings in open sentences in some variable v, i.e. expressions (whether predicate-leading or not) in which an n-place predicate is attached to n occurences of v. The general idea is that $\forall v$ followed by an open sentence in v is T if and only if the result of putting some subject uniformly in place of v in the open sentence is T *whatever* the subject unequivocally—even if wrongly—refers to; e.g. '$\forall x$ x is wise' is T if and only if 'Jim is wise' is T no matter which member of the domain 'Jim' refers to.In other words the truth of the resulting closed sentence must survive every uniform change in the referring part of the context whether or not the change preserves right usage. But there is a proviso: the chosen subject must not already occur in the open sentence. This is because we want such a sentence as '∀*x x* is the same age as Charles' to share the truth-condition of 'Everything is the same age as Charles', and so to be F even though 'Charles is the same age as Charles' comes out T, in some domains, whatever 'Charles' unequivocally refers to.So the rule is: [T∀] for any variable v, in any QC-context,domain and world, ∀v followed by an open sentence in *υ* is T or F according as the result of replacing *υ* uniformly by some subject no already contained in the open sentence is T in every unequivocal context differing from the QC-context at most as to the reference within that domain of the subject, or F on some such context.

In the two modal calculi ' S_5-context' replaces '- context' and 'QS_5-context' replaces 'QC-context'; with these changes the same rules carry over as in PC and QC respectivel;y. The single extra rule is: [T□ for any σ in any S_5- (QS_5-)context, domain and world *w*,□σ is T or F in w according as σ is T in every world or F in some world. ' is T in every world' means 'can be used to express a proposition which would be true whatever the facts, i.e. to express a necessary truth'. But whether this rule succeeds in making '□'synonymous with the English 'necessarily' is a harder question than may appear.

The syntax of the connectives, in that unrefined sense in which syntax assigns expressions to parts of speech or categories, is easily deduced from the truth-conditions. '&', for example, always joins two sentences, one or both of which may be an open sentence when '&' falls wihin the scope of '∀-' and it always makes a sentence out of them, open or closed. The important part of this syntactical information is that '&' between two sentences makes a sentence: it is, when it operates on(closed) sentences, a *binary sentence-forming operator*. Inspection of the other truth-conditions will show that all the connectives, and the predicate-leading construction, are sentence-forming in the following ways:

8.2(I) Any *n*-place predicate followed by *n* subjects makes a sentence; '=' between two subjects makes a sentence; if σ and τ are sentences, so are ~ σ,(σ & τ),□ σ; if υ is a variable, ∀υ followed by an open sentence in υ makes a sentence.

8.3 Formulae into schemata

The notation introduced in Chapter 7 was uninterpreted. Interpretation seeks to convert it into an instrument of testing arguments, the rules of 8.1 and 8.2 effect this conversion by means of two consequences: they ensure that all-formed formulae of PC,QC,S_5 and QS_5 are schemata or sentences, and they come near enough to fixing and revealing the meanings of the connectives. This section establishes the former consequence.

Let us start by considering those well-formed formulae which are in primitive notation and also contain a letter from one or more of the group called, at first only by courtesy, 'propositional', 'predicate', and 'subject'. The schematic interporetation confirms the titles, and so demonstrates that such well-formed formulae will be interpreted as schematic in some way. But whether they are schemata, i.e. sentence-schemata, will clearly depend on the interpretation of the connectives. For example if '&' meant 'therefore','*p* & *q*' would be an inference-schema. We can advance on step further by reflecting on the syntax of the connectives, given in 8.2 (I). Since '&' makes sentences out of sentences it will make (sentence-) schemata out of (sentence-) schemata, and in general it follows from 8.2(I) that

8.3(I) any predicate letter follwed by one or more subject letters makes a schema; '=' between two ssubject letters makes a schema;if (π) and (ϙ) are schemata, so are ~π ,(π & ϙ),□π;if υ is a variable, ∀υ followed by an open schema in υ makes a schema.

From 8.3 (I) we can tell straight away that '(*p* & *q*)'is a schema,since 8.1 has already interpreted '*p*' and '*q*' as schematic letters marking places for sentences, and such letters are schemata. But we cannot yet tell whether more complex formulae such as '$\forall xfx$ & (p & q)' are schemata. In order to prove the generalisation over all well-formed formulae, in the majority group,I shall use an argument by what is known as strong mathematical induction, and I shall go through the argument carefully, because there will be several curcial proofs by strong induction later in the book. We start by ordering all well-formed formulae according to the number of symbols they contain(it matters that there are none of infinite length , but not that many share the same length). The principle of strong induction, which is used but not proved in the argument (see pp. 266-9), holds that the conclusion wanted will follow from an intermediate conclusion, namely : for any n, if all well-formed formulae of length less than n are sentence-schemata, so are all of length n (thus the thought behind the principle is that if wherever you start, even at the nil length, you always get a schema at the next step, then you always get a schema). Since this intermediate conclusion is general and hypothetical, its proof proceeds by *taking* a length of formulae, *supposing* (the 'inductive supposition' or 'induction hypothesis ') that all well-formed formulae of less than that length are schemata, and *showing* that it follows regardless of the length chosen that all well-formed formulae of that length are schemata.

The proof is carried out in stages, relying at each stage on what the formation rules tell us about well-formed formulae and what the interpretation rules tell us about symbols. The inductive supposition is only needed in the later stages. First, we must notice that by the external formation rules every well-formed formula in primitive notation either (a) is a propositional letter or (b) is an atomic formulae containing a predicate letter or (c)-(e) has a primitive main connective. If any primitive well-formed formula of the chosen length falls under case (a), it is a schema by the interpretation of propositional letters. If any primitive well-formed formula of the chosen length falls under case (b), 8.3 (1) shows that it is a schema provided that its first component is a predicate letter and its others subject letters; and they are by the interpretation. As regards primitive well-formed formulae falling under the other cases ewe must consider each connective in trun. (c) If a well-formed formula of the chosen length has '='for its main connective, 8.3 (I) shows that it is a schema provided that a schema provided thart its component letters are subject latters; and they are by the interpretation. (d) If its main connective is '∀',8.3(I) shows that it is a schema provided that its first component is a variable and its second an open schema in that variable, Its first component is a variable by the interpretation. Its second component has two features: (i)it contains a schematic letter (for we are assuming still that the formula as a whole does); and(ii)it is a propositional function in the variable (pp.84-5),i.e.it becomes well-formed when a subject latter is substituted for each occurrence of the variable. But the formulae produced by such substitution is the same length as the propositional function and so shorter than the original formula,which prefixed'∀' and a variable. It is also well-formed. Hence by the inductive suppostion, which here comes into play for the first time, it is a schema. Hence the propositional function (i)contains a schematic letter and (ii) results from a (closed)schema by substituting variables for subject letters and this makes it an open schema.(e) Finally if a primitive well-formed formula of the chosen length has some other main connective,8.3 (I)shows that it is a schema provided that its component formula or formulae are schemata;and they are by inductive supposition, because they are well-formed and shorter than it. This completes the survey of cases and so proves the intermediate conclusion, whence it follows by the (assumed) principle of strong induction that all well-formed formulae which contain a schematic letter and are in primitive notation are schemata.

It remains to extend this result to well-formed formulae in primitive notation that contain no schematic letters, and to well -formed formulae not in primitive notation. The former can be formed in only one way, out of sub-formulae whose only connectives are'=' together with '∀'. As might be expected they come out as sentences not schemata under the interpretation rules. They cannot, therefore, be fitted by sentences in the sense introduced in 5.2. But it is useful to extend that sense in the following way.We count sentences as the limiting case of schemata, and say that every schema of the limiting kind is fitted just by itself . A consequence of this will be that the formula '∀-x ($x = x$)', for example, , has as its sole QC- instance and QS_5-instance, relative to a domain, the proposition that every member of the domain is identical with itself. This extension in the sense of'schema' allows clause(d) of the induction to cover such cases.

Finally, each well-formed formula in non-primitive notation abbreviates a well-formed formula in primitive notation, and therefore, by the induction, abbreviates a schema; and what abbreviates a schema is a schema.

8.4 Truth-conditions and meaning

If truth-conditions are going to amount to interpretation rules, they must both fix and reveal meaning.

Certainly not all truth-conditions reveal meaning. For example the rule'σ and τ' is **T** if and only if σ is **T** and τ is T' cannot be informative in that formulation, since its right hand side uses, and so relies on prior understanding of, the very construction it seeks to interpret—'and' between sentences. But the rules of 8.2 avoid this defect, by keeping the lannguage of interpretation, the metalanguage, free of symbols from the language to be interpreted, the object language.

Truth-conditions for sentences do not always fix meaning. For example the sentence 'If it's raining, it's raining' is **T** in unequivocal English under all conditions, **F** under none. Yet that fact does no distinguish it in meaning from any other sentence in which a necessary truth is expressible, e.g. 'Two plus two equlas four', and so does no fix its meaning. Truth-conditions for connectives protect themselves to some extent from this defect by taking sentences in sets. But the protection is insufficient. For example the English expression 'and two plus two equals four and' shares the turth condition of 'and' when put between sentences, viz. making a **T** sentence when flanked by two **T** sentences, an **F** sentence when flanked by **T** or **F** sentences at least one of which is **F**. Yet presumably the expression differs in meaning from 'and'. Admittedly this defference might be exposed by other truth-conditions, forming together a *theory* of truth, It has been suggested by Davidson that although truth-conditions do not all fix meaning individually, still "a theory of truth shows how we can go from truth to something like meaning"(DAVIDSON DCT p 84,cf. T & M p.9). Even so we do not get all the way. For example 'but' and 'and',between sentences, surely differ in English meaning; yet replacement of one by the other seems to affect appropriateness or felicity rather than truth, and it is hard to see how any truth-conditions could expose it. Such examples caused Frege to distinguish two aspects of meaning, sense ('sinn') and tone (Beleuchtung',' Färbung',DUMMETT p.2), only the former of which is fixed by truth-conditions.

Interpretation rules for the connectives can deal with tone in one of two ways: either by adding a rider that the connectives have no tone (cf.HUGHES &LONDEY p.20 on '⊃': "We are not concerned with or attempting to represent anything but material implication"), or by leaving tone, and so meaning , unfixed. Both solutions acknowledge the quite serious limitations of expressive power in logical languages. For example '&' differs from 'but' and 'and' not only in its more restricted syntax (it must join open or closed sentences) but also in its inability to convey the adversative tone of the former or the suggestion of temporal succession sometimes present in the latter (STRAWSON ILT p.80). Likewise'∀, cannot express the suggestion of 'severally' present in 'the general addressed each of the soldiers' but absent from 'the general addressed all the soldiers.' These examples could be multiplied.

The latter of the two solutions, ignoring tone, weakens the claim of logical interpretation rules to interpret: they leave one aspect of meaning unfixed. In communication this would matter. But our purpose is the more limited one of testing arguments by translating into symbols (cf.FREGE BS p. 3: "in my formalised language...only that part of judgments which affects the *possible inferences* is taken into consideration"), and for that purpose knowledge of truth-condition suffices, as I shall now show through a representative example. Suppose that 'and' in English has the same truth-condition as '&' in some logical language I,and suppose that we construcrt a variant of in which 'and' is substituted for '&', leaving this truth-condition constant (thus the variant logical language is permitted, for the nonce, to contain a word as well as symbols). Then take two sequents, one containing '&', the other resulting from it by substitution of 'and'. The crucial fact, which will become obvious in, is that *validity* turns only on truth-conditions. Because of that fact the '&'-sequent will be l-valid if and only if the '&'- sequent is valid in l's variant; that is, all l-instances of the one will have premisses which strictly imply their conclusions if and only if all l-variant-instances of the other do, Now although this does not entail that every l-veriant-instance of the 'and'-sequent is an I-instance of the '&'-sequent, it does nevertheless show that acceptance of that conclusion will *not lead us astray* in a test of correctness: treating some argument as an instance of the one sequent will certify it as correct if and only if teating it as an instance of the other would also so certify it. Hence we can safely say of any argument that it is an instance of, i.e. expressible in sentences fitting, the '&'-sequent if it is an instance of, i.e. expressible in sentences fitting, the 'and'-sequent; and therefore that it is expressible with '&' if expressible with 'and, provided only that '&' and 'and' have the same truth-condition. Other purposes call for other standards of accuracy in translation, and sameness of meaning is normally a part of the ideal. But in logic sameness of truth-condition susffices. It therefore does not matter if we are left ignorant of the tone of logical connectives, or if, as might happen under the first solution, we know that their tone differs from that of the English words they supplant.

8.5 Pure semantics

Logical interpretaiion rules are often presented in terms which stick more closely than 8.1 and 8.2 to the language of mathematics, and such presentaion is called formal or pure semantics, or model theory. Although the important thing for the purposes of this book is to get the logical symbols interpreted, not to dress the interpretation in mathematical clothes, there are two reasons for introducing pure semantics in the present section: many other elementary text-books, e.g. MASSEY and MATES, make at least a bow in its direction, and an extension of its concepts will provide the easiest, though a roundabout, way of proving soundness.

In two respects pure semantics differs strikingly from the formulations of 8.1 and 8.2: it deals with well-formed formulae not sentences, and it introduces the notion of a 'valuation' which itself stands in need of explication. Because of this latter feature the initial statement of formal semantics for a calculus is quite abstract, and does not reveal the functions of the symbols at all.

We are to consider structures consisting of three items,a domain (only needed for QC and QS_5),a set of worlds (only needed for S_5 and QS_5) and valuation. Such a structure is sometimes called a model(HUGHES & CRESSWELL pp. 72, 146) but that word is used in a diferent sense by MASSEY (p.248) and MATES (p. 60). **A valuation**,or value-assignment, in each model is a set of elements, and each element must be of one of the following kinds: (i) an ordered pair pairing a subject letter with a member of the model's domain,(ii) an ordered pair pairing a predicate letter with a set of ordered sets, each consisting of members of the domain followed by one world from the model's set of worlds, or (iii) an ordered triple grouping a well-formed formula, a truth-value , and a world from the set of worlds. In PC and S_5 we need only elements of the last kind, since there are no subject letters or predicate letters, and in PC and QC the elements are simplified by the excision of worlds. The effect of these general requirements is that a valuation consists of elements each of which pairs a subject letter with a member of the domain,or a predicate letter with a property or relation conceived as a set of ordered sets of members of the domain (perhaps relative to a world), or a well-formula with a truth value (perhaps relative to a world). The items so paired with letters and formulae are called values of the letters and formulae under the valuation.

Valuations must meet three other conditions, two general and one special to each calculus. The first general condition is that in each valuation no two values may compete for the same letter or formula:for example a valuation may contain the elements <‘*a*’, Napoleon> and <‘*b*’ Wellington>,or <‘*a*’ Nepoleon> and <‘*b*’,Napoleon> but not <‘*a*’,Napoleon> and <‘*a*’,Wellington>. Without this requirement a valuation would already be,in set- theoretic terms, a relation (set of ordered sets); with it, it becomes that kind of relation which is called a function. Because valuations are functions the usual metalogical symbolism for stating that <‘*a*’ Napoleon> or <‘*p*’, truth. This world> is an element of some valuation v is v(‘*a*’) = Napoleon’ or ‘v(‘*p*’, this world) = truth’; notice that ‘=’ is here a metalogical symbol. The second general condition is that valuations in a model must be complete, in the sense that they pair values with every well-formed formula and letter, except variables, in the logical language and if necessary relative to every world in the model’s set of worlds;so they are infinite functions which, in set theoretic language, map the set of well formed formulae and letters (sometimes formula-world pairs and letter-world pairs) onto a set of values. Thirdly, a valuation belongs to a particular calculus (is a PC-valuation etc.) by conforming to the value rules of the calculus. The value rules, which correspond to the truth conditions of 8.2 are as follows (I use‘v’ and ‘v_1’,‘w’ and ‘w_1’ and ‘δ’ as metalogical variables ranging over valuations, worlds and predicate letters respectively, ‘I’ and ‘o’ as metalogical abbreviations for ‘truth’ and 'falsity', and 'iff' for 'if and only if'):

PC For any PC -formulae (π) and ϙ and PC- vluation v ,v(π) = I or o and

V ~ v(~π) = I iff <v(π) =o

V & v((π & ϙ)) = I iff v(π) = v(ϙ) =I

QC For any a, a_1,... a_n, β, v, δ, ϕ containing no *a* or *υ*, QC-formulae π, ϙ, QC-valuation v and domain, v(π) = I or o, v(*a*) is a member of the domain, for some positive n v(δ) is a set of ordered sets each containing *n* members of the domain (the same or different), and

v ~and V & as in PC

VP v(δ a_1..... a_n) = I iff <v(a_1),... v(a_n) > is a member of v.(δ)

V = v(α= β) = I iff v(α) = v(β)

V∀- v(∀ϕ*υ*) = I iff v_1 (ϕα) =I for all v_1 which differ from v at most in pairing some other member of the domain with α.

S_5 For any S_5-formulae π and ϙ, world w in a set of worlds, and S_5-valuation v, v (π, w) = I or o and

V ~ v (~ π, w) =I iff v (π, w) = o

V & v ((π & ϙ), w) = I iff v (π, w) = v (ϙ, w) = I

V □ v (□π, w) = I iff v(π, w_1) = I for all worlds w_1 in the set

QS_5 For any *a*, a_1,...a_n, β, *υ*, δ, ϕ containing no *a* or, *υ*, QS_5-formulae π, ϙ, world w in set of worlds, QS_5-valuation v and domain, v (π, w) = I or o, v (α) is a member of the domain, for some positive *n* v (δ) is a set of ordered sets each containing *n* members of the domain (the same or different) followed by one world from the set of worlds, and

V ~ ,V& and V□ as in S_5

VP v(δα_1,. . . . . a_n , w) = I iff < v(a_1), ... v(a_n), w> is a member of v (δ)

V = v (*a* = β, w) = I iff v (*a*) = v (β)

V∀ $v(\forall v\phi v, w) = I$ iff $v_1(\phi\alpha, w) = I$ for all v_1 which differ from v at most in pairing some other member of the domain with *a*.

'Differs from *v*' is shorthand for "differs from v in its pairings with letters". Notice that in $\mathbf{QS}_5$ V=alone makes no provision for pairing different values with a formula relative to different worlds in a single valuation; see HUGHES & CRESSWELL pp. 192-6.

Each valuation can be thought of as constructed in two stages. It starts with an *initial* assignment pairing every letter (except variables) with a truth value or member of the domain or set of ordered sets of members of the domain as appropriate, perhaps relative to every world in the set of worlds; and then it *extends* the initial assignment to all well-formed formulae by the rules V~ etc.

How do these value rules tie in with the truth-conditions of 8.2? One notable difference is that even if the pure semantics tells us that "I" means "truth" and "**O**" means "falsity", it explains "valuation" only through truth-conditions of the metalogical sentences that result from "**v**(π) = truth" and "**v** (π) = falsity" by putting designations of a well-formed formula for "π" and a valuation for "v". We saw in 5.14 that, although truth-conditions can in principle reveal meaning, these ones cannot reveal both the meaning of "valuation" and the meanings of the connectives at one and the same time. Hence the value cannot interpret the connectives until "**I**", "**o**" and "valuation" (and also, if necessary, "domain" and "world") are independently explicated-until, that is, the pure semantics is converted into applied semantics. The simplest satisfactory conversion for PC explicates a pairing of **I** (or **o**) to a formula π as a declaration that π is synonymous with some **T** (or **F**) sentence (MASSEY p. 25). So construed the value rules would presuppose that formulae had been interpreted as sentences, not formulae.

To fit in with a schematic interpretation of the logical letters, and also to accommodate context and domains and worlds, a pairing of **I** (or **o**) to a formula must be a replacement of the formula by a **T** (or **F**) sentence, that accords with the **PC** fitting conventions, in a **PC**-context and domain and world. Then V ~, for example, cashes out as follows: in any replacement that accords with the **PC**-fitting conventions, of **PC**-formulae by **T** or **F** sentences in a **PC**-context and domain and world, ~ π is replaced by a T sentence if and only if π is replaced by an F sentence.

V ~ so explicated still differs from **T** ~ because it applies to formulae not sentences. But the effect is the same. By the PC fitting conventions every sentence **PC**-fits a PC-formula, and by the value rules so explicated every PC-formula is PC-fitted by a sentence. Hence for every sentence o there is a replacement in accord with the PC fitting conventions which replaces ~π by ~σ and π by σ, for some PC-formula π; and conversely for any **PC**-formula π there is some such replacement and sentence σ. This sameness of effect has a more general application. A simpler way of stating the explicated version of V~ is as follows: in any **PC**-context and domain and world, any sentence **PC**-fitting ~ π is **T** or **F** according as the *corresponding* sentence **PC**-fitting π is **F** or **T**, where the sentence corresponding to the first is the result of lopping '~' off the first, i.e. the one which stands to the first as π stands to ~π. In general therefore the device of using the word "corresponding" enables us, if we wish, to state truth-conditions in terms of schemata rather than sentences. The device could even be extended to propositions; we might have stated **T** without preliminaries as to context and domain in the form 'a **PC**-instance of ~π would be true or false given any world according as the corresponding **PC**-instance of π would be false or true given that world", where "corresponding PC-instance of π" means "proposition expressible in the same PC-context and domain in the corresponding sentence PC-fitting π" (cf. STRAWSON ILT p.30 footnote, p. 67).

In **QC** the pairing relation in a valuation becomes more variegated because it can also hold between subject letters and things, and between predicate letters and sets of ordered sets of things. If we were aiming, like MASSEY and MATES, at an interpretation of letters as dummies, we could explicate 'v(a) = Napoleon" as 'in va is declared synonymous with some subject which can be used to refer to Napoleon" and "v (δ)=the set in which each mother is paired once with each of her children" as "in vδ is declared synonymous with some predicate true just of mother-child pairs in that order". It is important to notice that the explications of the pairing relation are not the same in these cases, and not the same as for the pro-positional case. There the explication brought in sentences, here subjects and predicates. It seems reasonable to say that· in this applied semantics the metalogical word "valuation" gets interpreted as ambiguous. So it does in the explication which goes with schematic letters: 'is declared synonymous with' gives way to 'is replaced by', and a **QC**-valuation (in a domain) is a replacement that accords with the **QC** fitting conventions, in a **QC**-context and world (and that domain). Then the **QC** truth-conditions of 8.2 result, but adapted to **QC**-formulae and letters.

Similarly an S_5-valuation (in a world) is a replacement that accords with the S_5 fitting conventions, in an S5-context and domain (and that world); and a **QS**$_5$-valuation (in a domain and world) is a replacement that accords with the **QS**$_5$ fitting conventions in a **QS**$_5$-context (and that domain and world).

8.6 Metatheorems on truth

We saw in 8.3 that it is not quite obvious whether the definitions of non-primitive connectives serve to make formulae containing them well-formed. But indubitably they do serve to interpret the non-primitive connectives. The process is familiar from ordinary language-learning:by explaining that one word or construction is short for others we teach the meaning of the former to anyone who already understands the latter. Without definitions the symbols ' V ', '⊃', '≡', '∃' '◊' could be assigned any truth-conditions we pleased, but given the definitions their truth-conditions are fixed by those of the primitive connectives defining them. How they are fixed will now be shown by proving them as metatheorems, starting with '∨'.

Take a **PC**-context, domain and world, and sentences σ and τ and suppose that σ and τ are each **T** or **F** in that context, domain and world. There are four permutations of truth and falsity between σ and τ Case (i): σ and τ are both **T**. Then by **T** ~ ~σ and ~τ are both **F**; so by **T** & (~σ & τ) is **F**; so by **T**~ ~ (~σ & ~τ) is **T**. But the formula shortens to '~(~*p* & ~*q*)', shortens to '(*p* ∨ *q*)', and since these formulae are schemata for sentences it follows that any sentence ~ (~ σ & ~ τ) shortens to (σ ∨ τ); so σ V τ is **T**. Case (ii): σ is **T** and τ is F. Then by **T** ~ ~ σ is F and ~τ is T; so by T & (~σ & ~ τ) is F; so by T ~ ~ (~ σ & ~ τ) is T; so agani σ V τ is **T**. Case (iii): σ is **F** and τ is **T**. This works out fust like the previous case; again σ V τ is T.Case (iv): σ and τ are both **F**. Then by **T** ~~ σ and ~ τ are both **T**; so by **T** & (~ σ & ~ τ~) is T; so by **T** ~ ~ (~ σ & ~ τ) is F; so σ V τ is F. Putting the four cases together we come out with the following truth-condition; [Tv] for any σ and τ in any **PC**-context, domain and world, σ V τ is T or F according as at least one of σ and τ is **T** (and the other T or **F**) or both are **F**.

It is helpful to represent the above argument in a diagram called a (generalised) truth-table. Start by supposing, tacitly, some PC-context, domain and world. List in rows the four permutations of truth and falsity between sentences σ and τ (or it could be done through formulae, following the suggestion in 8.5). Then use the truth-conditions for '~' and '&' to compute in successive columns the **T**-or-**F** ratings, in the supposed context, of the complex parts of ~ (~ σ & ~ τ). Finally transfer those ratings to the abbreviation σ V τ. **Thus:**

σ	τ	~σ	~τ	(~ σ & ~ τ)	~ (~ σ & ~ τ)	σ ∨ τ
T	**T**	**F**	**F**	**F**	**T**	**T**
T	**F**	**F**	**T**	**F**	**T**	**T**
F	**T**	**T**	**F**	**F**	**T**	**T**
F	**F**	**T**	**T**	**T**	**F**	**F**

The above truth-table displays a metalogical arguement whose conclusion, metatheorem, can be recorded on its own in a diagram taking either of the following forms:

σ τ	σ V τ
T T	T
T F	T
F T	T
F F	F

σ V τ		τ: T	τ: F
σ	T	T	T
	F	T	F

Such a diagrammatic representation of a truth-condition is called a matrix (LEMMON *BL* p. 65, "basic truth table" HUGHES & LONDEY p.33): obviously it is available for recording primitive and nonprimitive truth-conditions alike. I shall not go through the arguments which prove the truth-conditions of '⊃' and '≡', given 8.2 and the definitions. Instead I sum up the **PC** interpretation rules by presenting the truth-conditions for all five **PC** connectives, primitive and non-primitive, in matrices:

T V, **T** ⊃, **T** ≡ and others

σ	~ σ
T	F
F	T

σ τ	σ & τ	σ V τ	σ ⊃ τ	σ ≡ τ
T T	T	T	T	T
T F	F	T	F	F
F T	F	T	T	F
F F	F	F	T	T

Each connective, when it is interpreted in these ways, gives a name to formulae (or sometimes sentences) having it as their main connective: for any well - formed formulae π and ϙ,~ π is called a negation, (π & ϙ) a conjunction, (π V ϙ) disjunction I (or alternation, **QUINE** *MofL* p. 10; but HUGHES & LONDEY p. 33 use 'alternation' in another sense), (π ⊃ ϙ) a material conditional, and (π ≡ ϙ) a meterial biconditional. In 6.13 some of these names, 'neration', 'conjuntion,' and 'material conditional' were applied to propositions, but not in quite the same sense: formulae and sentences are negations etc. in virtue of containing a certain symobol which has been given a certasin truth-condiion, whereas propositions are negations etc. *of* other propositions in virtue of the *possibility* of expressing the former in sentences which affix those symbols to sentences expressing the latter.

Matrices are available as a way of presenting truth-conditions because of a feature which is peculiar to PC connectives, that they are interpreted as **truth-functional**. This means that the truth or falsity, in a context, of any sentence having one of them as its main connective is a function of (is determined by) the truth or falsity, in that context, of its remaining parts. In the other calculi interpretation rules still determine truth and falsity: so a right hand column of 'T's and 'F's could be constructed for each connective if only a left hand column could. But the condition is not met, because truth and falsity are no longer determind *by* the truth and falsity of parts but by, for exsample, a sentence's being true-in-every-world or a predicate's being true of something. It follows that the arguments proving truth-conditions for the non-primitive connectives '∃' '◊' cannot be displayed in generalised truth-tables, and we shall have to return to prose.

For '∃' the proof is this. Take a QC-context, domain and world, an open sentence in some variable *υ*, and the closed sentence which results from it when v is uniformly replaced by some subject not already contained in it. There are two cases to consider: (i) ∃υ followed by the open sentence is T in the context, domain and world ; (ii) it is **F** in them. Since the argument is quite long it will save space to take the two cases jointly, bracketing the second. By Def ∃ ~ ∀υ ~ followed by the open sentence is **T (F)**. So by **T** ~ ∀υ ~ followed by the open sentence is **F (T)**. So by **T**∀ '~' followed by the closed sentence, with subject in place of v, is F in some (**T** in all) unequivocal contexts differing from the QC-context at most as to the reference within the domain of the subject.So by **T** ~ again the closed sentence itself is **T** in some (F in all) such differing contexts. This shows that if ∃*υ* followed by the open sentence is **T**(**F**), the closed sentence is **T** in some (**F** in all) such differing contexts. But the same joint argument works in the reverse direction too; so we can add 'and only if'. The metatheorem thus proved is: [T∃] for any v, in any QC-context, domain and world, $\exists\upsilon$ followed by an open sentence in υ is **T** or **F** according as the result of replacing v uniformly by some subject not already conained in the open sentence is **T** in some unequivocal context differing from the QC-context at most as to the reference within that domain of the subject, or **F** in every such context.

Proof of the truth-condition for '◊' is along similar lines. Take an S_5-(**Q**S_5-) context, domain and world, and a sentence σ, and suppose that ◊σ is **T**(**F**) in that context, domain and world. By Def ◊ ~ □ ~ σ is **T**(**F**) in them. So by **T** □ ~ σ is **F**(**T**). So by T□ ~δ is Fin some world (**T** in ever world). So by **T** ~ σ is **T** in some world (**F** in every world). The joint argument works in the reverse direction too. So the truth-condition is:[**T**□] for any sentence σ, ◊ σ is **T** or **F** in any S_5-(**Q**S_5-) context, domain and world according as σ is **T** in some world or **F** in every world, in that context and domain.

8.7 Other people's rules

I shall discuss seven ways in which other people's interpretation rules differ significantly from those of 4.1 and 8.2.

(I) Although we have seen in 6.5 that the use of formulae to reveal form is little affected by interpretation of letters as dummies rather than schematic, still that alternative has repercussions on 8.3 and 8.5. The proof that all well-formed formulae turn out as schematic will be replaced by a proof that they turn out as sentences, mostly with unfixed meanings. The model-theoretic language in 'v('*p*') = I', 'v('*a*') Napoleon'and the like will accordingly have to be fleshed out in terms of meaning not fitting e.g. as "in *v* "*p*" is declared synonymous with some sentence which is T' and "in *v* "*a*" is declared synonymous with some subject which can be used to refer to

Napoleon'. This accounts for the use in MATES (pp. 54-6) and MASSEY (p.19 note) of the word "interpretation" as an alternative to "assignment" or "valuation":pairings of values with a formula are explicated as interpretations if they are explicated as fixing *ad hoc* meanings to the formula's constituent letters. Interpretations, in this usage, are not determined by the interpretation rules; rather those rules, by interpreting (in one sense) letters as expressions of unfixed meaning, deliberately leave us free to interpret (in the new sense) each such expression on each occasion of its use. Hence interpreting letters and interpreting connectives become less alike in one way, more alike in another; less alike because only connective-interpretation is the business of the interpretation *rules,* more alike because in both caes to interpret is as to assign a meaning (wheres the interpretation rules for letters, whethear they make them schematic or dummies, do not assign them meanings.

(2) The word "interpretation" is subject to further vagaries. According to QUINE (*MofL* p. 29) "by interpretation of the letter "*p*" (or "*q*" etc.) may be meant specification of an actual [indicative sentence] which is to be imagined in place of the letter". Here letters are schematic and "interpreting" them is replacing them by sentences or other expressions which fit them. So when QUINE says (*MofL* p.35) thata truth-functional schema is called valid "if it comes out true under every interpretation of its letters" he means "if every T or F sentence PC-fitting it is T" which, restricted to eternal sentences and generalised over PC-contexts, domains and worlds, holds just when it is PC-valid in the sense of 6.13 (3); In Mates "true under all interpretations" for "valid" more nearly means what it seems to say, but still not quite. No formula is true under *all* interpretations: e.g. "$P \supset P$' is not T in a language in which "*P*' abbreviates "Paris" and "$\supset$" means "is larger than".Rather the sense is "$P \supset P$' is true under all l-interpretations' where l is some logical language containing T $\supset$ and the convention that "*P*' abbreviates sentences, so that all that remains for an "l-interpretation" to do is specify which sentence "*P*' abbreviates.

(3) Interpretation rules stated in the manner of the pure semantics of 8.5 are sometimes left in a perilously abstract state, through failure to explicate "valuation", "domain" and "world". There is nothing objectionable about such abstract semantics as a subject of mathematical study; it constitutes a kind of logistic system in which relations are explored not between formulae or sequents but between ordered pairs (or triples) each joining a formula and a value (and a world). It is even possible, and from this mathematical point of view desirable, to get by without identifying and of the values, and in particular without indicating that "I" and "o" are to abbreviate "truth" and "falsity". But abstract semantics is not yet semantics at all, since metalogical formulae like "v (π) = I" can only serve to interpret the connectives if the metalogical word "valuation" and the metalogical symbol "I" have themselves been first explicated.

(4) One possible way of explicating "*v*("*p*") = I would be "in *v* "*p*" is declared to be a name of truth, and another similar way would be "in *v* "*p*" is replaced by a name of truth". The temptation to regard the values of every logical letter as things named by the letter, or named by expressions replacing it, comes from the treatment of functions in mathematics. We have seen that when a binary relation is such that nothing has it to more than one thing it is called a (unary) function: squaring to, or having for a square, is an example among numbers, since the square-unlike the square root—of each number is unique. We can form a name or designation of the second thing by taking a "functor" or "function sign" (cf.p.255, MATES p.158) such as "-^{2}" and fitting into its gap a name of the first thing; for example since 9 is the (only) square of 3 the expression "3^2" can be used as a name of 9 (and of no other number; so can "$(-3)^2$ be used as a name of 9 and of no other number). Function-signs are thus subject-forming operators on subjects. Frege suggested that we might regard truth-functional sentence-connectives as a species of function-sign, forming names of truth-values from names of truth-values. The

mathematician says that x^2 has the "value" 9 for the "argument"3, and x-y has the "value" 5 for the "arguments" 7 and 2 in that order, i.e. for <7, 2>; just so Frege proposed to say that "(*p* & *q*)" has the value truth for the argument <truth, truth> (this is how the expression "truth-value" originated). It is then a short step to the notation "if *p* = T and *q* = T, *p* & *q* = T", which looks like one row in the truth table of "*p* & *q*" (LEMMON *BL* p.65). But there is a high price to pay for this assimilation. Sentence-connectives form sentences out of sentences; so they can be a species of function-signs, forming subjects out of subjects, only if sentences are a species of subjects-in particular they will be, according to Frege's suggestion, names of truth and falsity. Once out in the open the suggestion is seen to be wrong: if "Men eat frogs" were a name of truth, then "Men eat frogs is stranger than fiction' should be a way of saying that truth is stranger than fiction, but it is not even grammatical. So we must reject notations like "*p* = I"as ungrammatical, and we must be careful to explicate 'v('*p*') = I not as in v '*p*' in v '*p*' is (replaced by) a sentence naming truth" but rather as "in v "*p*" is (replace by) a sentence possessing truth, i.e. a T sentence' (see PRIOR, *OT* pp. 30-I). Hence the contrast stressed in 8.5 between "v("*p*") = I" and 'v('*a*') = Napoleon'; the latter does get explicated as in v *a* is replaced by aname of Napoleon, because '*a*' is to be interpreted as a subject letter replaceable by subjects not sentences. Hence too any attempt to find the same relation expressed in '*p*' is paired with truth' as in '*a*' is paired with Napoleon" will conflict with the intention to connect '*a*' a-nd '*p*' with expressions belonging to exclusive grammatical categories. Such conflict is threatened by MATES'claim (p.55) that sentence letters 'stand for' or 'denote' truth-values, and by MASSEY'S claim (pp. 25-6) that truth-values are the 'referents' of sentences.

(5) In mathematical usage values are non-linguistic entities—numbers, truth-values, people etc. But logicians who follow the schematic interpretation without much mathematical apparatus sometimes treat values as linguistic entities, namely

as those expressions which replace schematic letters when sentences are formed out of schemata. HUGHES & LONDEY, for example, write We can get a proposition from 'if *p*, then *q*' only by replacing *'p'* and *'q'* by propositions,...........*p'* is said to take propositions as values" (p.2); and here, it seems 'proposition' must mean 'indicative sentence' since it is sentences that replace letters(cf.p.280 footnote "values whose substitution for the predicate variables"). This usage, which understands 'value of' as 'replacement for', is confusing because of its divergence from that of the mathematician, who says for example that the value of x^2 for the 'argument' 3 is the number 9 not the numeral '9'. Just as one must be alive to the distinction between a number and the numerals that name it, so one must also be alive to the distinction between a truth-value, truth or falsity, and the sentences that (do not name but) possess it. HUGHES & LONDEY not only mislead here but are themselves misled; for on the same page 2 they speak of numbers rather than numerals as values of numerical subject letters, and falsely calim that such letters are *replaced* by numbers. (The same confusion infects an expression not used in this book, 'value of a variable'; see QUINE, RPM p.180).

(6) According to the formation rules.of 7.2 "*fab*" and "*fa*" are both well-formed; consequently "(*fab* ⊃ *fa*)" is well-formed; consequently it is interpreted as a schema fitted by sentences. But probably none of the sentence QC-fitting it can be used in a QC-context to express a proposition, true or false. For (i) the fitting conventions require that "*f*" should be replaced in each of its two occurrences by the same predicate, and (ii) the context requires that the predicate should be used unequivocally. The sentence "The car broke the wall ⊃ the car broke' meets condition (i), but not (ii) since "broke" shifts from a transitive to an intransitive meaning; the sentence "She drank the potion ⊃ she drank" meets condition (i), but probably not (ii) since "drank" shifts from implying no supplementation to implying the supplementation "something". So probably "*fab* ⊃ *fa*" has no **QC**-instances; or if it does it is probably not **QC**-

valid; and the same goes for the sequent <{"*fab*"},"*fa*">. In general it is best to avoid using the same predicate letter with a varying number of subject letters in a single formula or sequent, and to be content instead with the fact that the proposition expressed in the breaking example QC-instantiates '*fab* ⊃ *ga*' which is QC- invalid, and the proposition expressed in the drinking example QC-instantiates '*fab* ⊃ ∃*xfax*' which is **QC**-valid. Uncertainty about the status of formulae like '*fab* ⊃ *fa*' could be removed by banning them as ill-formed, through a formation rule requiring different styles of predicate letter for each number of following letters or variables. In this spirit "R" is sometimes reserved as a more-than-one-place, or as a two-place, predicate letter (LEMMON *BL* p. 180). The resources of the alphabet are of course unequal to providing different styles for every number of places, so that if such are wanted some device like superscript numerals has to be used, as in '*f*1*a*', '$\exists x f^2 bx$', '$f^4 bbbc$',. Then for example <{'$f^2 ab$'}, '$f^2 a$'> will contain an ill-formed formula, while <{'*fab*'}, '$f^1 a$'> will be no harder to interpret than its unfestooned counterpart <{'$f^2 ab$'}, '*ga*'>. Furthermore 'p', '*q*', '*r*' etc. can be replaced by "f^0", "g^0", "h^0" etc. This is the notation of MATES (pp. 45, 51) and MASSEY (p. 230) who require superscript numerals but indeminify their elision.HUGHES & LONDEY (p. 296) have a similar formation rule.

(7) Some authors replace truth-conditions by satisfaction conditions. This is particularly appropriate for systems in which there are well-formed formulae containing free variables, interpreted as open sentences or open schemata. Like predicates open sentences may be true or false *of* ordered sets of things but they cannot be T or F. Satisfaction is designed to encompass this kind of case. As a preliminary to stating satisfaction conditions the expression "is satisfied by' needs first to be explicated, as follows: a closed sentence is satisfied by all or no ordered sets (of members of a domain in a context and world) according as it is T or F (in the domain, context and world)—here the reference to ordered sets idles; an open

sentence is satisfied by an ordered set (of members of a domain in a context and world) if and only if the result of replacing its alphabetically first variable by a subject which refers (in the context) to the first member of the set, , its alphabetically second variable by a subject which refers to the second member, and so on through all its alphabetically distinct variables, is a closed sentence that is T (in the context, domain and world). In Quine's examples "The open sentence "*x* walks" is satisfied [in English] by each walker and nothing else. The open sentence "*x* > *y*" is satisfied by each descending pair of numbers and no other pairs". The quotation is from *PofL* pp. 36-42, in which interpretation rules for the predicate calculus are stated in this way; see also MASSEY p. 386. Satisfaction may also be written into the definition of validity, "π is an l-valid formula" becoming short for "In any l-context, domain and world all open and closed sentences l-fitting π are satisfied by all ordered sets of members of the domain".

Assuming Bivalence (see p. I65) a well-formed formula is valid by this definition if and only if its '∀'-closure is valid by definition 6.13 (3), where the '∀'-**closure** of a formula is the result of prefixing ∀*υ* for each v which occurs free in it, if any (MASSEY p. 305; cf. pp. 6-7 and the somewhat different definition of "closure" in MATES p. 134; "if any" indicates that the '∀'-closure of closed well-formed formula is itself; an "*E*"-closure similarly is the result of prefixing ∃v for each free occurrence of v, if any). The notion of being satisfied by an ordered set is related to thc model-theoretic notion, of being satisfied by a valuation; but the latter belongs to pure semantics.

Chapter-9

Derivation Rules for Sequents

Chapter 9

9.1 Natural deduction

The logician who looks for patterns of correct argument has many ways of starting his results. We saw in Chapter 6 that a metalogical assertion such as

(A) The sequent <{'*p* & *q*'}, '*p*' > is valid

refines

The inference-schema '*p* and *q*; so *p*' is valid.

The latter is perhaps more natually formulated, in the manner of Aristotle, as

Given that *p* and *q*, it follows that *p*

where we are left to supply the gloss 'This is T whatever sentences are put unifomly for '*p*' and '*q*' in it'. Other possibilities are

The inference from '*p* and *q*' to '*p*' is correct
'*p*' is deducible from '*p* and *q*'.

These last are ambiguous. If we understand the same tacit gloss, now operating through quotation marks, the second of them has the same force as is conveyed in the metalogical open sentence 'σ is deducible from $\ulcorner\sigma$ and $\tau\urcorner$' it is a schema about sentences, gloss elided. Alternatively we can read it without gloss as a sentence about the schemata '*p* and *q*' and '*p*' synonymous with

The schema '*p*' is deducible from the schema '*p* and *q*'.

(The basic case of this metalogical ambiguity is ' "*p*" is a sentence', which might be a (valid) schema about sentences or a (false) sentence about a schematic letter; some authors ban the former reading by refusing to let the required gloss operate through quotation marks).Finally, making the jump back to connectives, a pattern of correct argument might be reported in the words.

(B) The formula '*p*' is deducible from the formula '*p&q*'.

The purpose of this section is to explore the relation between (A), which is stated in language I have explained, and (B), which is not. The trouble with (B) is that it imputes the relation of deducibility, the converse of entailment, not to prop'ositions nor even to sentences (as in 'σ is deducible from ⌜σ and τ⌝') but to formulae. Deduction was explained in terms of truth and necessity; yet how can formulae be true or necessary ? At this point the logician has a choice. One alternative is to point to the fact that formulae get interpreted, either as schemata or as sentences. It would be possible to extend the idea of deduction to cover sentences,or extend it through sentences to cove schemata, hence giving a meaning to (B) in terms of the interpretation of its symbols. The aim would be to manage the extension in such a way that (B) turned out to say the same thing as (A) and therefore deducibility, like validity, would have to be made relative to a logical language.The other alternative is to forget the connection of formulae with sentences and schemata, forget their possible interpretations altogether, and define instead a sense of deduction between formulae which is in no way beholden to the ordinary sense.The study of this kind of deduction will then be perfectly abstract, non-semantic', and it will be an open question, to be settled at a later stage, how the new relation connects with validity in any ligical language.

As I forecast in the first two chapters current logical practice favours the second alternative, and in construing (B) ignores the tenuous thread running back from it to (A). We are invited to understand (B) as a metatheorem inferred from the rules of some abstract system. Quine's 'deduction' rules (*MofL* p. 20 ff.) are perhaps not thus abstract; but Mates 'inference rules' are so, in spite of the name as are Lemmon's 'derivation rules' (*BL* p.8). As a help towards freeing assertions like (B) from association with the ordinary idea of deducibility I shall follow Mates and Lemmon in appropriating the word 'derivable' for the relation (B) attributes; all connection between deriving and deducing or inferring must be ignored. Before the end of this section 'derivability' will have become the name of a property of sequents; but for the moment it is the name of a relation between formulae Although in (B) itself this relation hold from one formula to another there will be cases in which it holds from more than one formula, and cases in which it holds from the empty set of formulae. So it is to be defined as a relation from sets of formulae, perhaps empty, to formulae, and (B) is to be rewritten as

(C) '*p*' is derivable from {'*p* & *q*')

A system using the relation of derivability might introduce it, as the property of well-formedness was introduced, by a recursive definition, which might have various categorical clauses such as 'π is derivable from {π} (π well-formed)', 'π is derivable from {π & ϙ} (π & ϙ and well-formed)', and also the hypothetical clause If π is derivable from a set of formulae Δ and every member of Δ is derivable from some subset of a set of formulae /" then π is derivable from /" (compare the 'transitivity' of entailment, p. 31). These clauses would state metalogical rules, which would have metalogical consquence provable as metatheorems. One metatheorem in many systems is the so-called Deduction Theorem (MASSEY p.145, but in MATES p. 67 the Deduction Theorem is different, being semantic): if ϙ is derivable from the union of /" and {π} is derivble from /". The Deduction Theorem stands at a junction in the network of logistic systems. On the one hand it has as a special case that if ϙ is derivable from {π}' alone, π ⊃ ϙ is derivable form the empty set', and this suggests that we might replace all the categorical clauses of the form 'ϙ is derivable from {π}' by clauses of the form 'π ⊃ ϙ is derivable from the empty set, and we might state all the rules in terms of derivability from the empty set. That way leads to so-called 'axiomatic' systems which will be the subject of Chapter 10. On the other hand it is possible to promote various hypothetical metatheoms, perhaps including the deduction theorerems itself, into the status of unproved rules and correspondingly to denote the rather cumbersome transitivity rule and most of the categorical rules except is derivable from. This last is Lemmon's rule A (MATES P, MASSEY RP), and the Deduction theorem is Lemmom's CP (MASSEY Cd, but C in MATES is slightly different). Both become parts, by this second process, of what may be called, in a wide sense, a system of Natural Deduction.

In the modern development of logistic systems 'axiomatic' versions, in which all formulae mentioned in the rules are derivable from the empty set, came first in time; and systems of natural deduction arose in response to the search for alternative rules which, while leaving the same formulae derivable from the same sets of formulae, resmbled more closely the principles of reasoning used in actual deduction of conclusions from premisses, in the presentation of these systems there has been a tendency to exaggerate the resemblance, treating the rules as if they were not only *natural* but literally rules for *deduction*. In this spirt a student of natural deduction may be invited to 'assume' any formula say '*p* & *q*' as a premiss and to use the rule 'π is derivable from {π & ♀}' in order to 'deduce' the 'conclusion' 'p'. But this is unsatisfactory for two reasons. First if 'p' is an uninterpreted formula, it cannot literally be assumed or deduced: you might as well try to assume an ink-blot. Secondly. every natural deduction system contains at least one hypothetical rule which, like the Deduction Theorem, permits 'assumptions' to be cancelled; for example if '*p*' is derivable from the Deduction Theorem permits us to conclude that '$p \;\&\; q \supset p$'is derivable from no 'assumptions'. So it is necessary to keep track of 'assumptions' , and to know at each stage of a derivation not only what has been 'deduced' but also what it has been 'deduced' from. A simple chain of formulae, e.g.

$p \;\&\; q$
p
$p \;\&\; q \supset p$

hides these vital dependencies, and needs to be replaced by a chain showing at each stage the assumptions remaining uncancelled. One way of doing so is to list uncancelled 'assumptions' in the left margin, as follows:

$\{p \,\&\, q\}$	$p \,\&\, q$
$\{p \,\&\, q\}$	p
	$p \,\&\, q \supset p$

Putting these two criticisms together we can see that the first two stages in the above chain are not adequately licensed by the rules 'any formula may be assumed as premiss' and 'π is derivble from $\{\pi$ & ϙ$\}$'.

There are various ways of making good the deficiency. One, similar to Quine's in *MofL*, adds supplementary rules about cancelling and explanations of the word 'assume' etc. Another, along the lines of LEMMON *BL*, changes the rules to 'any formula is derivable from the empty set, depending on itself' and 'π is derivable from $\{\pi$ & ϙ$\}$, depending on the same formulae as π & ϙ depended on'. A third possibility, which I prefer even though it moves away from the original conception of natural deduction, is to treat derivability as running, so to speak, horizontally rather than vertically: each formula is to be derivable not from preceding formulae in the chain (if any) but from the set of formulae to its left, on which it 'depends'. Then the rules become 'Any formula is derivable from itself (i.e. is derivable from $\{\pi\}$)' and 'If π & ϙ is derivable from a set of formulae Γ, π is derivable from Γ'.

In this third method we have the now familiar pattern of recursive definition: a categorical rule masquerading as the 'rule of premisses' and a rule or eliminating '&' which is hypothetical like the Deduction Theorem. Each rule concerns the relation of derivability from some set of formulae Γ to some formula π. But what results differs still in two ways from the formulation to be used in this book. First, to say that derivability holds from Γ to π is the same as to say that it holds of the ordered set $<\Gamma, \pi>$. Such an ordered set is a sequent. So instead of regarding derivability as a relation among formulae we can regard it more simply as a property of sequents, and we can reformulate (C) as

(D) The sequent <{‘*p* & *q*’}, ‘*p* ’> is derivable.

Secondly, it is technically convenient (as forecast in 5.10) to define this property indirectly, rather than through a recursive specification. So the derivation rules will be directions for constructing items called sequent-derivations; and ‘derivable sequent’ will be defined as ‘sequent which appears last in some sequent-derivation’.

9.2 Formulating the rules

A sequent-derivation in a calculus is a finite and non-empty ordered set of sequents, constructed according to the following rules, which are summarised in Appendix Two.

In the propositional calculus there are to be five sequent-rules, one of them categorical, the rest hypothetical. The categorical rule is: [A] any PC-formula preceded by (the set consisting just of) itself may be entered in a sequent-derivation. By analogy with the formula system to come in Chapter 10 we may describe sequents licensed under categorical rules as sequent-axioms. Since A is the only axiom-licensing rule of the calculus (in **QC** another will be added) it is best to think of its name as standing for ‘**Axiom Rule**’. In Lemmon it means ‘Rule of Assumptions, which is misleading for the reasons given in 9.I. In stating the hypothetical rules it would be tedious to forgo metalogical symbolism altogether, and I shall help myself to ‘π’ and ‘ ϙ’ from the start. Many hypothetical sequent-rules come in pairs, one for introducing and one for eliminating some connective in the last formula in a sequent. The ‘&’-**Elimination** rule runs: [&E] for any formulae π and ϙ, if (π & ϙ) preceded by any (set of) formulae has been entered in a sequent-derivation, then π so preceded may be entered in it, and also ϙ so preceded may be entered in it. As the ‘and ’ indicates this rule contains two parts, the first of which, like A, was anticipated in 9.1 The ‘&’- **Introduction** rule is: [&I]

for any formulae π and ϙ, if π and ϙ each preceded by any (set of) formulae have both been entered in a sequent-derivation, then (π & ϙ) preceded by (the union of the sets of) those formulae may be entered in it. The union is formed by pooling: see p. 10. '~' -**Elimination** provides for eliminating double '~': [~ E] for any formula π, if ~ ~ π preceded by any (set of) formulae has been entered in a sequent-derivation, then π so preceded may be entered in it. The pair to this rule, '~'-Introduction, will be proved as a metatheorem in 9.4 and does not need to be included among the primitive rules; in Lemmon~E and ~I are lumped together under the name 'Double Negation rule'. The last of the five propositional rules, **Reductio ad Absurdum**, corresponds to the following principle of reasoning : if a set of premisses entail a contradiction, then one of the premisses—any one—can be negated ('blamed' as some say) and deduced from the remaining premisses. The rule states: [RAA] for any formulae π and ϙ, if (π & ϙ) preceded by (a set consisting of) π and any o ther formulae has been entered in a sequent-derivation, then ~π preceded by the (set of) other formulae may be entered in it. This is the only primitive rule to provide for reduction in the membership of the set of formulae with which a sequent begins. In Mates' system rule C has that role; in Masseys Cd; in Lemmon' s RAA shares it with CP. Since it is possible by use of RAA to reduce membership of an initial set of formulae in a sequent to nil, the sets mentioned in this and every other hypothetical rule may be empty. On the other hand the sets which come in by the only categorical rule, A, are one-membered; and although & I provides for their enlargement by pooling we can never get by this process beyond a finite membership. Everything generated by the rules is therefore a finite sequent .

Statement of the rules can be shortened by adding metalogical symbolism from set theory:'{ }' for sets, '< >' for ordered sets, and '∪' for union of sets. I shall also continue the practice begun in the last section of using 'Γ', 'Δ' as metalogical variables ranging over sets of formulae. Then the PC rules become: for any formulae π, ρ and sets of formulae Γ, Δ, in any sequent-derivation, if π is a PC-formula $<\{\pi\}, \pi>$ may be entered; if $<\Gamma, \pi \,\&\, \rho>$ has been entered, $<\Gamma, \pi>$ and also $<\Gamma, \rho>$ may be; if $<\Gamma, \pi>$ and $<\Delta, \rho>$ have been entered, $<\Gamma \cup \Delta, \pi \,\&\, \rho>$ may be; if $<\Gamma, \sim\sim\pi>$ has been entered, $<\Gamma, \pi>$ may be; and if $<\Gamma \cup \{\pi\}, \rho \,\&\!\sim \rho>$ has been entered, $<\Gamma, \sim\pi>$ may be.

The predicate calculus with identity includes the same five rules, now adapted to QC-formulae and sequents of them; and adds four new rules, two for '=' and two for '∀'. I shall distinguish the '∀'-introduction rule as ∀I-S , because it has an analogue ∀I-F in the formula system of Chapter 10. Among the new rules one, for '='-Introduction, is categorical, and moreover stipulates for the first time a one-formula sequent, a formula preceded by the empty set. It is: [=I] for any subject letter α, $\alpha{=}\alpha$, preceded by (the set containing) nothing, may be entered in a sequent-derivation. All the other new rules involve substitution, of subject letters for subject letters, subject letters for variables, and variables for subject letters. '='-**Elimination** goes like this: [= E] for any subject letters α, β, and formula π containig, if $\alpha = \beta$ and π each preceded by any (set of) formulae have both been entered in a sequent-derivation, then the result of substituting β for at least one occurrence of α in π, preceded by (the union of the sets of) those formulae, may be entered. As in the formation rules reference here to substitution can be replaced by reference to stencils; then the rule provides that if Γ followed by $\alpha = \beta$ and Δ followed by a stencil filled up with *a* have both been entered, $\Gamma \cup \Delta$ followed by the same stencil filled up with β may be entered. Notice that nothing prevents the letter *a* which fills up a stencil from already being present elsewhere in the unfilled stencil. When that happens, filling it up with β will have the effect of substituting β for some but not all the occurrences of *a* in the original formula; and that is allowed. For example it follows from the rule that if $<\{$'*a* = *b*'$\}$, '*a* = *b*'$>$ and $\{$'*faa*'$\}$, '*faa*'$>$ have been entered, then $<\{$'*a* = *b*','*faa*'$\}$, '*fba*'$>$ may be; in fact by choosing in turn the stencils '*f*—*a*', '*fa*—' and '*f*— —' we can successively enter the sequents ending '*fba*', '*fab*', '*fbb*'. In the rule for '∀ '-**Elimination** this liberty has to be curtailed. The reason is that we want every entered sequent to be well-formed; hence when $\forall \upsilon$ is eliminated from a sequent's last formula, no υ may remain. If the rule is formulated in terms of substitution, this means that 'every occurrence' must replace 'at least one occurrence', as in : [∀E] for any subject letter *a*, variable υ, and formula π, if any (set of) formulae followed by $\forall \upsilon\pi$ has been entered in a sequent-derivation, then that set followed by the result of substituting *a* for every occurrence of υ in π may be entered in it. And the stencil formulation is: if Γ followed by $\forall \upsilon$ prefixing a stencil filled up with υ has been entered, then Γ followed by the same stencil filled up with *a* may be, provided that the stencil contains no υ. In the final rule, for '∀'-Introduction, the same proviso is needed in order to block formulae that are ill-formed on account of vacuous quantification. Although this proviso gives no trouble in practice, because one quickly gets an eye for ill-formed formulae, it is joined in the '∀'-Introduction rule by another, absent from ∀E, which is more tricky. I begin by explaining its motivation. The general idea of the rule is to license a sequent $<\Gamma, \forall \upsilon\, \varphi>$ as enterable when $<\Gamma, \pi>$ has been entered and π differs from φ in containing a subject letter wherever (old proviso) φ contains υ. But there are two kinds of case we need to block if the rule is eventually to turn out sound, never leading from valid to invalid sequents. One case would arise if the rule were so framed as to permit passage from e.g. <{'*fa*'}, '*fa*'> to <{'*fa*'}, '∀*xfx*'>—it is obvious that the former sequent is valid but not the latter. To block this, it has to be stipulated that the letter 'bartered' for the variable υ, here '*a*', does not appear in the licensed sequent's *initial* set of formulae. The second case would arise if the rule were so framed as to permit passage from e.g. <{'∀*xfxx*'}, '*faa*'> to< {'∀*xfxx*'}, '∀*xfxa*'>. The former sequent is obviously QC-valid; but the latter is not, for it has as a QC-instance 'Everyone is the same age as himself; so everyone is the same age as Methuselah', an argument with true premiss and untrue conclusion. To block this, the ∀I rule will stipulate that the letter bartered for the variable *υ*, here '*a*', does not appear in the licensed sequent's *last* formula. The joint effect of these restrictions is that when any variable *υ* is introduced by the rule the subject letter bartered for it must appear *nowhere* in the sequent which emerges. This effect can be secured by stating the rule thus:[∀I-S] for any subject letter *a*, variable *υ*, and formula π containing *a* but not *υ*, if any (set of) formulae *not* containing *a*, followed by π, has been entered in a sequent-derivation, then that set followed by the result of substituting *υ* for *every* occurrence of *a* in π and prefixing ∀*υ* may be entered in it. In terms of stencils: if Γ followed by a stencil filled up with *a* has been entered, then Γ followed by ∀*υ* prefixing the same stencil filled up with *υ* may be, provided that Γ contains no *a* and the stencil contains neither *υ* nor *a*.

It cannot be denied that these predicate calculus sequent rules, and particularly ∀I-S, are harder to understand and manipulate than any of the formation and interpretation rules; in fact they are the hardest indispensable rules in the book. Metalogical symbolism, now with 'ϕ' ranging over stencils and 'Λ' for the empty set, certainly makes it possible to state them more briefly, which may help. They become: for any subject letter *a*, variable *υ*, stencil ϕ, and sets of formula Γ, Δ, in any sequent-derivation, <Λ, *a* = *a* may be entered; if <Γ, α = β > and <Δ, ϕα> have been entered, then <Γ∪ Δ, ϕβ> may be; if ϕ contains no *υ* and <Γ, ∀*υ*ϕ*υ*> has been entered, then <Γ, ϕ*a*> may be; and if ϕ contains no *υ* and neither ϕ nor Γ contains *a* and <Γ,ϕ*a*> has been entered, then <Γ, ∀*υ*ϕ*υ*> may be.

The sequent rules of S_5 and QS_5 result by adapting to S_5-formulae and QS_5-formulae the rules of PC and QC respectively and adding to each set a rule for '□' -**Elimination** and a rule for '□ '-Introduction. The former is quite unproblematic, and goes like this:[□E] for any formula π, if □π preceded by any (set of) formulae has been entered in a sequent-derivation, then π so preceded may be entered in it. '□'-Introduction, distinguished as I-S because it too will have an analogue in the formula system of Chapter 10, stands in the same relation to its counterpart elimination rule as ∀I-S did to the elimination rule for the universal quantifier, and hence needs a proviso corresponding to the requirement that a sequent licensed by ∀I-S should exclude all occurrences of the bartered subject letter. The corresponding requirement is that in a sequent licensed by □I-S all formulae must be **fully modalised**, which means that every propositional letter, every predicate letter, and every '=' which they contain must lie within the scope of ' ' □' ◊' (for e xample '□(*p*⊃*a*=*a*)' and '*p*⊃◊ (*a*=*a*)' are fully modalised, but '□ *p*⊃*a*=*a*' is not). The final formula in a sequent licensed by the rule is bound to be fully modalised, because '□' will be its main connective; so the proviso in the rule will concern the initial formulae. The rule is:[□I-S] for any formula π, if π preceded by any (set of) formulae, all fully modalised, has been entered in a sequent-derivation, then □π so preceded may be entered in it. Without the proviso nothing would prevent passage from the valid <{'*p*'}, '*p*'> to the invalid <{'*p*'}, '□*p*'>.

The same metalogical symbolism as before permits the S_5 and QS_5 modal rules to be stated in the form: for any formula π and set of formula Γ, in any sequent-derivation, if <Γ, □π> has been entered, then <Γ, π> may be; and if all members of Γ are fully modalised and <Γ, π> has been entered, then <Γ, □π> may be.

Finally, the symbolic definitions are all allowed to function as rules for constructing sequent-derivations. That is: for any π, ϙ and Γ, if ϙ results from π by one of the symbolic definitions, and <Γ, π> has been entered in a sequent-derivation, then <Γ, ϙ> may be entered in it.

The set of derivable sequents in each calculus is now to be defined in terms of these rules. A sequent is derivable in the propositional calculus, **PC-derivable** for short, when it is the last entry in a **PC** sequent-derivation, i.e. in some derivation constructed according to the five PC rules plus the definitions; a **QC-derivable** sequent is the last entry in some **QC** sequent-derivation; and similarly in the other cases.

9.3 Sequent-derivations

The purpose of derivation rules is to afford a method of proving derivability. The method is: construct a sequent-derivation in which the sequent to be proved derivable is the last entry. In this section I shall illustrate the method and then comment briefly on it.

Here is an example of a PC sequent-derivation, the order of its four sequents running from left to right:

(E) <{'*p* & *q*'}, '*p* & *q*'>, <{'*p* & *q*'}, '*q*'>,
<{'*r*'}, '*r*'>, <{'*p* & *q*', '*r*'}, '*q* & *r*'>

(E) is a sequent-derivation of PC (and also of QC, S_5 and QS_5 because it is a finite and non-empty ordered set of sequents, its first and third sequents are licensed by A, its second is a result (one of two that are possible of applying &E to its first, and its fourth is a result (again one of two posible) of applying &I to its second and third. The third sequent could have been placed earlier but the second sequent required prev-ious entry of the first, and the fourth required previous entry of the second and third. By definition a sequent- derivation is just an ordered set of sequents-constructed according to the rules, But in order to make for ease of contruction and of checking, it is useful to adopt some extra conventions that are not part of the definition. There will be five them (all in standard use). (i) Each sequent in a derivation will be entered on separate line. SO (E) becomes:

<{'*p* & *q*'}, '*p* & *q*'>
<{'*p* & *q*'}, '*q*'>
<{'*r*'}, '*r*'>
<{'*p* & *q*', '*r*'}, '*q* & *r*'>

(ii) The lines will be numbered, thus:

(1) <{'*p* & *q*'}, '*p* & *q*'>
(2) <{'*p* & *q*'}, '*q*'>
(3) <{'*r*'}, '*r*'>
(4) <{'*p* & *q*', '*r*'}, '*q* & *r*'>

(iii) Instead of writing out an expression for each sequent on its line, only the last formula in it will be written, each of the other formulae in it, if there are any, being indicated in the left hand margin of its line by means of an index number; and the index number will be the number of some earlier (or not latter) line in which that formula is the last fomula i.e. in which it is actually writen. So (E) becomes:

{1} (1) '*p* & *q*'
{1} (2) '*q*'
{3} (3) '*r*'
{1,3} (4) '*q* & *r*'

Here 'I' in the left hand margin of lines (1), (2) and (4) refers to the formula *written* in (1), viz '*p* & *q*', and '3' in the left hand margin of lined (3) and (4) refers to '*r*'. This convention makes the structure of a derivation much more perspicuous. The convention is possible—index numbers are always available—because according to the rules of 5.2 no formula can get into a properly constructed derivation except as the last formula of the sequent that introduces it. (iv) Next, the curly barackets and quotation marks will be elided, thus:

1 (1) *p* & *q*
1 (2) *q*
3 (3) *r*
1,3 (4) *q* & *r*

(v) Finally, most derivations will be *annotated* by citing in the right hand margin of each line the derivation rule of definition which justifies its entry at that point in the derivation, together with the numbers of any previous lines in the derivation to which the rule or definition has been applied. In (E) the first and third entries are justified by A, the second by applying & E to (I) and the fourh by applying &I to (2) and (3). So it becomes:

1	(1) *p* & *q*	A	
1	(2) *q*	&E	I
1	(3) *r*	A	
1,3	(4) *q* & *r*	&I	2,3

Notice that although line (4) is justified by line (2) and (3) its indexed formulae on the left are not 2 and 3 themselves but—as & I requires—the formulae indexed in them, viz, I and 3: its written formula 'depends' on what theirs 'depended' on. Notice too that whereas the citations on the right are discretionary annotation what mathematicians call and analysis of the derivation, the index numbers on the left are *part of the seq-uents entered*, and so cannot be omitted although they might be replaced by actually writing out the formulae they refer to.

Any reader to whom the idea of a derivation is quite new will need to supplement the above explanation by reference to some other book or by working through examples. I shall do no more here than to give a few furher examples of annotated derivations, two more from **PC**, and one each from **QC**, $\mathbf{S_5}$ and $\mathbf{QS_5}$.

(F)	I	(1) $p \& \sim q$	A	
		(2) $\sim (p \& \sim q)$	RAA	I
		(3) $p \supset p$	Def $\supset$2	

Here the first entry is <{'p & ~ p'}, 'p & ~ p'>, a sequent - axiom by A; the second is < |, '~ (p & ~ p)'>, which comes by RAA from the first entry because that sequent's last formula was a case of ϙ & ~ ϙ, allowing (the only) one formula from its initial set to be negated and written as last formula following the (empty) remainder of the set; the final entry is < |, '$p \supset p$'>, which comes from line 2 by applying Def $\supset$ to that line last formula. For the remaining examples I give less commentary; they need to be pondered line by line.

(G)	I 1	(1) $p \supset q$	A	
	2	(2) p	A	
	3	(3) $\sim q$	A	
	2,3	(4) $p \& \sim q$	&I	2,3
	I	(5) $\sim (p \& \sim q)$	Def $\supset$1	
	I,2,3	(6) $(p \& \sim q) \& \sim (p \& \sim q)$	&1	4,5
	I,2	(7) $\sim \sim q$	RAA	6
	I,2	(8) q	~E	7

This uses all the primitive PC rules except &E. Notice how the set of indexed formulae on the left is bulit up by application of &I and then diminished by an application of RAA. I shall return to (G) in the next section.

(H)	1	(1) *fa*	A	
	2	(2) ∀*x* ~ *fx*	A	
	2	(3) ~ *fa*	∀E	2
	1,2	(4) *fa* & ~ *fa*	&I	1,3
	1	(5) ~ ∀*x* ~ *fx*	RAA	4
	1	(6) ∃*xfx*	Def∃	5

It will be obvious by now that no entry is determined by its precursors; there are always alternatives, if only fresh applications of A. For example after line 4 in (H), even granted the decision to apply RAA, it was permissible to have entered

2	(5*a*) ~ *fa*	RAA	4

'blaming' I instead of 2 for the 'contradiction'.

(1)	1	(1) □*p* v □*q*	A	
	1	(2) ~ (~ □*p* & ~ □*q*)	Def v I	
	3	(3) ~ *p* & ~ *q*	A	
	3	(4) ~ *p*	&E	3
	5	(5) □*p*	A	
	5	(6) *p*	□E	5
	3,5	(7) *p* & ~ *p*	&I	4,6
	3	(8) ~ □*p*	RAA	7
	3	(9) ~ *q*	&E	3
	10	(10) □*q*	A	
	10	(11) *q*	□E	10
	3,10	(12) *q* & ~ *q*	&I	9,11
	3	(13) ~ □*q*	RAA	12
	3	(14) ~ □*p* & ~ □*q*	&I	8,13
	1,3	(15) (~ □*p* & ~ □*q*) & ~ (~ □*p* & ~ □*q*)	&I	2,14
	1	(16) ~ (~ *p* & ~ *q*)	RAA	15
	1	(17) *p* v *q*	Def v	16
	1	(18) □(*p* v *q*)	I-S	17

Here the application of □I-S is correct in line 18 because the (only) formula in the set indexed there is fully modalised. The converse sequent <{'□(p v q)'}, '□p v □q'> is not derivable (cf. ARISTOTLE, *De Int.* 9.19ª28-9) , although both <{'◊(p v q)'}, '◊p v ◊q') and its converse are derivable.

(J)	1	(1) $a = b$	A	
		(2) $a = a$	= I	
		(3) □($a = a$)	□I-S	2
	I	(4) □($a = b$)= E		1,3

All members of the initial set in line 3 are fully modalised, because there are none. In the application of = E the eliminated '=' is in '$a = b$', and the stencil, which happens to contain another '=' is '□(a = _)'.

I end with two comments about the use of derivations to prove derivability. (i) A derivation is not an argument (it contains no sentences). But it does, at least if annotated, show or *display* the steps by which to argue that all its entries deserves their place, and therefore that its last entry is derivable. Notice that what is thus proved in a derivation is not a sequent but *that a sequent is derivable* 'Provable' is not synonymous with the technical sense of "derivable" though is might be used as a lazy shorthand for "porvably derivable". (ii) The rules of 9.2 for constructing derivations have a feature not shared by Quine's rules of natural deduction, namely that any initial segment of a derivation is a derivation, or in other words if you cut off the last entry in a derivation you are always left with a derivation, down to the limit where only one entry remains (which must be a sequent-axiom). This feature is definitve of "logistic sysytem" (Massey p. 274). It follows from it, by the definition of "derivable", that not only the last but every entry in a derivation is a derivable sequent.

9.4 Metatheorems on derivability

An effective method could be devised for constructing a sequent derivation whose last entry is any desird sequent, if it is derivable (MATES pp. I47-50, not in Ist edition' cf. MASSEY p.300).Butthere is no effective method of constructing, for each derivable sequent, a short derivationtlet—all one the shortest-whose last entry it is; this requires practice, tactical instruction, and ingenuity.The appeal of the method,and also its advantage over the formula-derivations to be discussed in 10.3, arise mainly from the fact that most of the derivation rules for seq-uents mirror principles of reasoning which we all use, even if unconsciously. In this section I shall show how, on the basis of the rules of 9.2 together with the symbolic definions (mostly absent from LEMMON) it is possible to prove various meta-theorems which likewise mirror principles of reasoning. The metatheorems will not be directives for constructing sequent derivations; but in the next section I shall extend the idea of a sequent-derivation so that we can make use of them. In what follows '⊢' affreviates 'is derivable'.

Modus Ponento for Sequents [**MPP-S**]. For any and then ϙ, Γ, Δ, if ⊢ <Γ, π ⊃ ϙ> and ⊢ <Δ, π>, then ⊢ <Γ ∪ Δ, ϙ>.

Proof. Take some π, ϙ, Γ, Δ, and suppose that <Γ, π ⊃ ϙ> and <Δ, π> are derivable; that is (using numbered lines for a reason which will appear shortly):

(1)	⊢ <Γ, π ⊃ ϙ>	supposition
(2)	⊢ <Δ, π>	sipposition

Since the chosen ϙ, and therefore ~ ϙ, must be well—formed under the first suppostion, it follows from fule A that < {~ ϙ}, ~ ϙ> is derivable for the chosen ϙ; that is

(3) ⊢ < {~ ϙ}, ~ ϙ> A

Similarly it follows from & I that, for the chosen π, ϙ, Γ, Δ, if <Δ, π> and <{~ ϙ}, ~ ϙ> are derivable, so is <Δ ∪ {~ ϙ}, π & ~ ϙ>; therefore from lines 2 and 3 we can infer:-

(4) ⊢ <Δ ∪ {~ ϙ}, π & ~ ϙ> &I 2,3

From (I) by Def ⊃ we get

(5) ⊢ <Γ, ~ (π & ~ ϙ)> Def ⊃I

From & I it follows again that if 4 and 5 then 6 below; so from 4 and 5 we can infer

(6) $\vdash <\Gamma \cup \Delta \cup \{\sim \rho\}, (\pi \,\&\!\sim\!\rho) \,\&\!\sim (\pi \,\&\, \sim \rho)>$ &I 4,5

From RAA it follows that if 6 then 7 below; so

(7) $\vdash < \Gamma \cup \Delta, \rho>$ RAA 6

From ~ E it follows if 7 then 8 below ; so

(8) $\vdash <\Gamma \cup \Delta, \rho>$ ~ E 7

Thus for the chosen π, ρ, Γ, Δ, whatever they are—i.e. for any π, ρ, Γ, Δ if the suppositions are true, then $<\Gamma \cup \Delta, \rho>$ is derivable. Q.E.D.

It is no accident that this metalogical proof runs nearly parallel to derivation (G) in the last section. In fact it results from (G) by the following five operations: (i) replace '*p*' and '*q*' by the metalogical variables 'π'and 'ρ' repectively; (ii) replace the index numbers '1' and '2' in (G) by the metalogical variables 'Γ' and 'Δ' respectively; (iii) record lines I and 2 as 'suppositions': (iv) add to each line the metaligical abbreviation '$\vdash$' (v) prefix 'for any 'π, ρ, Γ, Δ' to the whole proof. But these changes are more than a formality; by inserting '$\vdash$', i.e. 'is derivable', in each line they convert the line from a sequent into a metalogical open sentence about sequents, and by prefixing metalogical quantifiers to the whole array they convert it from a set of sequents into a generalised argument about sequents, which could be expressed in English rather than the metalogical symbols that are used for brevity. Because this sort of conversion is always possible it will be instructive to write the remaining proofs of this section, like that of MPP-S, in numbered and annotated lines; but they are proofs about derivability, not derivations according to the definition of derivation in 9.2 Of course each proof may build on those that precede, using their results as well as the primitive rules and definitions.

Modus Tollendo Tollens [MTT]. For any π, ρ, Γ, Δ, if $\vdash<\Gamma, \pi \supset \rho>$ and $\vdash<\Delta, \sim \rho>$, then $\vdash<\Gamma \cup \Delta, \sim \pi>$.

One proof, using MPP-S, results by converting Lemmon's

derivation 55 on p. 62 of *BL.*

Modus Ponendo Tollens [MPT]. For any π, ϙ, Γ, Δ, if $\vdash\langle\Gamma, \sim(\pi \,\&\, ϙ)\rangle$ and $\vdash\langle\Delta, \pi\rangle$, then $\vdash\langle\Gamma \cup \Delta, \sim ϙ\rangle$; alsio if $\vdash\langle\Gamma, \sim(\pi \,\&\, ϙ)\rangle$ and $\vdash\langle\Delta, ϙ\rangle$, then $\vdash\langle\Gamma \cup \Delta, \sim\pi\rangle$.

Proof of first version. For any π, ϙ, Γ, Δ

(1)	$\vdash\langle\Gamma, \sim(\pi \,\&\, ϙ)\rangle$	supposition
(2)	$\vdash\langle\Delta, \pi\rangle$	supposition
(3)	$\vdash\langle\{ϙ\}, ϙ\rangle$	A
(4)	$\vdash\langle\Delta \cup \{ϙ\}, \pi \,\&\, ϙ\rangle$	&I 2,3
(5)	$\vdash\langle\Gamma \cup \Delta \cup \{ϙ\}, (\pi \,\&\, ϙ) \,\&\!\sim(\pi \,\&\, ϙ)\rangle$	&I 1,4
(6)	$\vdash\langle\Gamma \cup \Delta, \sim ϙ\rangle$	RAA 5

Modus Tollendo Ponens [MTP]. For any π, ϙ, Γ, Δ, if $\vdash\langle\Gamma, \pi \vee ϙ\rangle$ and $\vdash\langle\Delta, \sim\pi\rangle$, then $\langle\Gamma \cup \Delta, ϙ\rangle$; also if $\vdash\langle\Gamma, \pi \vee ϙ\rangle$ and $\vdash\langle\Delta, \sim ϙ\rangle$, then $\vdash\langle\Gamma \cup \Delta, \pi\rangle$.

The proof is straightforward by Def v, Def $\supset$ and MPP-S.

'~' **-Introduction** [~ I]. For any π, Γ, if $\vdash\langle\Gamma, \pi\rangle$, then $\vdash\langle\Gamma, \sim\sim\pi\rangle$.

Proof. for any π, Γ

(1)	$\vdash\langle\Gamma, \pi\rangle$	supposition
(2)	$\vdash\langle\{\sim\pi\}, \sim\pi\rangle$	A
(3)	$\vdash\langle\Gamma \cup \{\sim\pi\}, \pi \,\&\sim\pi\rangle$	&I 1,2
(4)	$\vdash\langle\Gamma, \sim\sim\pi\rangle$	RAA 3

Conditional Proof [CP]. For any π, ϙ, Γ, if $\vdash\langle\Gamma \cup \{\pi\}, ϙ\rangle$ then $\vdash\langle\Gamma, \pi \supset ϙ\rangle$.

Proof. For any π, ϙ, Γ

(1)	$\vdash\langle\Gamma \cup \{\pi\}, ϙ\rangle$	supposition	
(2)	$\vdash\langle\{\pi \,\&\sim ϙ\}, \pi \,\&\sim ϙ\rangle$	A	
(3)	$\vdash\langle\{\pi \,\&\sim ϙ\}, \sim ϙ\rangle$	& E	2
(4)	$\vdash\langle\Gamma \cup \{\pi, \pi \,\&\sim ϙ\}, ϙ \,\&\sim ϙ\rangle$	& I	1,3
(5)	$\vdash\langle\Gamma \cup \{\pi \,\&\sim ϙ\}, \sim ϙ\rangle$	RAA	4
(6)	$\vdash\langle\{\pi \,\&\sim ϙ\}, \pi\rangle$	& E	2
(7)	$\vdash\langle\Gamma \cup \{\pi \,\&\sim ϙ\}, \pi \,\&\sim\pi\rangle$	& I	5,6
(8)	$\vdash\langle\Gamma, \sim\{\pi \,\&\sim ϙ\}\rangle$	RAA	7

(9) $\vdash <\Gamma, \pi \supset \varphi>$ Def $\supset$ 8

'$\vee$' -**Introduction** [$\vee$I]. For any π, φ, Γ, if $\vdash <\Gamma, \pi>$ then $\vdash <\Gamma, \vee \varphi>$ and also $\vdash <\Gamma, \varphi \vee \pi>$.

Proof of first half. For any π, φ, Γ

(1) $\vdash <\Gamma, \pi>$	supposition	
(2) $\vdash <\{\sim \pi \& \sim \varphi\}, \sim \pi \& \sim \varphi>$	A	
(3) $\vdash <\{\sim \pi \& \sim \varphi\}, \sim \pi>$	&E	2
(4) $\vdash <\Gamma \cup \{\sim \pi \& \sim \varphi\}, \pi \& \sim \pi>$	&I	1,3
(5) $\vdash <\Gamma, \sim (\sim \pi \& \sim \varphi)>$	RAA	4
(6) $\vdash <\Gamma, \pi \vee \varphi>$	Def $\vee$	5

The other half of the proof is the same except that '$\sim \varphi$ & $\sim \pi$'replaces '$\sim$ *p* & $\sim \varphi$' throughout.

'$\vee$'-**Elimination** [$\vee$E]. For any π, φ, ρ, Γ, Δ, E, if $\vdash <\Gamma, \pi \vee \varphi>$ and $\vdash <\Delta \cup \{\pi\}, \rho>$ and $\vdash <E \cup \{\varphi\}, \rho>$, then $\vdash <\Gamma \cup \Delta \cup E, \rho>$.

For use of this metatheorem see LEMMON *BL* pp. 22-5; I omit its proof.

The preceding metaheorems concern derivability in all four calculi, but those which now follow belong to QC and Qs_5 only.

'$\exists$'-**Introduction** [$\exists$I]. For any α, υ, ϕ not containing υ, and Γ, if $\vdash <\Gamma, \phi\alpha>$, then $\vdash <\Gamma, \exists\upsilon\phi\upsilon>$.

The proof parallels (H) in the last section, with 'υ' for 'x' 'α' for 'a' and 'ϕ' for 'f' . The proviso that ϕ contain no υ is required for the use of $\forall$E in line 3 it. This proof is analogous to that of vI, as will be the proof of $\Diamond$I.

'$\exists$' **Elimination** [$\exists$E]. For any π, a, υ, ϕ, Γ, Δ (no υ in ϕ no α in π, ϕ or Δ) if $\vdash < \Gamma, \exists\upsilon\phi\upsilon>$ and $\vdash <\Delta \cup \{\varphi \vdash\}, \pi>$, then $\vdash <\Gamma \cup \Delta, \pi>$.

This difficult metaheorem is analogous to $\vee$E. The provisos in it are required for the use of $\forall$**I-S** in its proof which, although I omit it, can be divined from (L) on p. 136. There are some comments on use of the metatheorem on p. 247. In S_5 and Qs_5 '$\Diamond$'-rules analogous to the two '$\exists$'-rules are provable. I state them here without proof.

'◊'-**Introduction**[◊I]. For any π, Γ, if $\vdash$ <Γ, π> then $\vdash$ <Γ, ◊ π>.

'◊'-**Elimination**. [◊E]. For any π, ♀, Γ, Δ (π and Δ fully modalised), if $\vdash$ < Γ, ◊♀> and $\vdash$ <$\Delta \cup$ {♀}, π>, then $\vdash$ <$\Gamma \cup \Delta$, π >.

Among the infinity of other metatheorems that could be proved I choose one hard one, which is like MATES' Replacement Metatheorem (p.136) and also like HUGHES & LONDEY's Rule for Substitution of Equivalents (p.117). The pairs of formulae with which it deals I shall call interderivable', reserving 'equivalent', for a semantic rather than proof theoretic meaning (seep. 189). Two formulae p and ♀ are **interderivable** when the '$\forall$'-closure (p.111) of their biconditional is derivable from the empty set, i.e. when there are n variables v_1 . . . . v_n such that <Λ, $\forall v_1$ . . . $\forall v_n$ ($\pi \equiv$ ♀)> is a derivable sequent. If n=o, π and ♀ must be well-formed and the sequent is just <Λ, $\pi \equiv$ ♀>, but it is useful to have a definition that counts pairs like '*fx*' and '~ ~ *fx*' as interderivable too, even though they are not well-formed.

Interderivability metatheorem. When for any part of the last formula of a derivable sequent an interderivable part is substituted, the result is still a derivable sequent if still well - formed.

Here 'part' is to be understood in such a way that atomic formulae contain no parts; e.g. '*fa*' is not a part of '*fab*'. Absence of this restriction would further complicate the proof, which is lengthy anyhow, and in three stages. I give them for QS_5; they can readily be adapted to S_5, QC (as in MATES) or PC (as in HUGHES & LONDEY). In the first stage it is to be proved that for any π, ♀, ρ, v, and ϕ and ψ containing no v,

(a) If π is interderivable with ♀, so is ~π with ~ ♀

(b) If π is interderivable with ♀, so is π & ρ with ♀ & ρ, and so is ρ & π with ρ & ♀

(c) If ϕ is interderivable with ψv, so is $\forall v\phi v$ with $\forall v\phi v$

(d) If π is interderivable with ♀, so is $\Box\pi$ with $\Box$♀

Proofs. (a) The supposition is that for some n

(I) $\vdash\langle\Lambda, \forall v_1 \ldots \forall v_n\ (\pi \equiv \&$ ♀$\rangle$ supposition

It follows by n applications of $\forall$E that $\vdash \langle\Lambda, \pi_n \equiv$ ♀$_n\rangle$, where π_n and ♀$_n$ are the results of putting a_1 for $v_1, \ldots, a_n$ for v_n in π and ♀, and π and ♀ themselves contain none of $a_1, \ldots, a_n$.

For ease of reading I drop the subscripts and write this as

	(2) $\vdash\langle\Lambda, \pi \equiv$ ♀$\rangle$	$\forall$E n times	1
so	(3) $\vdash\langle\Lambda, (\pi \supset$ ♀$)$ & $($♀$\supset \pi)\rangle$	Def $\equiv$	2
	(4) $\vdash\langle\Lambda, \pi \supset$ ♀$\rangle$	&E	3
	(5) $\vdash\langle\{\sim$ ♀$\}, \sim$ ♀$\rangle$	A	
	(6) $\vdash\langle\{\sim$♀$\}, \sim \pi\rangle$	MTT	4,5
	(7) $\vdash\langle\Lambda, \sim$ ♀ $\supset \sim \pi\rangle$	CP	6

Similarly from line 3

(8) $\vdash\langle\Lambda,$ ♀ $\supset \pi\rangle$	&E	3
(9) $\vdash\langle(\sim \pi\}, \sim \pi\rangle$	A	
(10) $\vdash\langle(\sim \pi\}, \sim$ ♀$\rangle$	MTT	8,9
(11) $\vdash\langle\Lambda, \sim \pi \supset \sim$ ♀$\rangle$	CP	10

So from lines 7 and 11

(12) $\vdash\langle\Lambda, (\sim \pi \supset \sim$ ♀$)$ & $(\sim$ ♀ $\supset \sim \pi)\rangle$	&I	7,11
(13) $-\langle\Lambda, \sim \pi \equiv \sim$ ♀$\rangle$	Def$\equiv$	12

Restoring the subscripts, we then use n applications of $\forall$I-S to get

(14) $\vdash\langle\Lambda, \forall v_1 \ldots \forall v_n\ (\sim \pi \equiv \sim$ ♀$)\rangle$ $\forall$I-S n times 13

Q.E.D. The proofs of (b), (c) and (d) are along similar lines, and are left to the reader.

In the second stage (elided in HUGHES & LONDEY p.120) it is to be proved that for any well-formed formula π, the formula which results by substituting for any part of it an interderivable part is interderivable with it; or in other words, given any pair of interderivable formulae, a well-formed formula containing the first of the pair is interderivable with the formula which results by substituting the second. The proof is by strong mathematical induction on the length of formulae. Take some pair of interderivable formulae. Abbreviate 'formula π whose '$\forall$-closure is well-formed and which contains the first of the pair as a part' to '$\underline{\pi}$', and abbreviate 'formula which results from $\underline{\pi}$ by substituting the second of the pair for the first' to '$\underline{\pi}$'; similarly for φ etc. Then take some such formula.$\underline{\pi}$ Suppose (the inductive supposition) that every such $\underline{\varphi}$ shorter than $\underline{\pi}$ is interderivable with $\underline{\varphi}$. The cases to be surveyed divide into three kinds, the third subdividing. First the interderivable part in $\underline{\pi}$ may be the whole of $\underline{\pi}$. Then trivially $\underline{\pi}$ and $\underline{\pi}$ are interderivable. Secondly π or π may be in non-primitie notation. In that case they are interderivable if and only if their primitie versions are. Thirdly the interderivable part in π may be less than the whole of it, π and π being in primitive notation. Then because of the sense given to 'part'in the Metatheorem π cannot be atomic, and there remain four cases to consider. (i) $\underline{\pi}$'s main connective is '~' i.e. it is ~ φ for some φ whose '$\forall$'-closure is well-formed. Then the part for substitution is in $\underline{\varphi}$, so that $\underline{\sim \varphi}$ is $\sim \underline{\varphi}$. By the inductive supposition $\underline{\varphi}$, being shorter than $\underline{\pi}$, is interderivable with $\underline{\varphi}$. Hence by (a) of the first stage of the proof $\sim \underline{\varphi}$ s interderivable with $\sim \underline{\varphi}$. But $\sim \underline{\varphi}$ is $\sim \underline{\varphi}$, i.e. $\underline{\pi}$, (ii) $\underline{\pi}$ is $\underline{\varphi \;\&\; \rho}$, for some φ and ρ whose '$\forall$'-closures are well-formed. Then $\underline{\varphi \;\&\; \rho}$ is $\underline{\varphi}$ & ρ or φ & $\underline{\rho}$. By the inductive supposition $\underline{\varphi}$ is interderivable with $\underline{\varphi}$ and $\underline{\rho}$ with ρ. Hence by (b)φ & ρ is interderivable with both φ & ρ and φ & ρ. But $\underline{\varphi \;\&\; \rho}$ i.e. π, is one of these. (iii) $\underline{\pi}$ is $\forall \upsilon \phi \upsilon$ for some $\phi \upsilon$ whose '$\forall$' -closure is well-formed. Then $\underline{\forall \upsilon \phi \upsilon}$ is $\forall \upsilon \underline{\phi \upsilon}$. By the inductive supposition $\underline{\phi \upsilon}$ is interderivable with $\underline{\phi \upsilon}$ (this is the clause for the sake of which the supposition must extend beyond well-formed formulae). Hence by (c) $\forall \upsilon \phi \upsilon$ is interderivable with $\forall \upsilon \phi \upsilon$. But this is $\forall \upsilon \phi \upsilon$, i.e. $\underline{\pi}$. (iv) $\underline{\pi}$ is $\Box \varphi$ for some φ whose '$\forall$' closure is well-formed. The same argument applies as in (i), now appealing to(d). This completes the survey of cases, proving that for any pair of interderivable formulae and for any π containing the first of the pair whose '$\forall$'-closure is well-formed, if every formula containing the first of the pair whose 'A'-closure is well-formed and which is shorter than π is interderivable with the result of substituting the second, so is π itself with the result of that substitution. Then by the principle of strong mathematical induction if follows that *every* formula containing the first of the pair whose '$\forall$'-closure is well-formed is interderivable with the result of substituting the second. A well-formed formula is the '$\forall$'-closure of a well-formed formula (itself). Hence in particular every *well-formed* formula containing the first of the pair is interderivable with the result of substituting the second, which was to be proved in the second stage.

In the third stage it is to be proved that for any π and φ that are well-formed and interderivable, if a derivable sequent has π for the *whole* of its last formula, then the result of substituting φ for it is still a derivable sequent. Proof. Take some Γ and well-formed π and φ, and suppose that π and φ are interderivable and $<\Gamma, \pi>$ is derivable. Since π and φ are well-formed and interderivable,

	(1)	$\vdash <\Lambda, \pi \equiv \varphi>$	by definition of 'interderivable'
so	(2)	$\vdash <\Lambda, (\pi \supset \varphi) \& (\varphi \supset \pi)>$	Def $\equiv$ 1
	(3)	$\vdash <\Lambda, \pi \supset \varphi>$	& E 2
	(4)	$\vdash <\Gamma, \pi>$	supposition
	(5)	$\vdash <\Gamma, \varphi>$	MPP-S 3,4

The conclusions of the second and third stages can now be put together. Suppose that for some π, φ, Γ (i) φ results from π by substituting an interderivable part, (ii) $<\Gamma, \pi>$ is derivable, and (iii) $<\Gamma, \varphi>$ is well-formed. By (ii) π is well-formed, and by (iii) φ is well formed. So by the second stage π and φ are themselves interderivable. So by the third stage $<\Gamma, o>$ is derivable. Q.E.D.

In order to use this metatheorem we need to be supplied with pairs of interderivable formulae. Among such pairs are π and $\sim\sim\pi$, $\forall\upsilon\forall\mu\pi$ and $\forall\mu\forall\upsilon\pi$ and $\exists\upsilon\exists\mu\pi$ and $\exists\mu\exists\upsilon\pi$, for any π

which is such that the '∀'-closures of those formulae are well-formed; the proofs of interderivability are quite easy. So we get as consequences of the metatheorem that [~ Int] the result of inserting or deleting '~ ~' anywhere in the last formula of a derivable sequent, is a derivable sequent provided that insertion preserves well-formedness; and [∀Int and EInt] the result of re-arranging adjacent occurrences of '∀'-plus-varible or of '∃'-plus-variable in the last formula of a derivable sequent is a derivable sequent (cf. HUGHES & LONDEY p. 269); the occurrences must be adjacent, not separated even by a bracket. ~ Int looks a bit like Lemmon's Double Negation, the conjunction of ~ E and ~ I. But it is much more than that, for it covers occurrences of '~ ~' anywhere in a sequent's last formula, not just at the beginning. A better comparison would be with the symbolic definitions, which likewise apply to any part of a well-formed formula. ∀Int and ∃Int are examples of quantifier shift rules, or rules of passage, which allow the scope of a quantifier, under certain conditions, to be extended or diminished. In '∀*x*∀*yfxy*' for instance, the scope of the second '∀' is '∀*yfxy*'; and according to ∀Int it is interderivable with '∀*y*∀*xfxy*', in which the scope of the '∀' binding '*y*' has been widened. Formulae in which all quantifiers have greater scope than any other connective are called prenex; and every well-formed formula containing quantifiers is interderivable with some prenex formula. But the rules of prenexing (QUINE *MofL* pp. 124-9) are complicated since in many cases a quantifier shifted to the left must change from universal to existential or vice versa; e.g. though '∀*xfx* & *p*', '*p* & ∀*xfx*' and '*p* ⊃ ∀*xfx*' are interderivable with '∀*x*(*fx* & *p*)', '∀*x*(*p* & *fx*)' and '∀*x*(*p* ⊃ *fx*)' respectively, '∀*xfx* ⊃ *p*' is interderivable with '∃*x*(*fx* ⊃ *p*)', and the same is true with '∃' for '∀' and '∀' for '∃' (compare derivation (L) on pp136-7). More confusingly still, a quantifier outranked by '≡' cannot in general be prenexed without doubling; e.g. '∀*xfx* ≡ *p*' is interderivable with '∀*x*∃*y*((*fy* ⊃ *p*) & (*p* ⊃ *fx*))', but not with '∀*x*(*fx* ≡ *p*)' or '∃*x*(*fx* ≡ *p*)'. Once quantifiers have been prenexed their order is not indifferent; for ∀Int and ∃Int do not cover mixed runs of '∀' and '∃', which are freely rearrangeable only in sequents in which all predicate letters are one-place (QUINE *MofL* pp. 118-23).

9.5 Abridged derivations

It would be tedious and absurd if every sequent-derivation had to start again at the beginning, making no use of those that precede it. One way of avoiding that necessity while still keeping within the definition of 'sequent-derivation' given in 9.2 would be to count each derivation as part of a single long one, extending over a whole book, or course of lectures, or examination script, or whatever seemed to be the appropriate unit (accordingly derivation lines might be numbered in a single continuous series). But such a fused derivation would still need to contain many see-mingly redundant parts; for example the inclusion of (H) in it, which proved the derivability of <{'*fa*'}, '∃*xfx*'>, would not dispense us from going through exactly parallel proofs if we wished at some later stage to establish the derivability of <{'*gb*'},'∃*xgx*'> or <{'~ (*faa* & *q*)', '∃*y*~ (*fya* & *q*)'>. Metatheorems come to the rescue, in one of two ways. Either we can prove a Substitution Metatheorem, permitting entry of sequent in a derivation whenever it is a 'substituend' of some sequent already proved derivable; this, which is the way of Lemmon's Rule of Sequent Introduction (*BL* p. 58) I shall not adopt though I shall describe it in 9.7. The other way is to use, and if necessary to enlarge, the battery of metatheorems proved in 5.4. Eithre course involves changing the definition of "sequent-derivation" so as to permit the metatheorems to justify entries. But the change does not open up any new destinations that could not have been reached by the rules of 9.2; it only shortens journeys to the old destinations. This is because an entry justified by a metatheorem can always be reached more lengthily by going through the steps that were used in proving the metatheorem, steps which of course relied on nothing except rules already adopted. Hence in derivations metatheorems may function as Short Cut rules (MATES p.120, "admissible rules" LAMBERT & VAN FRAASSEN p.38).

I shall now illustrate the power of metatheorems to shorten derivations, and their dispensability. A licence to justify an entry by the Interderivability Metatheorem makes it possible to get to the last entry of the following derivation in five lines instead of twenty (and compare the nine-line derivation in MATES p.126):

(K)	I	(1)	$\sim \forall x \exists y \forall z fxyz$	A	
	I	(2)	$\sim \forall x \sim \forall y \sim \forall z fxyz$	Def∃	I
	I	(3)	$\exists x \forall y \sim \forall z fxyz$	Def∃	2
	I	(4)	$\exists z \forall y \sim \forall z \sim \sim fxyz$	~ Int	3
	I	(5)	$\exists z \forall y \exists z \sim fxyz$	Def∃	4

The effect is to shift '~' past three quantifiers, each of which changes from '∀' to '∃' or '∃' to '∀'. The next example illustrates the dispensability of metatheorems by recording, in boxes, the steps which MPP-S, ∃E, and CP shortcut (the shortest route using the 9.2 rules alone is in fact shorter than the route through the boxes, but still fifteen lines long).

(L)	1	(1)	$\forall x(fx \supset p)$	A		
	2	(2)	$\exists x fx$	A		
	3	(3)	fa	A		
	1	(4)	$fa \supset p$	∀E	1	
	5	(5)	$\sim p$	A		
	3,5	(6)	$fa \;\&\sim p$	&I	3,5	
	I	(7)	$\sim (fa \;\&\sim p)$	Def ⊃4		
	1,3,5	(8)	$(fa \;\&\sim p) \;\&\; \sim (fa \;\&\sim p)$	& I	6,7	
	1,3	(9)	$\sim \sim p$	RAA	8	
	1,3	(10)	p	~ E	9	MPP-S 4,5
	1,3,5	(11)	$p \;\&\sim p$	& I	5,10	
	1,5	(12)	$\sim fa$	RAA	11	
	1,5	(13)	$\forall x \sim fx$	∀I-S	12	
	2	(14)	$\sim \forall x \sim fx$	Def∃	2	
	1,2,5	(15)	$\forall x \sim fx \;\&\; \sim \forall x \sim fx$	&I	13,14	
	1,2	(16)	$\sim \sim p$	RAA	15	∃E 2,10

1,2	(17)	p	$\sim \exists$	16	
18	(18)	$\exists xfx \;\&\; \sim p$	A		
18	(19)	$\sim p$	$\&\exists$	18	
1,2,18	(20)	$p \;\&\; \sim p$	& I	17,19	
1,18	(21)	$\sim \exists xfx$	RAA	20	
18	(22)	$\exists xfx$	&E	18	
1,18	(23)	$\exists xfx \;\&\; \sim \exists xfx$	&I	21,22	
1	(24)	$\sim (\exists xfx \;\&\; \sim p)$	RAA	23	
1	(25)	$\exists xfx \supset p$	Def $\supset$	24	CP 17

It is unreasonable in general to use a metatheorem in a derivation without first proving it. Otherwise every derivation could be shortened to its last entry, justified by merely asserting the metatheorem whose proof parallels its other entries. Sequent-derivations may be abridged, but we have to be careful that the abridgments still *display* the method of proving that their last entries are derivable and it is doubtless sometimes a debtable matter whether that condition has been met.

9.6 Other people's rules

I shall mention nine ways in which other people's rules of derivation differ from those adopted in the present chapter.

(I) In MATES '$<\Gamma, \pi>$ is derivable' is replaced by 'π is derivable from Γ'. We have seen in 9.1 that this is a trifling difference.

(2) Authors prescribe various ways of "keeping track of assumptions". Usually, as in 9.3, the method involves citing "assumptions" in the left-hand margin of a derivation, so that a derivation not only displays the derivability of some sequent but consists of a string of sequents, one to each line (so MATES, MASSEY, LEMMON *BL*). In this method only the last formulae of successive sequents, the ones written on successive lines, mirror the pattern of actual reasoning. So it is not surprising that there exist even more "natural" methods of "deduction" in which successive lines are merely formulae; of this kind are the methods of QUINE (*MofL* chs.30,37) and FITCH (ch. 2, cf.

LAMBERT & VAN FRAASSEN).

(3) In the method of MASSEY, modelled on QUINE, the rules corresponding to ∀I-S and ∃E are so formulated that not every sequent in a derivation is derivable, with the result that not every intial segment of a derivation is a derivation. Rogue sequents have consequently to be "flagged", and rules have to be stated for telling when a derivation is "finished" (QUINE *MofL* pp.204-5, MASSEY pp.285-90).

(4) In QUINE, MASSEY and MATES the ruels for intr-oducing quantifiers are called UG and EG, for "universal generlisation" and "existential generalisation". The rules for eliminating quantifiers are called US and ES in MATES ('S' for 'specification'), UI and EI in QUINE and MASSEY ('I' for 'instantiation'-it is unfortunate that this conflicts with its use for 'introduction').

(5) If the primitive, i.e. undefined, connectives are different, not just notationally, the primitive, i.e. unproved, derivation rules must be different too, to secure the same set of derivable sequents. The general requirement turns out to be that a sequent system needs a rule for introducing and a rule for eliminating each of its primitive connectives.The syste m of 9.2 meets the requirement in spite of not containing ~I as primitive, because RAA fulfils the function of introducing '~'. ~I could of course be added, superfluously, to the list of rules, as LEMMON *BL* superfluously adds it; but it cannot replace RAA, if only because no other rule in 9.2 reduces the number of formulae in a sequent's initial set. In MATES, where in effect '~', '⊃' ,'∀' are sole primitive connectives, MPP-S is used for eliminating and C for introducing '⊃' and, because of a feature of C which distinguishes it from the Deduction Theorem, CP on p.129, there is only a single '~' rule; but this latter, MT, again differs from MTT on p.128. LEMMON uses only one definition, Def ≡, and so needs many more primitive derivation rules, though not quite so many as for his own reasons he actually provides.

(6) When MATES passes from the propositional to the predicate calculus (p.112) he discards all but A and C from his propositional rules and substitutes T, which amounts to 'if$<\{\pi_1,...\pi_n\},\varphi>$ is well-formed and PC-valid and each of $<\Gamma_1, \pi_1>,...<\Gamma_n, \pi_n>$ has been entered, $<T_1 \cup ... T_n\ \varphi>$ may be entered'; and MASSEY (p.276) concurs. This course does not threaten the soundness in QC of the predicate calculus system, since every QC-sequent which is PC-valid is also QC-valid (see pp.194-5). And for the same reason rule **T** could be introduced in S_5, QS_5 and, of course, PC itself. The motive for its introduction is the existence of methods for proving PC-validity directly, without recourse to propositional derivation rules. Hence, the argument goes, if the purpose of logistic systems is eventually to provide proofs of validity in certain logical languages, and **PC**-valid sequents that are well-formed in those systems are all valid in those languages, why not make use of the direct methods instead of bothering with propositional derivations which are not always short or easy to find? The resulting natural deduction systems of MATES and MASSEY are *impure* in that their reference to validity presupposes an interpretation of the symbols they manipulate (but they could be purified by substituting 'PC-select', for '**PC**-valid').

(7) Natural Deducton systems may contain a Rule of Substitution. Although this could of course be among the primitive rules, it is more often cited as a metatheorem, e.g. by Lemmon who gives a proof of it for the propositional calculus(S_2 on p. 55 of *BL*). The rule states, with deceptive simplicity, that any substituend (or "substitution-instance") of a derivable sequent is derivable. I shal not prove it, but on pp. 158-9. I shal explain the meaning of 'substituend of a formula', from which the extension to 'substituend of a sequent' is easy. The rule, once proved, can be used for shortening derivations by permitting entry of any sequent which is a substituend of some sequent previously proved derivable; and its use can supplant that of other metatheorems on derivability. For example if it is desired to prove the derivability of <{'*p*'}, '~ ~

p'> and also <{'*q*'}, '~ ~ *q*'>, then instead of first proving ~ I we can use the following abridged sequent- derivation:

(M)	1	(1)	p	A
	2	(2)	$\sim p$	A
	1,2	(3)	$p \& \sim p$	& I 1,2
	1	(4)	$\sim\sim p$	RAA 3
	q	(5)	$\sim\sim q$	substituend of (4)

Notice that the substitution in line 5 affects the initial set in that line, which becomes {'*q*'} as well as the written formula, which becomes '~ ~ *q*' LEMMON's Rule of Sequent Introduction (*BL* p. 58, cf. MATES p. 101) is a bit more complex, partly because steps of CP and MPP-S are needed to prove it from the Substitution Rule and partly because it is stated specifically as a rule of construction. It goes like this: if $<\{\pi_1, \ldots . \pi_n\}, \varphi>$ is a substituned of some sequent proved derivable in a previous derivation and each of $<\Gamma'_1, \pi_1> \ldots <\Gamma'_n, \pi_n>$ has been entered, $<\Gamma'_1 \cup \ldots \Gamma'_n, \varphi>$ may be entered.

(8) In place of '$<\Gamma, \pi>$ is derivable when it is the last entry in some derivation " MATES in effect substitutes '$<\Gamma, \pi>$is derivable when for some subset Δ of $\Gamma<\Delta, \pi>$ is the last entry in some derivation" (MATES pp. 98.113). Since infinite sets have finite subsets this admits infinite sequents as derivable (though they are not well-formed under the formation rules of the present book). The generality thus gained is not of practical value outside mathematics and would complicate the proof of soundness.

(9) LEMMON and HUGHES & LONDEY call proved rules "derived rules ", which loses the virtue claimed for the word "derivable" on p.113. that its links with the ordinary concept of deduction are tenuous and easy to ignore. Lemmon's usage may suggest that derived rules are deriveble in the same sense as derivable sequents are. They are not. A 'derived rule is a metatheorem, a metalogical truth about sequewnts provable from the primitive derivation rules. A sequent is not a met-

alogical truth, because it is not a truth it may be proved derivable but it cannot be derived in the *sense* 'proved' (p.126).

Chapter-10

Derivation Rules for Formulae

Chaptrer 10

10.1 Axiomatic systems

In 9.1 I sketched a logistic system which started with various catergorical rules and added the hypothetical rule if π is derivable from Δ and every member of Δ is derivable from some subset of Γ, π is derivable from Γ'. Then I exchanged it for a sequent system whose rules were fully stated in 9.2. The sequent system differed from its sketched precursor in two ways, one more important than the other. The less important difference was that I chose to substitute derivability as a property of sequents for derivability as a relation from sets of formulae to formulae, replacing 'π is derivable from Γ' by '$<\Gamma, \pi>$ is derivable'. The more important difference was that the sequent system, even for the propositional calculus, contained not one but four hypothetical rules and only a single categorical rule (two in **QC**). In the shall move away from the sketched system in the other direction, keeping its preponderance of categorical rules but discarding its application to sequents.

The change is effected in two steps. First the derivation rules, both categorical and hypothetical, are made to apply only to formulae which are derivable from the empty set of formulae, Λ. The fact that some formula π is derivable from tha empty set can still, of course, be stated by saying that a sequent is derivable, namely the sequent $<\Lambda, \pi>$; but it is simpler now to leave out reference to sequents and to say merely that π is a derivable formula. As in 9.I it was possible but unnecessary to think of '$<\Gamma, \pi>$ is a derivable sequent' as meaning 'π is derivable form Γ', so in the new system it will be possible but unnecessary to think of' 'π is a derivable formula' as meaning π is derivable from Λ'. The second step in the transfromation will be to frame rules for constructing derivations in such a way that every entry in a derivation must be a formula derivable from the empty set i.e a derivable formula. This means that the Deduction Theorem which refers essentially to formulae derivable from non empty sets will not be provable in the logistic system of this chapter—a feature which distinguishes it from Massey's System P (MASSEY p. 125 ff.).

Many authors use the word "theorem" in place of "derivable formula" (MATES pp. 127, 166, LEMMON BL p. 50, MASSEY p. 128, QUINE *MofL* p. 72); and many describe theorems that are derivable in virtue of categorical rules as 'axioms' (MATES p.165, QUINE *MOFL* p.72, MASSEY p.126; an alternative terminology restricts the word 'theorem' to derivable formulae that are not axioms, HUGHES & LONDEY p. 88). Consequently logistic systems in which only formulae and no (other) sequents are derivable are often distinguished as 'axiomatic'. But the name is misleading for two reasons. First, sequent systems also must contain what I have called sequent-axioms such as <{'*p*'}, '*p*'> i.e. formulea derivable from sets of formulae in virtue of categorical rules, and may even contain formula-axioms such as <*Λ*, '*a* = *a*'> i.e formulae derivable from the empty set in virtue of categorical rules; the former are like, and the latter actually are, axioms in the logician's traditional sense. Secondly, use of the words 'çaxiom' and 'theorem' may suggest too close an analogy with what MATES (p. 183) calls a deductive theory, QUINE (*MofL* p.74) a postfoundational axiom system, and MASSEY (p. 307) a postulate system. Deductive theories in this sense—Euclid's geometry is the most famous specimen - differ from logistic systems in two crucial respects. they are interpreted, and moreover must be interpreted in such a way that they consist of sentences not schemata; and their theorems are entailed by their axioms.By contrast the relation among formulae in a system of derivable formulae that the other theorems are derivable if the axioms are—holds whether or not the formulae are interpreted and regardless of what the interpretation may be;and even if a system's formulae are made by some interpretation into sentences, its axioms might fail to entail its theorems without reproach to the system, as such-failure would merely attest.

the system's unsoundness under *that* interpretation. A third, less definite, difference is that logistic systems are usually developed, as in this book, in the course of a *study* of entailment: they reveal, if sound, patterns of deductively correct inference.That is why derivation rules get called—too hastily,as we saw p.113—rules of inference. But in a deductive theory like Euclid's, interst centres on the special subject matter and inferences, though of course drawn, are not examined systematically, if at all.

Because the formula systems of this chapter are no more 'axiomatic' than the sequent systems of Chapter 9.1 shall avoid that name for them. But I shall defer to tradition in calling their categorically derivable formulae axioms, in spite of the big difference between uninterpreted formulae and the propositions taken as axioms in a deductive theory. Once 'axiom' has been permitted there would be no objection to 'theorem', though I shall continue to use 'derivable fourmula' instead. Most logicians now guard against confusion between derivable formulae and provable assertions about them by distinguishing the latter as 'metatheorms'; but HUGHES AND LONDEY are an exception, and the Deduction Theorem is commonly so called.

As in Chapter 5, I shall formulate the rules as rules for constructing a formula-dervation.

10.2 Formulating the rules

A formula-derivation in a calculus is a finite and non-empty ordered set of formulae, constructed according to the following rules which are summarised in Appendix Two.

As in the sequent system, there are to be five propositional rules, but this time four of them are categorical. The first is **Iteration for** '&' [It&] for and **PC**-formula π, $\pi \supset \pi \;\&\; \pi$ may be entered in a formula- derivation . Its mate **Simplification for** '&', is closely analogous to &I of the sequent system: [Simp&] for any PC-formulae π and ϙ, π & ϙ $\supset \pi$ may be entered in a formula-derivation. Analogy between elimination rules and simplification- rules will run right through the two sets of systems. The former are, in a way, more powerful. For one thing 'π & ϙ ⊃ ϙ is derivable' is not incorporated in Simp&, though it can be proved, eventually, in the formula system; whereas &E contained a part corresponding to that version too. For another thing, and more fundamentally, the formula system affords no means of gaining the generality of &E' s reference to sets of formulae 'Γ'; as forecast in 10.1 all such initial sets now have to be enpty. Notice that π and ϙ must be well-formed, to gurante that π & ϙ ⊃ π is; in the hypothetical & E this work was done by the supposition that <Γ, π & ϙ> is derivable. The third rule is **Commutation** for '&', so called because it corresponds roughly to the provable semantic rule 'if 'σ & τ' is **T**, so is 'τ & σ' which is a law of commutation; but the formula system requires a negated and categorical version as primitive, the unnegated and hypothetical version being eventually provable: [Com&] for any PC-formulae π and ϙ, ~(π & ϙ) ⊃ ~(ϙ & π) may be entered in a formula-derivation. The final axiom rule, which I call 'Summation for '&' on the analogy of Summation in *Principia Mathematica* (WHITEHEAD & RUSSELL p. 97), runs like this: [Sum&] for any PC-formulae π, ϙ, ρ, (π ⊃ ϙ) ⊃ (~ (ϙ & ρ) ⊃ ~ (π & ρ)) may be entered in a formula derivation. To these four is added a single hypothetical rule, **Modus Ponendo Pones for Fomulae**. This is just the special case of MPP-S in which both Γ an Δ are empty: [MPP-F] for any formulae π and ϙ, if π ⊃ and π have both been entered in a formula-derivation, then may be entered in it.

For abbreviating the statement of these rules I shall here, though not in Appendix Two, write '(π & ϙ) etc. as 'πϙ' etc. and '~' as a bar surmounting the formula within its scope. This, the notation of Quine (*MofL* p.9), brings great economy to the formulation of rules in a proposition formula system in which '~' and '&' are primitive. The five rules become: for any PC-formulae π, ϙ, ρ, in any formula-derivation, π ⊃ ππ, πϙ ⊃ π, πϙ ⊃ ϙπ, and (π ⊃ ϙ) ⊃ (ϙρ ⊃ πρ) may be entered; and if π ⊃ ϙ and π have been entered, then ϙ may be.

In the predicate calculus with identity the same five rules reappear, adapted to **QC**-formulae, and four new ones are added, two each for '='and '∀'. Of the four newcomers '=' - **Introduction** is the very same rule as in the sequent system, now expressed in the words: [= I] for any subject letter a, $a = a$ may be entered in a formula-derivation. The next rule, also categorical, I call **Simplification for** '=' because of a resemblance, admittedly slight, with Simp&: each contain an occurrence to the left of '⊃' the symbol it is named after, and no occurrence to the right (hence each can be used in conjunction with MPP-F for eliminating its symbol, and Simp = stands to = E as we found that Simp stands to & E). The rule is : [Simp =] for any subject letters α and β and QC-formulae π and ϙ, $\alpha = \beta \supset (\pi \supset$ ϙ$)$ may be entered in a formula-derivation if ϙ differs from π only in containing β in at least one place where π contains α. In the language of stencils the rule becomes: $\alpha = \beta \supset (\phi\alpha \supset \phi\beta)$ may be entered provided that $\phi\alpha$ is a QC-formula. Of the two '∀'-rules **Simplification for** '∀' continues the process of converting hypothetical elimination rules for sequents into categorical rules for foumulae. One formulation would be: [Simp∀] for any subject letter α, variable υ, formula π containing υ and QC-formula ϙ, $\forall\upsilon\pi \supset$ ϙ may be entered in a formula-derivation if ϙ differs from π only in containing α in every place where π contains υ. As in the sequent system this is unlike Simp= in requiring substitution of α for υ throughout π. So its stencil version must insist on a stencil not already containing υ, and must take the form: for any α, υ and ϕ, $\forall\upsilon\phi\upsilon \supset \phi\alpha$ may be entered provided that $\phi\alpha$ is a QC-formula and ϕ containd no υ. The final rule, '∀'-**Introduction**, is hypothetical, and like ∀I-S requires that the formula licensed should contain no occurrence of the 'bartered' subject letter. In terms of substitution: [∀I-F] for any subject letter α, varible **QC**-formula π containing no α, and QC-formula ϙ containing α but not υ, if $\pi \supset$ ϙ has been entered in a formula-derivation, then $\pi \supset \forall\upsilon$ followed by the result of substituting υ for every occurrence of α in ϙ may be entered in it. In terms of stencils: if $\pi \supset \phi\alpha$ has been entred, then $\pi \supset$

$\forall\upsilon\phi\upsilon$ may be, provided that π contains no α and ϕ contains neither υ nor α.

In 10.4 I shall show how on the basis of ∀I-F the simpler but less powerful metatheorem 'if $\vdash\phi\alpha$, then $\vdash\forall\upsilon\phi\upsilon$' can be proved ($\phi$ still containing no α or υ). Notice, though, that this is by no means the same as proving the categorical metatheorem '$\vdash\phi\alpha \supset \forall\upsilon\phi\upsilon$'. There is a contrast here with Simp∀, which is categorical and can be proved in the sequent system from the hypothetical as follows:

(1)	$\vdash\langle\{\forall\upsilon\phi\upsilon\}, \forall\upsilon\phi\upsilon\rangle$	A	
(2)	$\vdash\langle\{\forall\upsilon\phi\upsilon\}, \phi\alpha\rangle$	∀E	1
(3)	$\vdash\langle\Lambda, \forall\upsilon\phi\upsilon \supset \phi\alpha\rangle$ CP	2	

provided $\phi\alpha$ is well-formed and ϕ contains no υ. An attempt to reproduce this proof with '$\phi\alpha$' and '$\forall\upsilon\phi\upsilon$' exchanged would founder in line 2, where ∀I-S would require that the initial set of formulae contain no *a*. In fact the categorical metatheorem cannot be proved from the rules of either the formula system of the sequent system which is just as well because for most α, υ, ϕ, $\phi\alpha \supset \forall\upsilon\phi\upsilon$ is QC-invalid, and so a logistic system containing the rule would be QC-unsound. This is a suitable point therefore at which to draw attention to the vital difference, in any system, between metatheorems of the form '$\vdash\pi \supset$ ϙ' and of the form 'if $\vdash\pi$, then $\vdash$ϙ'. The latter can be inferred from the former in a system containing MPP but the former cannot in general be inferred from the latter (different again is the categorical form '$\vdash\langle\{\pi\}$, ϙ$\rangle$', which some would write as '$\pi \vdash$ ϙ'; this entails and is entailed by '$\vdash\pi \supset$ ϙ' in systems containg A, MPP and the Deduction Theorem).

With full metalogical abbreviation as before the four extra predicate calculus rules become: for any subject letters α and β variable υ, stencil ϕ and QC-formula π, in any formula-derivation, $\alpha = \alpha$ may be entered; if $\phi\alpha$ is a QC-formula, $\alpha = \beta \supset (\phi\alpha \supset \phi\beta)$ may be entered; if $\phi\alpha$ is a QC-Formula and ϕ contains no υ, $\forall\upsilon\phi\upsilon \supset \phi\alpha$ may be enterd; if ϕ contains no υ and neither ϕ nor π contains α and $\pi \supset \phi\alpha$ has been entered, then

$\pi \supset \forall \upsilon \phi \upsilon$ may be.

The formula-rules of S_5 and QS_5 result by adapting to S_5-formulae and QS_5 formulae the rules of **PC** and **QC** respectively, and adding to each set a pair of rules analogous to Simp∀ and ∀I-F **Simplification for** '$\Box$', which is categorical is [Simp $\Box$] for any s_5-(QS_5-) formula π, $\Box\pi \supset \pi$ may be entered in a formula-derivation. '$\Box$' -Introduction for Formulae remains hypothetical and carried over from the serquent system the reqirement that every formula licenes by it should be fully modalised (see p. 121). Its statement is: [$\Box$ I-F] for any S_5-(QS_5) formulae π and ψ, if $\pi \supset \psi$ has been entered in a formula-derivation, then $\pi \supset \Box\psi$ may be enterd in it, provided that π is fully modalised. Without the proviso nothing would prevent passage from the S_5-valid '$p \supset p$' to the S_5-invalid '$p \supset \Box p$'. As in QC the simpler and less powerful metatheorem 'if $\vdash\psi$, then $\vdash\Box\psi$ (ψ fully modalised)' is provable from $\Box$**I-F**; and in contrast with ∀**I-F** the categorical '$\vdash\psi \supset \Box\psi$ is also provable, provided still that ψ is fully modalised (see p. 153).

Abbreviated, the modal rules are: for any S_5-formulae π and ψ in any formula-derivation, $\Box\pi \supset \pi$ may be entered; and if π is fully modalised and $\pi \supset \psi$ has been entered, then $\pi \supset \Box\psi$ may be Similarly for QS_5.

Finally, the symbolic definitions are allowed to function as rules for constructing formula-derivations. That is : for any π, ψ, if ψ results from π by one of the symbolic definitions, and π has been entered in a formula-derivation, then ψ may be entered in it.

The set of derivable formulae in each calculus is now to be defined in terms of these rules. A formula is derivable in the propositional calculus, **PC-derivable** for short, when it is the last entry in some **PC** formula-derivation, i.e. in some derivation constructed according to the five PC rules plus the definitions; a **QC-derivable** formula is the last entry in some QC formula-derivation; and similarly in the other cases.

10.3 Formula- derivations

A formula-derivation, like a sequent-derivation, does not infer that a formula is derivable by argument from premisses, but rather displays that fact in a structure made according to rules. For better display I adopt the following fairly standard conventions: (i) each formula in a derivation will be written on a separare line; (ii) the lines will be nunbered; (iii) the derivation rule or definition which justifies each entry will be cited to its right.

Here are some derivations by way of example. In the first I resume the convention introduced in 10.2 of writing '(π & ϙ)' as 'πϙ' so as to make the shape of each formula plainer. The reference '(N)' continues the series begun in Chapter 9.

(N) (1)	$(p \supset pp) \supset ({\sim}(pp \mathbin{\&} {\sim}p) \supset {\sim}(p \mathbin{\&} {\sim}p))$	Sum&	
(2)	$(p \supset pp) \supset ((pp \supset p) \supset (p \supset p))$	Def ⊃ twice	1
(3)	$p \supset pp$	It &	
(4)	$(pp \supset p) \supset (p \supset p)$	MPP-F	2,3
(5)	$pp \supset p$	Simp &	
(6)	$p \supset p$	MPP-F	4,5

Notice that It&, used in line 3, requires the same formula thrice repeated, while Simp&, used in line 5, permits without requiring that. The layout is simpler than in sequent-derivations because, each line being a formula rather than a sequent, no sets of formulae need to be cited in the left hand margin (or: the citation is 'Λ' throughout). But it is typical or 'axiomatic' methods that (N) is twice the length of (F) on p.124 which ended '<Λ, '$p \supset p$'>'. Also, results in the formula systems rely much more heavily on use of preceding derivations. Whereas for example the rules of 9.3 permit a nine-line sequent- derivation ending '<Λ, '$fa \supset \forall x fx$'>', the formula '$fa \supset \forall x fx$' can be reached in a formula-derivation only through a complex set of propositional moves leading to '$(\forall x {\sim} fx \supset {\sim}fa) \supset (fa \supset {\sim} \forall x {\sim} fx)$', whence it emerges by Simp∀, MPP-F and Def∃ (cf. '∃'-Introduction on p. 152) Similarly the sequent whose validity shows that '=' expresses a transitive relation, <Λ, '$a = b \supset (b = c \supset$

$a = c)$'>, can be reached in eight lines in a sequent derivation, but its last formula needs a much longer formula-derivation, even though two very similar-looking versions are axioms and so arrive in one line each:

(O) (I) $a = b \supset (a = c \supset b = c)$ Simp =
(P) (I) $a = b \supset (c = a \supset c = b)$ Simp =
(in (O) the stencil is' = c', in (P) 'c = _').

In S_5 and QS_5 there is the same problem of length. But on interesting S5-derivable formula emerges fairly quickly:

(Q) (I)

.

.

.

(6) $\Diamond p \supset \Diamond p$ by steps as in (N)
(7) $\Diamond p \supset \Box\Diamond p$ $\Box$I-F 6

Line 7 is correct because '$\Diamond p$' is fully modalised.This formula is sometimes called the "characteristic S_5 axiom," because its derivability distinguishes S_5 from various weaker modal systems. That it is not an axiom of S_5 in the present book illustrates the familiar fact that one and the same system can be axiomatised in different ways.

10.4 Metatheorems on derivability

In this section I select some among the infinitely many metatheorems provable in the formula systems of 10.2. Because the metalogical proofs of these rules virtually copy, as in Chapter 9, the steps of derivations, they tend to be lengthy and to rely on their precursors: and for these reasons I shall leave several of them incomplete.

Syllogism [Syll]. For any well-formed π, ϙ, ρ, $\vdash(\pi \supset$ ϙ$) \supset (($ϙ $\supset \rho) \supset (\pi \supset \rho))$; also if $\vdash\pi \supset$ ϙ, then $\vdash($ϙ $\supset \rho) \supset (\pi \supset \rho)$; also if $\vdash\pi \supset$ ϙ and $\vdash$ϙ $\supset \rho$, then $\vdash\pi \supset \rho$.

This is three different metatheorems under the same name, the first of them categorical like Sum&, the other two hypothetical. HUGHES & LONDEY call the first 'Syll' and the last 'Derived Rule 2' (p. 106). The proof of the categorical version is this : for any well-formed π ϙ, ρ,

(1) $\vdash (\pi \supset$ ϙ$) \supset (\sim ($ϙ $\& \sim \rho) \supset \sim(\pi \,\&\! \sim\rho)$ Sum &
(2) $\vdash (\pi \supset$ ϙ$) \supset (($ϙ $\supset \rho) \supset (\pi \supset \rho))$ Def $\supset$ twice 1

The hypothetical versions can then be reached by appending:

(3) $\vdash \pi \supset$ ϙ supposition
(4) $\vdash ($ϙ $\supset \rho) \supset (p \supset \rho)$ MPP-F 2,3

and then

(5) $\vdash$ ϙ $\supset \rho$ supposition
(6) $\vdash \pi \supset \rho$ MPP-F 4,5

Both categorical and hypothetical versions have uses, and so it is with most of the other metatheorems I shall state.

Double Negation for Formulae [DN-F]. For any well - formed π, $\vdash \sim\sim \pi \supset \pi$; also $\vdash \pi \supset \sim\sim \pi$; also $\vdash \pi$ and only if $\vdash \sim\sim \pi$.

I shall prove the two categorical versions (lines 6 and I3 below); the other follows easily from them as in Syll. For any well-formed π.

(1) $\vdash \pi \supset \pi$ proof parallels (N) on p.147
(2) $\vdash \sim(\pi \,\&\! \sim \pi) \supset \sim(\sim \pi \,\&\, \pi)$ Com &
(3) $\vdash (\pi \supset \pi) \supset \sim(\sim \pi \,\&\, \pi)$ Def $\supset$2
(4) $\vdash \sim(\sim \pi \,\&\, \pi)$ MPP-F 1,3
(5) $\vdash \sim(\sim\sim \pi \,\&\! \sim \pi)$ sepecial case of (4)
(6) $\vdash \sim\sim \pi \supset \pi$ Def $\supset$5
(7) $\vdash \sim\sim\sim \pi \supset \sim \pi$ special case of (6)
(8) $\vdash (\sim\sim\sim \pi \supset \sim \pi) \supset (\sim(\sim\pi \,\&\, \pi)$
$\supset \sim(\sim\sim\sim \pi \,\&\, \pi))$ Sum&
(9) $\vdash \sim(\sim \pi \,\&\, \pi) \supset \sim(\sim\sim\sim\pi \,\&\, \pi)$ MPP-F 7,8
(10) $\vdash \sim(\sim\sim\sim\pi \,\&\, \pi)$ MPP-F 4,9

(11) $\vdash \sim(\sim\sim\sim\pi \;\&\; \pi) \supset \sim(\pi \& \sim\sim\sim\pi)$	Com&	
(12) $\vdash \sim (\pi \;\&\; \sim \sim \sim \pi)$	MPP-F	10,11
(13) $\vdash \pi \supset \sim \sim \pi$	Def ⊃12	

Transposition [Transp]. For any well- formed π, $ϙ$, $\vdash(\pi \supset ϙ) \supset (\sim ϙ \supset \sim \pi)$; also $\vdash(\sim ϙ \supset \sim \pi) \supset (\pi \supset ϙ)$; also $\vdash\pi \supset ϙ$ if and only if $\vdash \sim ϙ \supset \sim \pi$.

I porve the first version: for any well-formed π, $ϙ$

(1) $\vdash \sim \sim \pi \supset \pi$	DN-F	
(2) $- (\pi \supset ϙ) \supset (\sim \sim \pi \supset ϙ)$	Syll	1
(3) $\vdash \sim (\sim \sim \pi \;\&\; \sim ϙ) \supset \sim (\sim ϙ \supset \sim \sim \pi)$	Com&	
(4) $\vdash(\sim \sim \pi \supset ϙ) \supset (\sim ϙ \supset \sim \pi)$	Def⊃twice	3
(5) $\vdash (\pi \supset ϙ) \supset (\sim ϙ \supset \sim \pi)$	Syll	2,4

Here Syll is used in two versions, the first hypothetical version in line2, which therefore cites one preceding line, and the second hypothetical version (HUGHES & LONDEY's DR2) in line 5, which therefore cites two preceding lines. The proof of the converse categorical version of Transp is similar, but uses the converse categorical version of DN-F. Transp is otherwise called 'Contraposition'. From this point I shall abandon proofs for a bit, merely stating results in the order in which they come out. With the help of Transp it is quite easy to prove that for any well-formed π, $ϙ$, ρ, $\vdash\pi \;\&\; ϙ \supset ϙ \;\&\; \pi$ (Pure Com&), $\vdash(\pi \supset ϙ) \supset (\pi \;\&\; \rho \supset ϙ \;\&\; \rho)$ (Pure Sum &) and $\vdash \pi \;\&\; ϙ \supset ϙ$ (an alternative Simp&). Then we can get.

Simplification for '⊃' [Simp⊃]. For any well-formed π, $ϙ$, $\vdash\pi \supset (ϙ \supset \pi)$; also if $\vdash\pi$, then $\vdash ϙ \supset \pi$.

Next an ingenious and difficult proof leads to

Association for '&' [Assco&]. For any well-formed π, $ϙ$, ρ, $\vdash((\pi \;\&\; ϙ) \;\&\; \rho) \supset (\pi \;\&\; (ϙ \;\&\; \rho))$; also $\vdash(\pi \;\&\; (ϙ \;\&\; \rho)) \supset ((\pi \;\&\; ϙ) \;\&\; \rho)$; also $\vdash(\pi \;\&\; ϙ) \;\&\; \rho$ if and only if $\vdash\pi \;\&\; (ϙ \;\&\; \rho)$.

The structure of the proof can be divined from HUGHES & LONDEY p. 131 where a proof of the corresponding Assoc ∨ is given in the formula system of WHITEHEAD & RUSSELL, which has '$\sim$' and '$\vee$' as primitive connectives. It is not surprising that Whitehead and Russell failed to find the proof of Assoc $\vee$ and so included it needlessly among their axiom-rules.

Inportation and Exportaion. For any well-formed π, ϙ, ρ) [Imp] $\vdash(\pi \supset (ϙ \supset \rho)) \supset (\pi \;\&\; ϙ \supset \rho)$; also [Exp] $\vdash(\pi \;\&\; ϙ \supset \rho, \supset (\pi \supset (ϙ \supset \rho))$; also $\vdash\pi \supset (ϙ \supset \rho)$ if and only if $\vdash\pi \;\&\; ϙ \supset \rho$.

Proof of Imp. For any well-formed π, ϙ, ρ.

(1) $\vdash\sim (\pi \;\&{\sim\sim}(ϙ \;\&{\sim}\rho))\supset{\sim}({\sim\sim}(ϙ \;\&{\sim}\, \rho) \;\&\; \pi)$ Com&

(2) $\vdash(\pi \supset (ϙ \supset \rho)) \supset {\sim}({\sim\sim}(ϙ \;\&\; {\sim}\rho) \;\&\; \pi)$ Def $\supset$ twice 1

(3) $\vdash (ϙ \;\&\; {\sim}\rho) \supset {\sim}{\sim} (ϙ \;\&\; {\sim}\rho)$ DN-F

(4) $\vdash((ϙ \;\&\; {\sim}\rho) \supset {\sim}{\sim} (ϙ \;\&\; {\sim}\rho)) \supset$
$({\sim} ({\sim}{\sim} (ϙ \;\&{\sim}\rho) \;\&\; \pi)\supset{\sim}((ϙ \;\&\; {\sim}\rho) \;\&\; \pi))$ Sum &

(5) $\vdash {\sim}({\sim\sim}(ϙ \;\&{\sim}\rho) \;\&\; \pi)\supset{\sim}((ϙ \;\&\; {\sim}\rho) \;\&\; \pi)$ MPP-F 3,4

(6) $\vdash(\pi \supset (ϙ \supset \rho)) \supset {\sim} ((ϙ \;\&\; {\sim}\rho) \;\&\; \pi)$ Syll 2,5

(7) $\vdash{\sim}((ϙ \;\&\; {\sim}\rho) \;\&\; \pi) \supset {\sim}(\pi \;\&\; (ϙ \;\&\; {\sim}\rho))$ Com &

(8) $\vdash(\pi \supset (ϙ \supset \rho)) \supset {\sim}(\pi \;\&\; (ϙ \;\&\; {\sim}\rho))$ Syll 6,7

(9) $\vdash((\pi \;\&\; ϙ) \;\&\; {\sim}\rho) \supset (\pi \;\&\; (ϙ \;\&\; {\sim}\rho))$ Assoc &

(10) $\vdash {\sim}(\pi \;\&\; (ϙ \;\&\; {\sim}\rho)) \supset {\sim}((\pi \;\&ϙ)\&{\sim}\rho)$ Transp 9

(11) $\vdash (\pi \supset (ϙ \supset \rho)) \supset {\sim} ((\pi \;\&\; ϙ) \;\&{\sim}\rho)$ Syll 8,10

(12) $\vdash(\pi \supset (ϙ \supset \rho)) \supset (\pi \;\&\; ϙ \supset \rho)$ Def $\supset$ 11

The proof of Exp is similar. Then the 'if and only if' version comes by applications of MPP-F.

Permutation [Perm]. For any well- formed π, ϙ, ρ, $\vdash(\pi \supset (ϙ \supset \rho)) \supset (ϙ \supset (\pi \supset \rho))$; also if $\vdash\pi \supset (ϙ \supset \rho)$, then $\vdash ϙ \supset (\pi \supset \rho)$.

This comes quite easily from Imp. and Exp. **All** the foregong metatheorems are provable in all four calculi. I shall now state a few that are provable only in **QC** and **QS$_5$**.

'$\exists$'Introduction for Formulae. For any α, υ, and ϕ not containing υ, if $\phi\alpha$ is well-formed, then $\vdash\phi\alpha \supset \exists\upsilon\phi\upsilon$; also if $\vdash\phi\alpha$, then $\vdash\exists\upsilon\phi\upsilon$.

Proof of categorical version: for any such α, υ, ϕ,

(1) $\vdash \forall \upsilon \sim\phi\upsilon \supset \sim\phi\alpha$	Simp∀	
(2) $\vdash \sim\sim \forall\upsilon \sim \phi\upsilon \supset \forall\upsilon \sim \phi\upsilon$	DN-F	
(3) $\vdash \sim \exists\upsilon\phi\upsilon \supset \forall\upsilon \sim \phi\alpha$	Def ∃	2
(4) $\vdash \sim \exists\upsilon\phi\upsilon \supset \sim\phi\alpha$	Syll	1,3
(5) $\vdash \phi\alpha \supset \exists\upsilon\phi\upsilon$	Transp	4

Pure'∀' Introduction for Formulae. For any α, υ, and ϕ containing neither, if $\vdash\phi\alpha$, then $\vdash\forall\upsilon\phi\upsilon$.

Proof: for any such α, υ, ϕ,

(1) $\vdash \phi a$	supposition	
(2) $\vdash \phi\alpha \supset ((p \supset pp) \supset \phi\alpha)$	Simp ⊃	
(3) $\vdash (p \supset pp) \supset \phi\alpha$	MPP-F	1,2
(4) $\vdash (p \supset pp) \supset \forall\upsilon\phi\upsilon$	∀I-F	3
(5) $\vdash p \supset pp$	It &	
(6) $\vdash \forall\upsilon\phi\upsilon$	MPP-F	4,5

The trick here is to choose some axiom which is like '$p \supset pp$' in containing no α—any such will do. The metatheorem differs from '∃'-Introduction in having, as explained on p. 146, no categorical version. Two other useful metatheorems are.

Distribution for '∀' and '∃'. For any α, υ, and ϕ and ψ containing no υ, [Dist∀] if $\phi\alpha$ and $\psi\alpha$ are well- formed, $\vdash\forall\upsilon(\phi\upsilon \supset \psi\upsilon) \supset (\forall\upsilon\phi\upsilon \supset \forall\upsilon\psi\upsilon)$; also [Dist∃] if $\phi\alpha$ and $\psi\alpha$ are well-formed, $\vdash\forall\upsilon(\phi\upsilon \supset \psi\upsilon) \supset (\exists\upsilon\phi\upsilon \supset \exists\upsilon\psi\upsilon)$; also if $\vdash\forall\upsilon(\phi\upsilon \supset \psi\upsilon)$ then both $\vdash\forall\upsilon\phi\upsilon \supset \forall\upsilon\psi\upsilon$ and $\vdash\exists\upsilon\phi\upsilon \supset \exists\upsilon\psi\upsilon$.

Proof of the categorical versions: for any such $\alpha,\upsilon,\phi,\psi$

(1) $\vdash \forall\upsilon\phi\upsilon \supset \phi a$	Simp∀	
(2) $\vdash (\phi a \supset \psi a) \supset (\forall\upsilon\phi\upsilon \supset \psi a)$	Syll	1
(3) $\vdash \forall\upsilon (\phi\upsilon \supset \psi\upsilon) \supset (\phi a \supset \psi a)$	Simp∀	
(4) $\vdash \forall\upsilon(\phi\upsilon \supset \psi\upsilon) \supset (\forall\upsilon\phi\upsilon \supset \psi a)$	Syll	2,3
(5) $\vdash \forall\upsilon(\phi\upsilon \supset \psi\upsilon)\ \&\ \forall\upsilon\phi\upsilon \supset \psi a$	Imp	4
(6) $\vdash \forall\upsilon(\phi\upsilon \supset \psi\upsilon)\ \&\ \forall\upsilon\phi\upsilon \supset \forall\upsilon\phi\upsilon$	∀I-F	5
(7) $\vdash \forall v(\phi\upsilon \supset \psi\upsilon) \supset (\forall\upsilon\phi\upsilon \supset \forall\upsilon\psi\upsilon)$	Exp	6

(1) $\vdash \forall v(\phi v \supset \psi v) \supset (\psi a \supset \psi a)$	Simp$\forall$	
(2) $\vdash (\phi a \supset \psi a) \supset ({\sim}\psi a \supset {\sim}\phi a)$	Transp	
(3) $\vdash \forall v(\phi v \supset \psi v) \supset ({\sim}\psi a \supset {\sim}\phi a)$	Syll	1,2
(4) $\vdash \forall v(\phi v \supset \psi v) \supset \forall v\, ({\sim}\psi v \supset {\sim}\phi v)$	$\forall$I-F	3
(5) $\vdash \forall v({\sim}\psi v \supset {\sim}\phi v) \supset (\forall v\, {\sim}\psi v \supset \forall v {\sim}\phi v)$	Dist$\forall$	
(6) $\vdash \forall v(\phi v \supset \psi v) \supset (\forall v\, {\sim}\psi v \supset \forall v\, {\sim}\phi v)$	Syll	4,5
(7) $\vdash (\forall v {\sim}\psi v \supset \forall v {\sim}\phi v) \supset ({\sim}\forall v\, {\sim}\phi v \supset {\sim}\forall v\, {\sim}\psi v)$	Transp	
(8) $\vdash (\forall v\, {\sim}\psi v \supset \forall v {\sim}\phi v) \supset (\exists v \phi v \supset \exists v \psi v)$	Def$\exists$ twice	7
(9) $\vdash \forall v(\phi v \supset \psi v) \supset (\exists v \phi v \supset \exists v \psi v)$	Syll	6,8

Because of the close analogy between the quantifier rules Simp$\forall$ and $\forall$I-F, and the modal rules, Simp$\Box$ and $\Box$I-F, modal metatheorems analogous to the above three are provable in S_5 and **QS**$_5$, namely:

'$\Diamond$'-Introduction for Formulae. For any π, if π, is well- formed, then $\vdash \pi \supset \Diamond\pi$; also if $\vdash \pi$, then $\vdash \Diamond\pi$.

Pure '$\Box$'-Introduction for formulae. For any π, if $\vdash \pi$, then $\vdash \Box\pi$; also if π is well-formed,and fully modalised, $\vdash \pi \supset \Box\pi$.

Distribution for '$\Box$' and '$\Diamond$'. For any π and ϙ, [Dist$\Box$] if π and ϙ are well- formed, $\vdash \Box(\pi \supset ϙ) \supset (\Box\pi \supset \Box ϙ)$; also [Dist $\Diamond$] if π and ϙ are well- formed, $\vdash \Box(\pi \supset ϙ) \supset (\Diamond\pi \supset \Diamond ϙ)$; also if $\vdash \Box(\pi \supset ϙ)$, then both $\vdash \Box\pi \supset \Box ϙ$ and $\vdash \Diamond\pi \supset \Diamond ϙ$.

The one failure of analogy with QC, forecast on p. I46, is that Pure'$\Box$'-Introduction has a categorical version. Its proof is: for any well- formed and fully modalised π

(1) $\vdash \pi \supset \pi$	proof parallels (N)	
(2) $\vdash \pi \supset \Box\pi$	$\Box$I-F	I

It is because of the possibility of proving this metatheorem that the 'characteristic S_5 axiom' '$\Diamond p \supset \Box\Diamond p$' is derivable in the S_5 and **QS**$_5$ systems, as is '$\Box p \supset \Box\Box p$' the chàracteristic axiomd of the weaker modal system S_4; moreover from the former we can prove e.g. by'$\Diamond$'-Introduction and Syll, the derivability of '$p \supset \Box\Diamond p$' (p. 161), the characteristic axiom of another weaker system B; see HUGHES & CRESSWELL pp. 46, 49,57.

In **QS**$_5$ metatheorems are provable concerning the

relationship between modal connectives and quantifiers. The three which follow are the most interesting (see BARCAN p. 2, and BURIDAN p. 130).

Barcan Metatheorem, For any v, and ϕ not containing v, if $\forall v \phi v$ is well-formed, $\vdash \forall v \Box \phi v \supset \Box \forall v \phi v$; also if $\vdash \forall v \Box \phi v$; then $\vdash \Box \forall v \phi v$; also if $\exists v \phi v$; is well-formed, $\vdash \Diamond \exists v \phi v \supset \exists v \Diamond \phi v$; also if $\vdash \Diamond \exists v \phi v$, then $\vdash \exists v \Diamond \phi v$.

Proof of first version: for any v, and ϕ not containing v, if $\exists v \phi v$ is well- formed, then for any a not in ϕ.

(1)	$\vdash \Box \phi a \supset \phi a$	Simp$\Box$	
(2)	$\vdash \forall v(\Box \phi v \supset \phi v)$	Pure $\forall$I	1
(3)	$\vdash \forall v \Box \phi v \supset \forall v \phi v$	Dist$\forall$	2
(4)	$\vdash \forall v \Box \phi v \supset \Box \forall v \phi v$	$\Box$I-F	3

I omit proof of the other versions, as of the next rule.

Converse Barcan Metatheorem. For any v, and ϕ, not containing v, if $\forall v \phi v$ is well- formed, $\vdash \Box \forall v \phi v \supset \forall v \Box \phi v$; also if $\vdash \Box \forall v \phi v$, then $|\!\uparrow \forall v \Box \phi v$; also if $\exists v \phi v$ is well-formed, $\vdash \exists v \Diamond \phi v \supset \Diamond \exists v \phi v$; also if $\vdash \exists v \Diamond \phi v$, then $\vdash \Diamond \exists v \phi v$.

Buridan Metatheorem. For any v, and ϕ containing, if $\exists v \phi v$ is well-formed, $\vdash \exists v \Box \phi v \supset \Box \exists v \phi v$, also if $\vdash \exists v \Box \phi v$, then $\vdash \Box \exists v \phi v$; also if $\forall v \phi v$ is well-formed, $\vdash \Diamond \forall v \phi v \supset \forall v \Diamond \phi v$; also if $\vdash \Diamond \forall v \phi v$, then $\vdash \forall v \Diamond \phi v$.

Proof of first version: for any v, and ϕ not containing v, if $\exists v \phi v$ is well formed, then for any a not in ϕ

(1)	$\Box \phi v \supset \phi v$	Simp$\Box$	
(2)	$\forall v(\Box \phi v \supset \mathrm{f}v)$	Pure $\forall$I	1
(3)	$\exists v \Box \phi v \supset \exists v \phi v$	Dist$\exists$	2
(4)	$\exists v \Box \phi v \supset \Box \exists v \phi v$	$\Box$I-F	3

I omit proof of the other versions. There is no converse Buridan metaheorem, and such formulae as '$\Box \exists x fx \supset \exists x \Box fx$' are not QS_5- derivable (nor QS_5-valid).

10.5 Abridged derivations

It will be proved in outline on p.192 that π is a valid formula of one of the four caluli if $<\Lambda, \pi>$ is a valid sequent of that calculus. This being so, and given also the soundness of the formula and sequent systems, there are always two logistic methods available for proving the validity of a formulaπ: find a formula-derivation ending π, or find a sequent-derivation ending $<\Lambda, \pi>$. In practice the latter method is nearly always the handier of the two. Neverthelwes it is worth describing ways of improving the former method, by abridgment of formula-derivations. (i) We shall need the same kinds of short cut as in sequent-derivations, namely use of substitutio or other metatheorems or both. And of course there is the same justification as before for relaxing the definiton of 'formula-derivation' so as to license these abridgments: every entry reachable by them could have been reached without them. It is also customary, and highly desirable, to permit other abridgments: (ii) entries justified by categorical rules can be elided when it is sufficiently obvious what they are, and (iii) two or more applications of MPP-F or Syll can be run together. Here is an example in which short cuts of all three kinds are used.

(R)			
	(1) $\sim\sim(q \,\&\sim p)\supset(q \,\&\sim p)$	DN-F	
	(2) $\sim\sim(q \,\&\sim p)\supset\sim p$	Syll	I, pure Com& Simp&
	(3) $p\supset\sim(q \,\&\sim p)$	Transp 2	
	(4) $p\supset(q\supset p)$	Def $\supset$ 3	

After line I entries of '$(q \,\&\sim p)\supset(\sim p \,\& q)$' and '$(\sim p \,\& q)\supset\sim p$' are elided, so that the annotation of line 2 refers not to them but to the categorical version of Pure Come& and the categorical rule Simp& which justify them: line I together with the former yields '$\sim\sim(q \,\&\sim p)\supset(\sim p \,\& q)$' by Syll, and that together with the latter then yields line 2 by another application of Syll; these two applications arc run together so as to make linio I plus the two elided formulae yield line 2 directly. More important than the saving by elision is the use of metatheorems DN-F, Syll, Pure Com& and Transp, without which the derivation would need more nearly forty than four lines. In the next example Syll affords a modest abridgment of formula-derivation (N) from p. 147:

(S)	(1) $p \supset pp$	It&	
	(2) $pp \supset p$	Simp&	
	(3) $p \supset p$	Syll	1,2

These are considerable economies. The trouble is that facility in using and following them demands practice, without which the methods of Chapter 9 are undoubtedly easier. Just how far to let abridgment go is, as in sequent- derivations, a matter for discretion. It would be possible for example, and perhaps sufficiently perspicuous, to contract (S) still further into the single line.

(1) $p \supset p$ Syll It&, Simp&

or as others would write it (cf.QUINE *MofL* p.73)

(1) It & ⊃ (Simp & ⊃ ($p \supset p$)) Syll

10.6 Other people's rules

(I) There are various ways of changing the axiom-rules while leaving exactly the same formulae derivable. Eight alternative sets of such rules for propositional systems in which only '~' and '&' are primitive (called KN systems after the Polish notation) have been examined by PORTE. They include a set due to Curry which differs from that of 10.2 in substituting '⊢(π ⊃ ϙ) ⊃ (ρϙ ⊃ ρπ)' for Sum&, which was '⊢(π ⊃ ϙ) ⊃ (ϙρ ⊃ πρ)'; and a set due to Rosser which replaces Com& and Sum& by the single rule '⊢(π ⊃ ϙ) ⊃ (ϙρ ⊃ ρπ)'(ROSSER p. 55; also in COPI, 177). To prove that these changes do not affect the set of derivable formulae it is necessary to show that the primitive rules of each system, are either primitive or provable in the others—a laborious business.

(2) If the primitive connectives are different the minimum list of primitive derivation rules must be defferent too. Modus Ponendo Ponens is commonly the only primitive hypothetical

rule in versions of the propositional calculus (though its '$\pi \supset \varphi$' will have different definitional expansions according as '&' or '∨' is primitive, and no expansion if '⊃' is). AN systems, in which only '~' and '∨' are primitive in the propositional calculus, can start with rules corresponding to A_1, A_2 and A_5 of HUGHES & LONDEY (p. 102), or with a shorter set in which A_3 and A_5 are combined as Rosser combines Com& and Sum& (see PRIOR FL p.305, 6.12 (6)). CN system, with '~' and '⊃' primitive, may start from the three propositional rules in MATES (p.165, I-III) or from three corresponding to the rules in QUINE (*MofL* pp.72-3,(1)-(3); both these sets are due to Lukasiwicz. Many other possibilites are noted by Prior (*FL*, appendix I) including several with only a single axiom-rule. Proof that all these make the same formulae derivable is again by showing that the primitive rules of each are either primitive or provable in the other; except that in such cases what is primitive in one system must be writen out in the system's primitive notation before submitting to proof in another system.

(3) Various alternatives to the two ∀-rules are known. One replaces ∀I-F by its purse version and adds the categorical rule '$\vdash \forall \upsilon(p \supset \phi\upsilon) \supset (p \supset \forall\upsilon\phi\upsilon)$, if π and $\forall\upsilon\phi\upsilon$ are well formed and π contain no υ'. Mates dispenses with a hypothetical '∀'-rule by admitting free variables in well-formed formulae and stating his rules under the rubric 'the '∀'-closures of the following are axioms' (MATES p. 165). Then instead of justifying argument from, say, "$\vdash$ '*fa* ⊃ *fa*' to "$\vdash$ '∀*x*(*fx* ⊃ *fx*)' " the rules ensure that the same argument which shows that $\vdash$'*fa* ⊃ *fa*' shows also that the '∀'-closure of '*fx* ⊃ *fx*' is derivable, i.e. that $\vdash$ '∀*x*(*fx* ⊃ *fx*)'.

(4) A common alternative to the '□'-rules which keeps the same formulae derivable , i.e. which is a set of S_5 rules, retains Simp □ and replace □I-F by its pure form together with three categorical rules stating that $\vdash \Box(\pi \supset \varphi) \supset (\Box\pi \supset \Box\varphi)$□ i.e. Dist □, $\vdash \Box\pi \supset \Box\Box\pi$ and $\vdash \pi \supset \Box\Diamond\pi$ (or '$\vdash \Diamond\pi \supset \Box\Diamond\pi$' in placr of the last two, MASSEY p. 106). The motive for the larger set is comparsion with other modal systems: if '$\vdash \pi \supset \Box$

$\Diamond\pi$' is dropped from it we get the system S_4; if '$\vdash \Box\pi \supset \Box\Box\pi$' is dropped, the system B; and if both are dropped, the system T, otherwise called M.

(5) Formula systems may, like sequent systems, contain a Rule of Substitution stating the every substituend of a derivable formula is derivable. The rule can, with difficulty, be proved as a metatheorem in the system of 10.2, just as its analogue was provable in the systems of 9.2. But in formula systems a very common alternative, adopted by HUGHES & LONDEY (p.102), QUINE (*MofL* pp. 72-3) and Massey (p. 126), is to make the Rule of Substitution primitive and to replace the axiom-rules by a finite list of formulae that are axioms. In the propositional calculus it is fairly easy to see how this transformation leaves the same formulae derivable. We start by defining a PC- substituend thus:

> "φ is a PC- substituend of π' is to mean 'φ is the result of one more successive operations in which a PC- formula is substituted for a propositional letter uniformly throughout π'.

(where uniformity as usual demands the same formula for tha same letter and permits it for different letters). Since propositional letters are themselves PC-formulae the following are all PC- substituends of 'p & $q \supset p$': itself, 'p & $p \supset p$', 'q & $r \supset q$', '$(q \supset r)$ & $\sim p \supset (q \supset r)$'; and so on. It follows from this definition that the axiom- rule Simp& is true if and only if every **PC**-substituend of 'p & $q \supset p$' is derivable (and obviusly such a formula as 'q &$p \supset q$' would serve here in place of 'p & $q \supset p$' since it has the same PC-substituends, though such a formula as '$(p$ & $p)$ & $q \supset (p$ & $p)$' would not since it has fewer). From this it is fairly clear, though the matter would take some proving, that Simp& has the same effect in propositional calculus as the conjunction of "p & $q \supset p$" is derivable, with the hypothetical Rule of Substitution if, is a PC- substituend of π and π is derivable, so also is 'φ'. Hence it is possible to reformulate the derivation rules of the propositional calculus by adding that rule of Substitution to MPP-F as a second primitive hypothetical rule and replacing the axiom-rules by "The following are derivable: '$p \supset pp$', '$pq \supset p$', '$pq \supset qp$', '$(p \supset q) \supset (qr \supset pr)$'".

The same change is easily made in S_5; in QC and QS_5 it becomes much more complex because of the need to permit substitution for subject letters and variables and predicate letters. The Rule of Substitution itself is simple enough: every QC-substituend of a QC-derivable formula is QC-derivable (and similarly for **QS**$_5$). But the business of defining QC-substituend" is fairly formidable. Here is one way. We allow a stencil to contain gaps marked by defferent numerals, e.g. '$\forall x(fx$①② & g②①$a)$'. We say that such a stencil is *filled* when some letter is uniformly inserted once into each gap marked '①'some letter, the same or differnt, is uni formly inserted once into each gap marked ②and so on. We define an atomic stencil as a stencil that becomes an atomic formula when all its gaps are filled by subject letters, and a well-formed stencil, e.g. a **QC**-stencil, as a stencil that becomes a well-formed formula, e.g. a **QC**-formula, when all its gaps are filled by subject letters (the latter is close to Mates definition of 'stencil' itself (MATES p. 178). Then.

> 'φ is a **QC**- substituend of π' is to mean 'φ is the result of one or more successive operations in which a QC- formula is substituted for a propositional letter, or a subject letter for a subject letter, or a variable for a variable (provided that no variable V is substituted for a different variable already in the scope of $\forall v$ or $\exists v$), or a QC- stencil for an atomic **QC**-stencil (provided that no stencil containng v is substituted for a defferent atomic stencil already in the scope of $\forall v$ or $\exists v$), uniformly throughout.

For alternative ways of stating this definition, and for use of the preficate calculus Substitituion Rule, see MATES pp. 179-80 and LEMMON *BL* pp.150 -2. Because the definition is so complicated it is not surprising that most logicians prefer to avoid making the Rule of Substitution primitive in the predicate calculus, and use instead universal axiom- rules like those of

10.2, so called axiom-schemata.

(6) Some authors, including HUGHES & LONDEY (p. 102), present derivation rules for formulae as a recursive definition of 'derivable formula' rather than directions for constructing a formula-derivation. For example in place of 'ρ may be entered $1 \supset \rho$ if and π have been' MPP-F becomes 'ρ is derivable if $\pi \supset \rho$ and π are'. See pp. 144, 180.

(7) Although we may think of a derivable formula as one that is derivable from te empty set, the formula systems of 6.2 do not define 'derivable' from except in this special case. It could be defined for PC, however, in the following way (cf.MASSEY p. 144). Add to the PC derivation rules 'any well' formed formula may be entered in a formula 'derivation as an' assumption. Then define 'π is derivable from Γ' to mean "There is a formula-derivation whose last entry is and whose assumption are the memberss of Γ" (or: of a subset of Γ")', and define 'π is a derivable formula' to mean 'π is derivable from 1'. The same formulae remain **PC**- derivable as by the rules of 10.2. Because of $\forall$1-**F** and $\Box$1-**F** more complex manoeuvres would be needed to work the extension into the other three formula systems; see for example MASSEY pp. 206, 414-5.

Such an extension allows formula-derivations to be used in proving the derivability of sequents. For example the following formula-derivation has 'p &q' as sole assumption and 'p' as last entry, and so proves that 'p' is derivable from 'p & q', i.e. that $\vdash \langle \{`p \;\&\; q'\}, `p' \rangle$:

(1) p & q	'assumption'	
(2) p & $q \supset p$	Simp&	
(3) p	MPP-F	1,2

Notice that the "assumption" here is a formula, not the propostion that that formula is derivable; so what is proved is that 'p' is derivable from 'p & q' not that 'p' is derivable— from nothing—if 'p & q' is. Finally the formula-derivation becomes a sequent-derivation if we use the device of Chapter 9 for " keeping track of assumptions":

I	(1) $p \,\&\, q$	'assumption'	
	(2) $p \,\&\, q \supset p$	Simp&	
I	(3) p	MPP-F	1,2

The rules of Chapter 9 allow the same sequent to be proved derivable more briefly, by means of

1	(1)	$p \,\&\, q$	A	
1	(2)	p	&E	1

and that is why they are preferable,even though the presence of RAA and CP in the, requires, as the formula rules do not, some device for keeping track of assumptions.

(8) Methods of annotating derivations, and methods of abridgment, vary a good deal. Here is a formula-derivation using the rule '$(q \supset r) \supset (p \vee q \supset p \vee r)$ is an axiom (WHITEHEAD & RUSSELL's Summation,HUGHES & LONDEY A_5), the Rule of Substitution, and the definition '$(\pi \supset \varphi)$ is short for, $(\sim \pi \vee \varphi)$', which I call for the nonce 'Df ⊃'. First I set out the derivation in full in the style of 10.3; then as it would be formulated and abridged by three other authors.

Style of 10.3:

(1) $(q \supset r) \supset \ (p \vee q \supset p \vee r)$	Summation	
(2) $(q \supset r) \supset \ (\sim p \vee q \supset \sim p \vee r)$	Substitution	1
(3) $(q \supset r) \supset ((p \supset q) \supset (p \supset r))$	Df ⊃	2

WHITEHEAD & RUSSELL p. 100:

$$[\text{Sum}\ \frac{\sim p}{p}]\quad \vdash :.\ q \supset r. \supset : \sim p \vee q. \supset\ \sim p \vee r \quad (1)$$

$$[(1).(\text{Df}\supset)]\quad \vdash :.\ q \supset r. \supset : p \supset q. \supset. p \supset r$$

HUGHES & LONDEY pp. 105, 108:

Sum $(\sim p/p)$: $(q \supset rf) \supset ((\sim p \vee q) \supset (\sim p \vee r))$ (1)

(1) × Df ⊃ : $(q \supset r) \supset ((p \supset q) \supset (p \supset r))$ (2)

PRIOR, *FL* p. 27:

Sum p/Np × Df⊃ = (1)

(1) *CCqrCCpqCpr*

Another style is proof trees, in which the tips of the branches are axioms and the final formula is at the base of the trunk. Here is a proof in that style ending with the "characteristic B axiom" '$p \supset \Box \Diamond p$'.

```
————————DN-F————————simp□
~~□~p⊃ □~p            □ ~p⊃ ~ p
——————————————————————Syll————It&————Simp&
~~□ ~ p ⊃ ~p          ◊p ⊃ ◊p & ◊p ◊p & ◊p ⊃ ◊p
——————————Transp      ——————————————Syll
p ⊃ ~ □ ~ p           ◊p ⊃ ◊p
——————————Def◊        ——————————□I-F
p ⊃ ◊p                ◊p ⊃ □◊p
  ——————————————————————Syll
          p ⊃ □ ◊ p
```

Every formula must have a bar above it, marked with a rule justifying its entry on the basis of what is entered, if anything, above it. So only categorical rules justify bars with nothing above them. Formula-derivations with "assumptions" can be represented by trees in which some tips have no superposed bar, and sequent-derivations can be written that way too, except that some means has to be found for showing when an "assumption" has been can-celled by RAA or CP, e.g. the square brackets in this example.

```
                                [◊p]
                                ———□I-S
[p]                             □◊p
————◊I                          ——————CP cancelling '◊p'
 ◊p                             ◊p ⊃ □◊p
 ———————————————————————————————MPP-S
                       □[◊p]
                       ———CP cancelling 'p'
                       p ⊃ □◊p
```

But it would be closer to the spirit of Chapter 9 to write sequent trees with strings of formulae, indicating sequents, on each line, e.g. like this:

$$
\dfrac{\dfrac{\dfrac{}{p \vdash p}\text{ A}}{p \vdash \Diamond p}\Diamond\text{I} \qquad \dfrac{\dfrac{\dfrac{}{\Diamond p \vdash \Diamond p}\text{ A}}{\Box\Diamond p}\Box\text{I-S}}{\vdash \Diamond p \supset \Box\Diamond p}\text{CP}}{\dfrac{p \vdash \Box[\Diamond p]}{\vdash p \supset \Box\Diamond p}\text{CP}}\text{MPP-S}
$$

(9) I end with a comment on the name "Transformation Rule" for what I call hypothetical derivation rules. Hughes & Londey adopt it in preference to "Rule of Inference" on the ground that the latter "would tend to impose an iterpretation" (HUGHES & LONDEY p.96, compare p.113 above.) But the name has two drawbacks of its own. It stresses a distinction *within* the derivation rules—between categorical and hypothetical—which is also present but unmarked within the formation rules. And it suggests that the relation between formation rules and derivation rules is like that between the rules for setting the board at chess and the rules for moving pieces; whereas in unextended axiomatic systems it is the axioms rather than the formation rules which correspond to rules for setting the board, since well- formed formulae that are not derivable never get on to the board at all.

Chapter-11

Modal

Chapter 11

The Predicate language described so far is the fundamental logical language. Like an old family house, it does not have all the modern conveniences and not everything in it works as well as it could, but one can live in it and it offers the scope necessary for further improvement. The efforts of logicians, philosophers and linguists detailed in the Reading List will give you some idea of the improvements which have been suggested. What I have tried to do in this book is to portray the structure of the original house before too many builders moved in.

As is often the case with additions to old houses, there is likely to be disagreement about their value and about how well they fit in. In this chapter, I will sketch an important new wing of the edifice, though it is by no means universally agreed to be an improvement, Less metaphorically, this chapter introduces elements of a logical language which can be grafted onto Sentential and Predicate. Because of its importance, I did not think even a basic account of the languages of logic would be complete without it. But what follows is only meant as an introduction. In particular, most of the discussion will be confined to the blending of the new elements with Sentential rather than predicate, as this gives you an uncluttered view of the issues.

11.0 A Sample Argument

Below is an argument in natural language. Do you think it is valid ?

(M) It is possibly the case that Jones is a bachelor.
It is necessarily the case that if Jones is a bachelor then Jones is not married.
Therefore, it is possibly the case that Jones is not married.

It certainly seems valid. Can it be translated into a language of logic which preserves this appearance ? The first thing to note is that nothing in the argument seems to require the *full* resources of Predicate. There are no quantifiers in the argument and it could be partially translated in either of the following ways.

(M_1) It is possibly the case that FA.
It is necessarily the case that (Fa ⊃ ¬Ga)

It is possibly the case that ¬ GA.

(M_2) It is possibly the case that P.
It is necessarily the case that (P ⊃ ¬ Q)

It is possibly the case that ¬Q.

Since Predicate isn't called for, we will stick with the Sentential version (M_2). However, we are still short of a full translation. Nothing in Sentential (or Predicate) was designed to cope with such notions as "possibly" or necessarily", yet the validity of the argument here seems to depend crucially on them. If these notions were dropped, then the argument would be a simple instance of ⊃E, and this cannot be all there is to it. The conclusion of the argument is not

Jones is not married

but

it is possibly the case that Jones is not married.

Suppose we create two new symbols to go with those already in Sentential thereby creating a new language. Thay are

'◊'meaning "it is possibly the case that"
'□'meaning "it is necessarily the case that".

We could then represent the argument in this way

(M_3) ◊ P
□ (P ⊃ ¬Q)

◊ ¬ Q

These new symbols are commonly called *modal operators*, and they are treated, for purpose of scope, like the negation in Sentential. However it is one thing to introduce symbols and another to give an explanation of them. Suppose, for example, you tried to test (M_3) for validity by constructing a truth table. The argument contains two basic sentences, so it would begin like this:

P	Q		◊ P
T	T		T
T	F		T
F	T		
F	F		

But here you are stuck. As the table indicates, it is reasonable to think it true that P is possible when you already know that P is true. This is the ground for the Ts in rows one and two. However, the fact that P is false is not a reason to think it false that P is possible. One of the main uses of the idea of possibility is to say something *true* about what may well be false as things stand, In any case, if rows three and four were assigned Fs, then the table for P and ◊ P would be exactly the same. This would mean that the new symbol would be adding absolutely nothing to the argument, and that is just wrong. (And if we put Ts in these rows, the truth table for ◊P would make it a tautology! This is no more acceptable.) The original argument (M) turns on the relationship between possibility and necessity. As was noted above, (M) is not merely another way of presenting ⊃ E.

Though I did not get as far as including it in the table, the '□' symbol is no less recalcitrant. Consider a row in which P⊃ Q is false. In such a row, it is reasonable to think that □ (P⊃ ¬ Q) is false, since if a sentence is false we would not count it as necessarily true. However, when (P⊃ ¬ Q) is *true,* we are again stuck. If adding the '□' to the sentence produces another truth, then the table for (P ⊃ ¬ Q). Will be indistinguishable from the one for plain $P \supset \neg Q$. In which case, the '□' is redundant.

Introducing the symbols is a first step, but all the work lies ahead.What is missing is some account of these new symbols which tells us how they are to be treated in the evaluation of arguments.

11.1 Modalities

Instead of beginning directly with the new symbols, we will take a step back and examine sentences in English such as

(a) it is possibly the case that Jones is a bachelor.

This sentence can be paraphrased as

(b) Jones might be a bachelor.

In fact, many would think that (b) is a more natural way of expressing the thought that underlies (a). But what is that thought?

The word' 'possibly' in (a) and the word 'might' in (b) are the key to understanding these sentences. These words were classified by early logicians (and grammarians) as *modalities* because it was held that they characterize the mood with which a thought is expressed. The idea is, I suppose, that some thoughts get expressed rather forcefully as assertions in the indicative, e.g.

the cat is on the mat.

But that an essentially similar thought can be expressed in a different mood as the more conditional

the cat might be on the mat
(it is possible that the cat is on the mat)

or, further still as the even more forceful

the cat must be on the mat
(it is neccessary that the cat is on the mat).

We don't have to swallow this whole story to accept the classification of certain words and phrases as modals. These include: 'possibly', 'necessarily', 'could have' 'might have' and 'must have'. However, we have to be able to say much more about the contribution of modalities to sentences than that they give the mood with which a thought is expressed. In this further discussion we will continue to focus on (a) and (b).

11.2 Kinds of Modality

There are two ways in which sentences (a) and (b) can be taken. To appreciate them try the following thought experiment. Imagine that you had asserted either of them and then suppose that someone were to show you a certificate clearly showing that Jones is married.I realize that forgeries are possible, but let us suppose that the cèrtificate is genuine and that you accept it as absolutely certain proof Jones is married . Would you still be prepared to think (a) and (b) true? if you would *not* be so prepared then you were taking them as *epistemic*. That is, if the marriage certificate convinced you that you were mistaken in saying that Jones might be a bachelor, then this is because the possibility is question has to do with the state of your knowledge. ('Epistemic' comes from the Greek word meaning "knowledge"). In the absence of any real information about Jones's marital state, it is only sensible to say that he *might* be a bachelor. When the certificate is presented to you, this increases your stock of knowledge and it is no longer reasonable to think that Jones might be a bachelor. It is no longer reasonable, that is, *when the kind of possibility in question is epistemic*. But thre is another way in which (a) and (b) can be taken.

If, even while you accept that Jones is married, you are still prepared to assert that he might be a bachelor, then you have this second kind of possibility in mind. There is no universally accepted label for this kind of possibility, but labels aren't needed to get hold of the notion. When you think that the married Jones might nonetheless be a bachelor, you are probably thinking one or more of the following sorts of thing.

(1) Jones could have led a different life. For example, if he had become a priest, an idea he in fact entertained when he was younger, he would not now be married.

(2) The world might not have contained the institution of marriage when Jones was born. For example, suppose that the ideas of certain groups of people in the 1960s took hold and by the time Jones was of age, there was no longer any institution of marriage.

With (1) or (2) in mind, it becomes reasonabe to think that the modality in "Jones might be a bachelor" is independent of the state of our knowledge about Jones's marital state. It is a kind of modality which depends on how the world could be and not on what we happen to know about it. For this reason, it is tempting to think of non-epistemic modality as *real* modality' but' since this is not a widely accepted label, we will continue to think of this second kind merely as *non-epistemic*.

Given that there are two general ways in which modalities can be understood, epistemically and non-epistemically, which of them is behind argument (M) and which of them gives us insight into the way in which '□' an '□' work ? These are surprisingly diffcult questions to answer. Before we can even begin we need to do a bit more groundwork.

11.3 Modal Speakers

In earlier chapters,I asked you to imagine that Sentential was a language spoken by a tribe of logicians. With it they are able to make claims about Situations. For example, supposing things to be like this:

Situation (16)

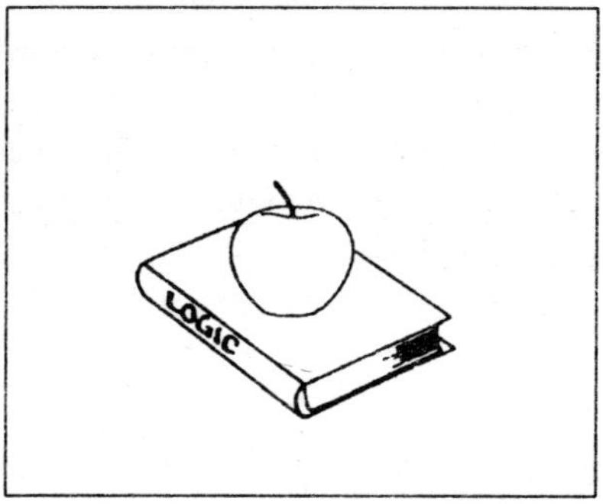

and supposing P to express the thought that the apple is on the book and 'P' to express the thought that the apple is not on the book, then the first claim truly describes the Situation and the second does not.

What I would now like you to imagine is that there are certain individuals in this tribe who, when looking at Situation (16), see more than is portrayed in the above picture, In fact, they see Situation (16) this way.

As my portrayal shows, these individuals see that the apple is on the book, but they also cannot help seeing a number of

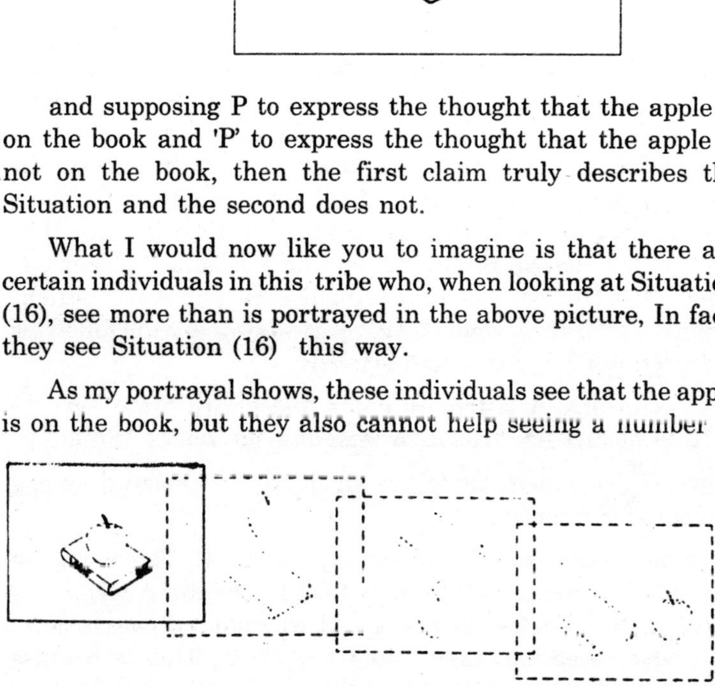

fainter scenes in which the apple and the book occupy different relative locations.

(The drawing captures only three of the very many fainter scenes which these individuals would claim to see.)

If you asked any of them whether P was true, they would

unhesitatingly say "Yes". They would as quickly agree that ¬P is false. In these judgements they agree with other members or the tribe. However, if you asked them whether □ P was true, they would say " No" and if you asked them whether ¬P was true, they would say "Yes". The other members of the tribe, the ones who cannot see the fainter scenes are simply mystified by these answers. In view of the idea behind '□' and, '◊' we will call those individuals who find the above answers obvious and natural *modal logicians*, and we can explain their behaviour in the following way.

The fainter scenes which they see, so to speak, *in* Situation (16) are alternative arrangements of the items in the actual Situation. They think of these Alternative Situations as *ways the world might have been*, as possibilities. When they are asked whether □ P is true, or whether ◊'P is true, they rely on their appreciation of these Alternative Situations in giving answers, For example, they say that □ P is false because they can see Alternative Situations in which P is false. They say that ◊ ¬P is true because they recognise Alternative Situations in which ¬ P is true. Underlying these answes are the following interpretations of the modal symbols.

□ A means 'A is true in *every Alternative Situation'*

◊ 'A means' A is true in *at least one Alternative 'Situation'*

where A is a schematic letter which can be replaced by any sentece of Sentential.

What would Modal logicians say about ◊ P? This is true in the Actual Situation (16) but not in any of the Alternatives pictured. Nonetheless, if you asked whether ◊ P was true in the above Situation, they would say "Yes". This is because they count the Actual Situation, the one which is not faint, as an Alternative Situation. In their view, if the apple is, in fact, on the book, then it is only reasonable to think it possible that the apple is on the book. Nonetheless even though the Actual Situation is counted as an Alternative, it is still the case that it is special. The Modal logicians in this example have as robust a sense of reality as their non-modal fellows, and they recognize that the truth of non-modal sentences depends solely on the way things are in the Actual Situation.

What does this talk of Alternative Situations tell us about modality ? Does it comnit us to regarding '□' & '◊' as epistemic or non epistemic ? And what does it tell us about the way these symbols work in arguments? These very important questions deserve treatment in separate sections.

11.4 Alternative Situations and Kinds of Modality

It is pretty clear that, in the example above, the modality is non- epistemic. Given that the Modal logicians were portayed as *knowing* that the apple is on the book, and given that they still regard P as true, they must understand □ ◊ P non-epistemically. However, this is just a feature of the way the example was presented, and it does not show that the explanation of modality in terms of Alternative Situations commits one to the view of modality as non-epistemic.

For instance. suppose that one of the Modal logicians is extremely sceptical of the deliverances of his senses. In his view, the apperance of things in Situation (16) does not constitute knowledge of where the apple is , and he marks his doubt by claiming that it is possible that the apple is *not* on the book ' ◊' P). The sceptic would still accept that the truth of ◊P comes down to: '◊' P is true in at least one Alternative Situation. Where he would differ from the Modal logicians described earlier is that he would have a different conception of the Alternatives. He regards as Alternatives all those Situations which are not ruled out by what he knows. The Alternatives are understood epistemically. In particular, since he does not regard himself as knowing which Alternative is the Actual Situation, he is prepared to count all of the scenes portrayed as on par.

What this shows is that the explanation of modality in terms of Alternative Situations can serve *both* as the explanation of epistemic *and* non-epistemic modality; though, in any particular case, we can tell which kind of modality is in question by discovering what kinds of Alternative are allowed.

Nor is this all that talk of Alternative Situations buys us. Fix in your mind the responses of the Modal logicians who regard ◊' P as non-epistemic. They are the ones who know perfectly well that the apple *is* on the book, but they still regard it as possible that it is not so placed. That is, they regard the fainter Situations that I drew as genuine Alternatives to the Actual One. However, even within the non epistemic realm of possibility, there are distinctions to be made. For example, as I've drawm it, is an Alternative Situation in which the book is floating freely above the apple. We can imagine that some Modal logicians would, and others would not, count this as an Alternative. Those who wouldn't would argue as follows: the world as we know it is governed by certain physical laws or regularties. In so far as the items on the desk are governed by the law of gravity, as they are in the Actual Situation, it is not reasonable to think of an Alternative Situation from which gravity is absent. For these logicians, it is *not* possible that a book can float freely above the desk, whereas, for others, this and even more "bizarre" Alternatives are possible. Modal logicians who think that the laws of physics constrain the range of Alternatives can be said to have a notion of *physical* possibility.

There are other notions of non-epistemic modality, though, for reasons which will be obvious, I have to go outside simple drawable Situations to give them. Consider these two sentences:

(i) It is not possible that John got to London from Oxford in ten seconds.

(ii) It is not possible that Smith killed Jones.

Someone who regards these two as true, could very well claim that they were to be understood in the following ways.

(i) There are no Alternative Situations in which John travels from Oxford to London in ten Seconds.

(ii') There are no Alternative Situations in which Smith killed Jones.

In each case, however, the constraints on choices of Alternatives are different. It is certainly physically possible to travel from Oxford to London in ten seconds: just imagine that British Rail devote all their resources to Star Trek-like molecular transportation. Even so, the person who made the claim in (i) is not likely to be impressed by this. In its most natural reading, (i) should be understood as about what is *practically* possible; (i) implies that only those Alternatives which are practical are to be countenanced in (i′)

In (ii), we can assume that there is no physical or practical reason why Smith could not kill Jones. What is at issue here is what mat be called *moral* Alternatives. The underlying thought in (ii′) is that the only Alternatives countenanced are those constrained by the various moral principles which it is presumed that Smith holds. The point made in (ii) is that it is not *morally* possible for Smith to have killed Jones.

What all this shows is that there are any number of ways in which we can understand "possibility" and "necessity". There is the basic division into epistemic and non-epistemic and a number of further divisions of which the physical, practical and moral are examples. In all these cases, we can express the modality in terms of Alternative Situations: they provide a way of thinking about modality which is not tied to any one kind.Thc distinction between kinds of modality can be captured, but only by adding constraints on the choice of Alternatives. Armed with a concepion of modalitty in terms of Alternative Situations. wc have now to see what can be said about modality and inference.

11.5 Modality and Validity

Alternative Situations do not trade under that name in the logical literature, so the first thing we must do is bring our discussion into line by expanding our horizons. In your imagination, think of the whole of our world and its history down to such specific things as where you are seated (I will assume you are seated). This is the Actual World. Imagine next a world in which everything is exactly as it is in the Actual World except that, instead of being seated, you are standing. Notiçe, I did not say that you got up. Rather, in theis second world, you were not seated in the first place. This second world is not very different from the Actual World but, in being different at all, it is distinct from the Actual World. We will call this second world a Possible World. (It is a sort of larger-scale Alternative Situation.) Imagine now the whole spectrum of Possible Worlds, each one of which differs in small or large respects from the Actual World. It should be clear that there are going to be a great many Possible World and we will say:

'◊ A' means 'A is true in at least one Possible World'
'□ A' means 'A is true in every Possible World'.

As with Alternative Situations, we will count the Actual World as itself a Possible World. In sum everything we said about modality in terms of Alternative Situations can now be spelled out in terms of Possible Worlds.

What we have to do now is to see whether, using the idea of Possible Worlds, we can find out enough about modality to help us understand its role in inference. The hope is that we can do this *without* having to be all that specific about which sorts of world count as possible. Some grounds for this hope can be found in the fact that we were able to judge this argument.

(M) It is possible that Jones is bachelor.
It is necessary that if Jones is a bachelor, then he is not married.
Therefore, it is possible that Jones is not married.

valid without being clear what kind of modality is in question.

The first thing to do is to rewrite (M) in terms of Possible Worlds. This gives the following:

(M/PW) There is a Possible World in which Jones is a bachelor. Every Possible World is such that if

Jones is a bachelor then he is not married.

Therefore, there is a Possible World in which Jones is not married.

This Possible World version lends itself naturally to translation into a special sort of Predicate. All we have to do is allow ourselves the idea of quantification over Possible Worlds. The translation of this version is

$$\frac{\begin{array}{l}(\exists w)\ Pw \\ (\forall w)\ (Pw \supset {}'Qw)\end{array}}{(\exists w)\ {}'Qw}$$

where: w is a variable for Possible Worlds and 'Pw' means 'P is true in world w'.

The validi ty of (M/PW) can be taken to show that the modal argument about Jones is valid. By transmuting this modal argument into talk about Possible Worlds, we end up with a method for validating it without having to decide precisely what kind of modality is involved.

We can extend this method to arguments which mix modal and non-modal claims by the following expedient: treat the Actual World as a designated Possible World. That is, think of the Actual World as picked out by the designator w* . The claim that Jones is, in fact, married then comes out as

Pw* (It is true in the Actual World that P).

On this understanding, it is easy to see why the following is valid.

Jones is married.
Therefore, it is possible that Jones is married.

This would be rendered as

$$\frac{Pw^*}{(\exists w)Pw}$$

and is a straightforward example of ∃I.

11.6 A Note of Caution

It is clear that Possible World talk is extremely useful in connection with modality. Nonetheless, one must not get carried away. The use of Predicate in the above discussion is not all it seems. You may have noticed that I spoke of (M/PW) as a 'rewrite' of the original argument. I used this word because I did not want to say that (M/PW) translates (M). Strictly speaking, the Modal translation of (M) is the following.

$$\Diamond P$$
$$\Box(P \supset {'Q})$$
$$\overline{\Diamond\ {'Q}}$$

The Predicate language was then used, not to give a further translation, but to provide us with *a way of talking about this translation*. Predicate is used as the *metalanguage* of modality. It is important to keep this in mind because we do not want any controversy about Possible World talk to infect t he undoubtedly uncontroversial use made of modality in everyday reasoning.

The modal arguments we have discussed are very simple and I have used them mainly to introduce you to the ways of thinking of Modal logicians. The full treatment of modality even within Sentential would require

(1) a deeper investigation of Possible World talk and its relation to modal argumentation, and

(2) a discussion of how Possible Worlds are related to one another.

Work on (1) can be expected to shed light on the differences between kinds of modality.We would expect that the differences between modalities would show up somewhere in inference even though relatively simple arguments like (M) are valid whether the modality is epistemic or non-epistemic.

The second of these requirements is especially pressing if we are to deal with the following sort of argument.

It is possible that it is possible that Jones is married.
Therefore, it is possible that Jones is married.

Here we have a case of *iterated* modalities and people have different intuitions about which inferences involving them are valid.

Finally, and perhaps most important of all, no understanding of modality would be complete if it did not include an account of how it functions within Predicate. Remember, even though we used the Predicate idiom to talk *about* Possible Worlds, the modalities themselves were functioning only within Sentential. This is an advanced topic guidance for which can be obtained from the Reading List. When you consult it you will find that a considerable amount of ink has been spilled over issues raised by the mixing of modality and quantification.

The Main Points of Chapter 11

(1) An argument was presented which was intuitively valid, but whose validity seems to rest on such notions as 'possibility' and 'necessity'.

(2) Two new symbols were introduced into Sentential. These symbols are called *modal operators*. They are

□ (it is necessarily the case that)
◊ (it is possibly the case that)

(3) When modal operators play a crucial role in Sentential arguments, we can no longer use the truth-table method to decide validity. In an effort to find some method of evaluation we embarked on a lengthy discussion of the nature of modality.

(4) There are two general kinds of modality: *epistemic* and *non-epistemic*. There are also many specific kinds of modality of which physical, practical and moral are instances.

(5) Using Situations, a useful tool for discussing modality was introduced. This was the notion of Alternative Situations.

When this is generalized into the more well-known notion of *Possible Worlds*,we can use some of the insights of Predicate to see why certain, relatively simple, modal arguments are valid.

(6) For a complete treatment of modality, we need to see what happens when modal operators are introduced into Predicate, and we need to better understand the nature of, and relations between. Possible Worlds.